Norbert Zimmerman

TITANIC

Chronology of a Disaster

"We built the ship so that it could swim. We didn't build it so it could run into an iceberg or a cliff. Unfortunately, that's what happened."

(Alexander Carlisle, Director of the Harland & Wolff shipyard)

Bibliographic information of the German National Library

The German National Library lists this publication in the German National Bibliography; detailed bibliographic data are available on the Internet at http://dnb.d-nb.de.

ISBN-13: 9783753406473

© 2021 Norbert Zimmermann for text and layout

No reproduction, storage, broadcast, transmission or processing by any present or future available method is permitted without the prior written consent of the author.

Production and publisher:

BoD - Books on Demand, Norderstedt

Contents

Introduction 7

A Myth is Born

Planning a Legend 11
The Construction of the TITANIC 23
German Workmanship at the TITANIC 38

The Last Voyage of the TITANIC

The Maiden Voyage of the TITANIC Begins 44
Lucky Coincidences of Fate 56
The Ice Warnings 61
The Iceberg Collision 67
The Evacuation of the Ship 79
This Happened when the TITANIC Sank 116

Titanic Destinies

The Tragedy of the Allison Family 127
The Legendary Straus Couple 135
The Elegant Sinking of Benjamin Guggenheim 139
The Wedding Ring of Gerda Lindell 143
The Tragic Story of the Goodwin Family 147
Thomas Millar and the Story of the Two Pennies 153
The Sad Death of Frederick Fleet 157

The Destroyed Honor of Masabumi Hosono	162
Scandinavian Destinies	166
Margaret Rice and Her Five Children	172
The Fate of the TITANIC Officers	177
The Oldest Survivors of the TITANIC	198

The Scapegoats of the Disaster

Stanley Lord and the CALIFORNIAN	259
The Ruined Reputation of Bruce Ismay	268
The "Incompetent" Captain Smith	280
Interesting Conspiracy Theories and Bad Omens	286
Passenger and Crew List of the TITANIC	294
Sources	361

Introduction

More than 108 years have passed since the sinking of the RMS TITANIC, but the fascination of the magnificent ship that sank on her maiden voyage is still unbroken today. When the full dimensions of the disaster became known in April 1912, the world sank into a kind of shocked paralysis. This "unsinkable" ship had sunk? Impossible! But unfortunately, true...

Even when the 712 survivors of the TITANIC were still on the rescue ship, CARPATHIA, on their way to New York, the press was already overflowing with reports of the sinking of the luxury liner. However, there were no eyewitnesses to be interviewed yet, but the whole world wanted to know what had happened, so many newspapers made up stories about the tragic sinking without further ado. When the survivors finally arrived in New York, many fairy tales and lies had already taken on a life of their own and could now be read as "facts" in the press.

In many ways, the disaster marked the end of an era. Only two years later, World War I shook the entire order that had been in place until then, and the sinking of the TITANIC understandably moved into the background. Not until the first Hollywood films about the sinking of the TITANIC appeared in the 1950s, did the tragic ship regain a place in people's consciousness.

A huge part of the fact that the history of the TITANIC came back into people's focus was without a doubt due to Edward Kamuda (10th November 1939 – 13th April

2014) who founded the Titanic Historical Society on Sunday, 7th July 1963, together with five friends. This was the first organization to study the sinking and the history of the TITANIC.

Now, the so-called TITANIC enthusiasts had also found a contact point, and until today, there are numerous TITANIC societies or clubs worldwide. Due to the blockbuster "TITANIC" by James Cameron, which won eleven Oscars, the topic TITANIC experienced a real boom from 1997 on, also in Germany. Finally, German-language TITANIC books were available, and the TV stations also broadcast several TITANIC shows.

The TITANIC boom has now been history for a long time, and most of the numerous "fans" of that time are no longer active. They were more fans of the movie than they were really interested in the history of the TITANIC. However, the history of the legendary ship is still fascinating.

After the wreck of the TITANIC was officially discovered on Sunday, September 1st, 1985, a lot has changed in the TITANIC research. Just by reading old TITANIC books, it is immediately noticeable that due to newer research on the wreck and partly very surprising archive findings, much of what is written in these books has become obsolete.

This book tells the story of the TITANIC starting with her planning and completion in Belfast, Ireland, up to her departure in Southampton. The author of the book also shows the mysteries surrounding the collision of the TITANIC with the iceberg and describes what, according to the current state of TITANIC research, happened in the last hours before the sinking.

This book also looks at the later scapegoats of the disaster and how much these people actually were partly responsible for the sinking of the ship.
Part of the history of the TITANIC is the sometimes very tragic fates of the people on board the luxury liner. Some of these very emotional and tragic stories are told in this book. It would have filled a whole book to tell all the stories, so here are just a few.

This book also reports on the latest research on the ship's break-up, which James Cameron made public in his book "Mission Titanic".

The author hopes that this book is now up to date with the latest TITANIC research.

Norbert Zimmermann in February 2021

A Myth is Born

Planning a Legend

The era in which the TITANIC was planned and built fell in a time of social and political change. Since the German-French War in 1870/71, there had been no war in Europe, and the so-called second wave of the industrial revolution had brought a certain prosperity, which almost without exception, benefited the rich. It was the age of the "Belle Époque," and in the High Society there was a great deal of optimism about the cultural and political future. (The extent to which rich contemporaries were off track with their optimistic assessment was shown in August 1914 when the First World War broke out, changing the entire map of Europe forever. Many historians already call the sinking of the TITANIC the real end of the Belle Époque ...)

For the common people in Europe, the "Belle Époque" was not that beautiful because the richness, of course, completely missed them. It was, rather, earned on their back. The ordinary workers in the factories started to organize themselves in trade unions in order to be paid and treated by their employers at least a little more decently. Of course, this also met with bitter resistance.

Women in the USA and Great Britain took to the streets for their own right to vote, which New Zealand was the first country to introduce in 1893. They did not shy away from using violence to draw attention to their demands. The so-called "suffragettes" kept the state power, which was of course firmly in male hands, in suspense from about 1903. This reacted partly with brute force against the women, and very many of the suffragettes ended up in prison.

Those of the lower class who could somehow manage it tried to escape from the poverty and hopelessness by emigrating to the so-called "New World". A large part of the emigrants to the USA were from the very poor Ireland, which was shaken by huge conflicts between Catholics and Protestants, but the Scandinavian countries were also very much represented.

In those days, the ship was the only transport medium to the "New World," and so there was a real rivalry between the different shipping companies for dominance on the oceans around the lucrative passages across the Atlantic. The ships were designed to transport as many emigrants as possible, as they were the most profitable.

Although the ships attracted the rich passengers with a lot of luxury in First Class, the real profit was made in Third Class, the so-called "steerage".

At the beginning of the last century, this highly competitive market was fought over by the rising imperial Germany with the *Hamburg Amerika Linie* (later *HAPAG*) and the *Norddeutsche Lloyd*, as well as the British lines *Cunard Line* and *White Star Line*, which felt increasingly threatened by German competition.

The whole thing was additionally fueled by the American financier, J. P. Morgan (17th April 1837 - 31st March 1913), to whose group *IMM* (*International*

Mercantile Marine) the traditional *White Star Line* meanwhile belonged. However, the *White Star Line* still retained its headquarters in Liverpool, England.

But how could it be possible that J. P. Morgan was able to secure such a position in the shipping industry? As a hard-calculating businessman, Morgan saw the enormous economic opportunities that were available to him in this industry. In 1900, together with a group of 20 shareholders, he provided the sum of $20 million with which the two important American shipping companies, *Atlantic Transport Line (ATL)* and the *International Navigation Company,* were bought up.

This coup gave Morgan a fleet of 40 ships at a stroke, most of which were freighters. But that was not enough for Morgan because after that, he set his sights on Great Britain. In April 1901, he paid $12 million in cash for the *Leyland Line* shipping company, which was the largest transatlantic freighter line with 40 ships at the time. Barely ten months later, he ventured out on a very big fish: the prestigious *White Star Line*!

After tough negotiations, Morgan bought the traditional company with its eight large passenger ships for what was then a gigantic $40 million in cash and shares, thus shocking the kingdom. Almost incidentally, Morgan also acquired the *Dominion Line* for the pocket money of $4.5 million. The *Dominion Line* brought six passenger and cargo ships into this connection.

Within just one year, Morgan and its partners had thus acquired a fleet of about 100 ships, which represented about a third of the tonnage that was then sailing between Europe and North America. On Thursday, 20th February 1902, the two German shipping companies, *Hamburg-Amerika Linie* and *Norddeutscher Lloyd*, concluded a ten-year contract with Morgan. Both shipping companies had no intention of selling to Morgan but wanted to pursue a common policy with him to avoid excessive competition.

On Wednesday, October 1st, 1902, J. P. Morgan announced the formation of the *International Mercantile Marine Company*, which he endowed with a capital of $170 million.

The financier J. P. Morgan saved the USA from national bankruptcy in 1895 and 1907 as the leader of several powerful investor groups. © public domain

The *IMM* had the following shipping lines under his rule at the time of the TITANIC:

- *American Line*
- *Red Star Line from Belgium*
- *Dominion Line*
- *The Leyland Line*
- *White Star Line*
- *Atlantic Transport Line*
- *International Navigation Company*

White Star Line's largest and longtime competitor, the *Cunard Line*, refused to sell to *IMM*, and Morgan and its president kept pressure on the British Parliament until it approved a loan of GBP 2.5 million (equivalent to about GBP 243 million in 2015) for the construction of new ships and annual subsidies of GBP 150 000.

In response, in 1903, *White Star Line* began planning for the construction of the Olympic class liners in strict secrecy with all parties involved. Shortly afterwards, contracts were signed with Harland & Wolff for the construction of a huge dock in Belfast, construction of which began in 1904.

> **The history of the Belfast shipyard Harland & Wolff began in 1851, when the shipyard Thompson & Kirwan was founded for the construction of wooden ships as the first forerunner of the shipyard. Two years later, Robert Hickson founded a company for building iron ships. One year later, Edward James Harland from Newcastle, England, took over the management of the Hickson shipyard and became its owner in 1858.**

Harland received financial support from Gustav Christian Schwabe, then junior partner of John Bibby, Sons & Co., Ltd, in Liverpool. From there, Harland received the order to build three ships (VENETIAN in 1859, SICILIAN in 1860 and SYRIAN in 1860). The construction of these ships resulted in 15 follow-up orders for further sailing ships (GRECIAN, ITALIAN, EGYPTIAN, DALMATIAN etc.) for the shipyard.

In order to be able to cope with the lucrative orders, the German engineer, Gustav Wolff (the nephew of Gustav Christian Schwabe) officially joined the company as a partner on Wednesday, January 1st, 1862, and the shipyard was founded as Harland & Wolff Ltd.

Through Gustav Schwabe, a particularly lucrative partnership developed, as he persuaded the founder of *White Star Line*, Thomas Henry Ismay, to order the ships of his shipping company from Harland & Wolff. This was also the beginning of the shipyard's great rise.

Through an agreement between Harland & Wolff and the *White Star Line*, Harland did not build for any direct *White Star* competitor, and the shipping company in turn had its new ships built exclusively by Harland & Wolff.

The golden era of Harland & Wolff had its beginning there. For many decades, the shipyard was one of the best in the world, at times even the best.

But this era finally came to an end due to the severe shipyard crisis in England in the 1960s and 1970s, and so Harland & Wolff was incorporated into the British Shipbuilders Corporation in 1977 and was privatized again six years later. Nowadays, however, their main business is no longer shipbuilding but rather the repair and overhaul of ships.

The shipyard Harland & Wolff at the beginning of the last century. © Collection of the author

The former Harland & Wolff headquarters in Belfast in 2017. On the right-hand side of the picture, you can still see the famous Harland & Wolff cranes. © private photo of the author

The Belfast City Hall also commemorates Harland & Wolff and the TITANIC. © private photo of the author

In 1907 *Cunard* put the two turbine steamers LUSITANIA and MAURETANIA into service. When the two ships began their service, they were the largest ships in the world with over 30,000 gross register tons.

With an average speed of 26 knots, the MAURETANIA won the so-called Blue Ribbon, awarded for the fastest crossing of the Atlantic, and held this record for 22 years.

Her sister ship LUSITANIA, which had previously held the Blue Ribbon for some time, achieved sad fame when she was sunk by the German submarine U-20 during the First World War on Friday, 7th May 1915. Above all, the circumstances of her sinking are still highly controversial today.

The legendary Lusitania was sunk by the German submarine U-20 during the 1st World War. © public domain

> It is not much known that there was already a "first" *White Star Line*, founded by John Pilkington and Henry Threlfall Wilson in Liverpool, England. The shipping company initially chartered sailing ships (TAYLEUR, BLUE

JACKET, RED JACKET, ELLEN and IOWA) for the trade between Great Britain and Australia. The shipping company symbol was a white star on a red background. A terrible blow for the "first" *White Star Line* was the sinking of the TAYLEUR on her maiden voyage in a storm on the Irish coast in 1854, in which over 300 people died (somehow maiden voyages, no matter from which *White Star Line*, did not seem to be under a particularly good star...)

In 1863 the *White Star Line* bought its first steamship with the Royal Standard. In order to open up new routes, the management of *White Star* tried to merge with other shipping lines, but all efforts finally failed, so they concentrated on the connection between Liverpool and New York.

In 1867, the "first" *White Star Line* was forced to file for bankruptcy. Their main bank, The Royal Bank of Liverpool, went bankrupt, which in turn led to the bankruptcy of *White Star Line*, which had recently invested heavily in new ships.

Two years later, Thomas Henry Ismay, former director of the *National Line*, founded the *Oceanic Steam Navigation Company* to provide a regular liner service from Liverpool to New York. Prior to this, Ismay had purchased the old shipping company symbol and the trading name of the bankrupt *White Star Line* for GBP 1000.

J. Bruce Ismay, the president of the *White Star Line*, and his financier, J. P. Morgan, had not been interested in the prestigious "Blue Ribbon" for a long time, because they had agreed to focus on comfort and luxury instead of speed of their ships like *Cunard*. Ismay had a dream of building a fleet of three luxury liners, and with Morgan's money, this vision came within reach.

> **According to a popular legend, the decision to build the ships was made at a dinner of Bruce Ismay and Lord William James Pirrie at Downshire House in London in July 1907. However, this seems to be only a legend that has lasted for a very long time. The names of the three ships should never be forgotten: OLYMPIC, TITANIC and BRITANNIC.**

For many decades, the third ship, BRITANNIC, has been rumored to have been originally called GIGANTIC, but was renamed BRITANNIC after the tragic sinking of the TITANIC. According to reports, however, old Harland & Wolff shipyard documents dating from October 1911, six months before the TITANIC disaster, already mentioned the name BRITANNIC. This would disprove the popular rumor that the name BRITANNIC was only assigned after the disaster.

Like her famous sister, the BRITANNIC was not granted a long life.

Converted to a hospital ship and without ever having fulfilled her actual purpose as a passenger ship, she hit a German mine during the First World War on Tuesday, November 21st, 1916, between the islands of Kea and Makronisios and sank. In contrast to her famous sister

TITANIC, most of the passengers, mostly soldiers, could be saved and "only" 30 people died. The sinking of the BRITANNIC meant the end of the Olympic class on which the *White Star Line* had placed so many hopes at that time.

The *White Star Line* did not recover from the famous sinking of two of their ships. And in 1934 they finally merged with their biggest competitor, *Cunard Line*, to form the *Cunard White Star Ltd.* One year later, the scrapping of the OLYMPIC began, which had acquired the impeccable reputation as "Old Reliable" over many years. After the Second World War, *Cunard* bought all *White Star* shares and as of 1950, the name *White Star* disappeared. The *Cunard Line* still exists today, and its fleet includes the Queen Mary 2.

The hospital ship BRITANNIC during World War I. © public domain

The Construction of the TITANIC in Belfast

After the *Cunard Line* unveiled the MAURETANIA and the LUSITANIA, White *Star Line* sent an official order to Harland & Wolff on Tuesday, 30th of April 1907, that they begin construction of the new Olympic class liners: hull #400 which was to be named OLYMPIC, and the hull number #401 which was to be named TITANIC.

This new order confronted Harland & Wolff with an organizational problem: the dimensions of the two ships were beyond the capacity of the shipyard! Extensive modifications became necessary in the shipyard, whose docks had already been enlarged since 1904.

The Thompson Graving Dock in Belfast in 2017 © private photo of the author

In order to be able to realize the ambitious project of the new giant liner, three slipways (a slipway - also known as a "Helgen" –originally refers to the space in the shipyard where a ship is built, more precisely the sloping surface where it is subsequently launched) had to be demolished in Belfast and replaced by two new, giant slipways.

Harland & Wolff also developed the scaffolding for the construction of the two huge ships themselves. It was 80 meters high, 290 meters long and equipped with 16 overhead cranes. It could be reached via four lifts and sloping corridors. After two years of construction and a total cost of GBP 100,000 (today about 10 million Euros) the new slipways were finally finished.

The two ships had an identical basic structure with three propellers each, two sets of four-cylinder piston steam engines, each of which was to move one propeller, and a 420-ton low-pressure turbine which would then drive the middle propeller with steam from the main aggregates.

A special highlight was the four funnels, of which the last one was only used as a kind of extractor hood. So, it was not a dummy, as it is written in so many books. Today, four funnels seem a little bit over-sized, but at that time it was thought that four funnels would make a ship look even bigger and more majestic, but they were not really necessary.

The steam came from the 29 main boilers, which consisted of 24 so-called double ended and five single ended boilers.

The construction and arrangement of the bulkheads on the TITANIC were controversially discussed after the disaster. The TITANIC had 16 watertight compartments, formed by 15 watertight bulkheads along the hull. Six of them extended to D Deck, eight to E Deck and one to F Deck. Each bulkhead had an automatic watertight door, which was kept open by a friction clutch and could be operated from the bridge by a magnet. This allowed the captain to close all the compartment doors immediately from the bridge by simply flipping the switch.

These bulkheads were a great invention and were also the topic of the prestigious magazine "The Shipbuilder" in 1911: *"The watertight compartments of the OLYMPIC and TITANIC are very extensive and designed in such a way that two main compartments can be flooded at a time without endangering the safety of the ship"*.

On Wednesday, December 16th, 1908, the first keel plate of the OLYMPIC was laid, and the same process would begin for her sister TITANIC on Monday, March 22nd, 1909.

> **In most publications about the TITANIC, Wednesday, 31st March 1909, is mentioned as the day of keel laying, but in the notebook of the shipyard Harland & Wolff, which can be found in the National Archives of Northern Ireland in Belfast, Monday, 22nd March 1909, is mentioned as the date.**

A rare picture: The sister ships OLYMPIC and TITANIC side by side. © public domain

Every single phase of the ship´s construction was to be documented by the photographer Robert Welsh, who was especially hired by Harland & Wolff. We owe the great images of the two sister ships to this photographer and, fortunately, they still exist today.

In March 1910 there was a personnel change, about which there are still controversial discussions today: After almost 40 years of service, Chief Designer Alexander Carlisle left the Harland & Wolff shipyard for health reasons! In the last few years there has been increasing speculation that his departure was due to a controversy Carlisle might have had with his brother-in-law, Lord William James Pirrie.

The controversy is reported to have been about the number of lifeboats on board the TITANIC. Carlisle asked for 64 lifeboats, which would have corresponded to the number of passengers on board, but Bruce Ismay intervened, and in conjunction with Pirrie, pushed through 16 lifeboats plus four collapsible boats. In the very successful documentary "TITANIC - Birth of a Legend," from 2005, this theory was taken up again and presented in such a way that Alexander Carlisle left Harland & Wolff because of this controversy. But this does not seem in accordance with the known facts.

Alexander Carlisle's replacement as the designer of the TITANIC was Lord Pirrie's nephew, Thomas Andrews, who had already worked on the plans before and now took over the complete leadership.

37-year-old Andrews had already attended the Royal Belfast Academical Institution at the age of eleven, and when he was 16 years old, he started working for Harland & Wolff. Initially he worked in the carpentry workshop for four months, followed by two months on the ships of the shipyard. He then spent the last 18 months of his five-year training in the drawing office. As early as 190,1 he became head of the design department and in 1907, he became one of the technical directors of the shipyard.

In his private life he was married to Helen Reilly Barbour, the daughter of a director at Harland & Wolff since June 24th, 1908. On November 27th, 1910, his daughter Elizabeth Law Barbour Andrews, called Elba, was born.

Andrews was very popular and highly regarded by the yard's employees, due to the fact, that despite his family connections, he did not enjoy preferential treatment in training.

A group of around 550 slipway workers had the task of laying down and placing the rib structure of TITANIC, literally building the skeleton of the luxury liner (the ribs reached from the ship's floor to the top deck). This task was completed at the end of April 1910. Shortly before, the interior work on the deck beams, the decks and the outer skin plating had been completed at the OLYMPIC, after the ribs had been set there in November 1909.

On Wednesday, October 19th, 1910, the plating of the TITANIC was completed by a specially developed hydraulic riveting system. The steel plates were then riveted shingle-like, one above the other, in rows of three. The riveting procedure was carried out as follows: It was partly riveted with pneumatic riveting hammers and partly by hand, whereby the rivet was heated to white heat by a so-called "Heater Boy" over a coal fire. The latter threw it to the "Catch Boy", who caught it in a wooden bowl and pushed it with pliers through the hole of two overlapping steel plates. The "Holder Up" then held the head of the rivet in place with a heavy hammer, while the fourth man, the "Basher", hit the rivet flat from the other side of the steel plate. After the rivet had cooled down, the plates were firmly joined together.

At the end of November 1910, the decision was made to slow down the work on the TITANIC in favor of completing the OLYMPIC. The TITANIC is no longer able to make her maiden voyage in 1911, but in 1912. In the end, the construction of the TITANIC will be delayed by a full 30 weeks!

The test runs of the OLYMPIC revealed several problems, one of which was the strong vibration of the ship. It was also noticed that the hull of the ship was "wheezing", which means that instead of being straight, it bent inwards and outwards, which was not supposed to happen in calm seas. Once these problems were localized, more steel was used in the construction of the two ships, as it was thought that this would help to stabilize them.

In the TV documentary, "The TITANIC's Weakness," TITANIC Historian Tom McCluskie commented as follows:

"Even then, dangerous cracks continued to form. Double plating was added to the stress points. On the outside and inside, they made some modifications to the ship. Similar modifications were also made to the TITANIC, which is currently under construction. One of the most striking: The Promenade Deck! Open on the OLYMPIC, closed on the TITANIC. Nothing is reported about the cracks or vibrations, only that White Star is recreating a French café, the Cafe Parisien. They claimed that they did it because of the luxury cabins and the Cafe Parisien. Andrew's notes show that it stabilized this part of the ship."

For Wednesday, May 31st, 1911, the *White Star Line*, together with Harland & Wolff, had come up with something very special: The launch of the TITANIC as well as the handover of the OLYMPIC to the *White Star Line* took place on the same day!

The launch of Olympic had taken place seven months before on Thursday, October 20th, 1910.

The Belfast Newsletter wrote about the launch: "*Above the bow of the ship, the flag of the White Star Company fluttered, and a code signal was emitted which spelled the word 'success'.*"

J. P. Morgan, who was also present at the celebrations, had been hopeful about this day´s success. Lord James Pirrie and J. Bruce Ismay made a last-minute inspection of the pressure gauge for the hydraulic launchers. The hull of the TITANIC then slid, accompanied by rockets and cheers from the more than 100,000 spectators, as planned, over 22,000 tons of tallow, lubricating oil and soap into the Lagan River.

The whole process of launching took only 62 seconds (just like on the OLYMPIC), and then the ship was towed by tugs to the fitting-out quay, where the interior was fitted out.

As usual with the *White Star Line*, the TITANIC was not christened. Contemporaries described it this way: "*They build them and push them into the water!*"

The "Shipbuilder" also celebrated the designers of the two sister ships:

"*The designers of the OLYMPIC and TITANIC, the celebrated company Harland & Wolff Limited, had an unprecedented wealth of experience in building large passenger ships and the new White Star liner ships add yet another triumph to this success story.*"

Immediately before the launch, however, a tragic incident occurred. After the workers had moved away from the hull of the ship, the obligatory counting of the men revealed that the worker James Dobbin was missing.

As it turned out, a wooden pile of the construction for the launch had collapsed, trapping Dobbin's leg. Although his colleagues found it quite quickly and pulled it out, Dobbin died a day later from his serious injuries.

According to a list by Harland & Wolff dated Wednesday, April 10th, 1912, the day of Titanic´s maiden voyage, there were eight deaths, 28 seriously injured and 218 minor accidents during the construction of the TITANIC.

After a short stop at her home port of Liverpool, the OLYMPIC continued on, to Southampton, where she was prepared for her maiden voyage to New York, to which she finally left on Wednesday, June 14th, 1911, under the command of Edward John Smith.
J. Bruce Ismay was also on board the OLYMPIC to get a personal impression of the new ship. This impression turned out to be more than positive and increased anticipation for the TITANIC.

On her maiden voyage, the OLYMPIC reached a very remarkable average speed of 21.17 knots which she was able to increase to 22.32 knots on her way back.
The *White Star Line* and Harland &Wolff were very impressed with the new ship.

On Tuesday, June 20th, 1911, still during the maiden voyage of the OLYMPIC, an enthusiastic Bruce Ismay telegraphed the order for a third sister ship to Harland & Wolff.

The OLYMPIC became very popular, and therefore, it shocked the *White Star Line* when its new flagship collided with the armed and outdated cruiser HMS Hawke during her fifth crossing while leaving the port of Southampton on Wednesday, September 20th, 1911.

Original Olympic postcard © collection of the author

Both ships suffered serious damage, as the bow of HMS HAWKE was severely damaged, while OLYMPIC suffered a twelve-meter-long crack in the stern. This incident made an immediate inspection and simultaneous repair of OLYMPIC in Southampton necessary.

An official investigation was initiated into this serious incident, which concluded that the collision was the fault of Captain Smith and the OLYMPIC, because Pilot George Bowyer underestimated the pull of the great liner.

However, this judgment is still highly controversial to this day because the fact that the steering wheel of HMS HAWKE probably had a technical defect and therefore jammed at the decisive moment was lost in the investigation. According to some experts, it also seems that at this point of the port in Southampton, it was simply too narrow for a ship the size of OLYMPIC and HMS HAWKE, so that a collision was inevitable.

The Hole in the "Olympic," the Damage Below the Waterline being Much Greater Than That Above   The Bow of the "Hawke," the Damage being so Great That the Ram Has Been Mashed Flat

Pictures from the Popular Mechanics Magazine Edition December 1911 © public domain

At least it would have been too embarrassing for the British Navy if they had to admit a technical defect of one of their cruisers. So, it was probably easier to blame the *White Star Line*, which in addition, was equipped with American money. At least some historians are of this opinion.

On Friday, October 6th, 1911, the damaged OLYMPIC had to go to the Belfast drydock, and many workers of the TITANIC were withdrawn for a six-week, very extensive repair work. The long-awaited maiden voyage of the TITANIC, which was originally scheduled for Wednesday, 20th March 1912, was then set for Wednesday, April 10th, 1912.

Meanwhile, the construction of the TITANIC entered its final phase. And in January 1912, the 16 wooden lifeboats and the four so-called Engelhardt collapsible boats were installed on board the TITANIC - at that time nobody could have guessed what a big and important role they later would play...

A month later, on Thursday, February 8th, 1912, at a meeting of the Ulster Liberal Association in Belfast, the future Prime Minister, Winston Churchill, and Lord Pirrie escaped serious riots, directed against both of them, only by a very narrow margin.

Lord William James Pirrie, who held the office of Lord Mayor of Belfast for some time, was an advocate of Irish independence (Home Rule Bill) which turned the Belfast population against him. That evening the situation escalated, and Pirrie was booed in the streets and mocked and attacked by his own shipyard workers. This was a heavy shock for Pirrie, who also retired from politics for health reasons and never saw the TITANIC again.

> **During his time as Lord Mayor of Belfast, Pirrie was raised to the nobility by the then King Edward VII and became Baron Pirrie of the City of Belfast. Since 1908, Pirrie was also a knight of the Order of Saint Patrick.**

After the end of the First World War, Pirrie was, among other things, chief accountant of the merchant shipbuilding industry. At the age of 74, he was promoted by King George V to Viscount Pirrie of the City of Belfast in 1921.

On Saturday, June 7th, 1924, William James Pirrie died, at the age of 77, during a ship voyage. Till today, he has left a deep mark on Belfast, and his memory is held in high regard.

Painting by Lord William James Pirrie at the Belfast City Hall.
© private photo of the author

On Saturday, February 24th, 1912, the OLYMPIC lost a propeller blade on the starboard side during her Atlantic crossing and had to return immediately to Belfast for a repair. The TITANIC, whose construction was already nearing its end at this time, had to leave her dry dock, as all other berths were much too small to be able to carry out the work on the OLYMPIC.

On Wednesday, March 6th, 1912, the propeller blade of the OLYMPIC was finally replaced, while on Sunday, March 31st, 1912, the equipment of the TITANIC was completed. Concerning the OLYMPIC's propeller blade, it is worth mentioning that it received a propeller blade from the TITANIC, which is one of the hooks in a theory of targeted insurance fraud that has been circulating for years (see chapter, Interesting Conspiracy Theories and Bad Omens).

> On Friday, March 29th, 1912, the Association of Naval Architects met in London and discussed the limited number of lifeboats on ships and the outdated regulations, dating from 1894, including the OLYMPIC and the TITANIC. It was emphasized that the ships were ready to be retrofitted with more boats if the regulations changed. Considering what was to Happen two weeks later, it almost seems like a macabre joke...

On Sunday, 31st March, the TITANIC was officially registered under the number 131428.

On Tuesday, April 2nd, 1912, the TITANIC completed her sea trials, which had been canceled the day before due to strong winds. The required maneuverability of the ship at different speeds and the performance of the rudder were tested. In addition, an emergency stop was carried out. During this test run, the TITANIC needed a little less than half a mile to stop at a speed of 20 knots, which is a very interesting figure for the later accident. Afterwards the ship returned from its test run to Belfast Lough.

After this whole procedure, the observers from Harland & Wolff disembarked, and the TITANIC received her passenger certificate. It was a long way to get there because the representative of the British Ministry of Trade, Francis Caruthers, had inspected the TITANIC more than 2,000 times before he certified the seaworthiness of the luxury liner.

The ill Lord William James Pirrie was represented by his nephew Thomas Andrews, who boarded the ship in Belfast as a representative of the Harland & Wolff shipyard, in order to be available on the spot in case of any difficulties.

The TITANIC leaving Belfast on April 2nd 1912 © Anka Schlayer collection

German Workmanship at the TITANIC

The German part of the history of the TITANIC was quite unknown for a long time and has only actually been discussed in the last years. In the following is a short presentation of the German workmanship of the TITANIC (and OLYMPIC and BRITANNIC):

Floating Crane of Benrather Maschinenfabrik AG

For the construction of the ships, a floating crane was used at the shipyard, which came from the *Benrather Maschinenbaufabrik AG* in Düsseldorf-Benrath. This crane had a reach of 52 meters and could lift a weight of 250 tons. In the still preserved books of account, the payment of 106,672.47 Imperial Reichsmark in 1908 is included. The building order had the number 29208.

However, there were some problems with the complicated construction of the crane in Belfast, as the shipyard workers refused to install the outermost tip of the boom, as they considered the ascent too high and therefore too risky. This posed a major problem for the shipyard but was solved by Chief Draftsman Roderick Chisum. He suggested that the shipyard management request assistance from the German company in Benrath to erect the crane.

Shortly afterwards, the men from Germany were on site and began the work. As a special incentive, it had been agreed that the fitters would be allowed to hoist the Imperial German flag over the crane if they could finish the work within the time limit set for that purpose. This seemed to have worked, because sometime later, the Imperial German flag blew over Belfast! When one considers that a few years later, both countries were to face each other as bitter enemies of war, this is an interesting side note.

After a merger with *Bechem & Kettmann*, the former *Maschinenfabrik AG* in Benrath meanwhile called itself *Duisburger Maschinenfabrik*. In 1910 the companies *Ludwig Stuckenholz* from Wetter and the *Märkische Maschinenbauanstalt* were added, and the company name changed again to *Deutsche Maschinenfabrik AG*, better known as *DEMAG*.

Pianos by Steinweg & Söhne

The Hamburg company *Steinweg & Söhne* supplied not only five so-called B-Grands, each 2.11 meters long, but also three pianos of the model "K", which means concert piano. Presumably, they were used for the First- and Second-Class Dining Rooms, as well as for the front staircase of the First Class on the level of the Boat Deck. The company is now known by its translated name *Steinway & Sons*.

39

Sports Equipment from Rossel, Schwarz & Co AG

The Wiesbaden-based company *Rossel, Schwarz & Co AG* was responsible for one of TITANIC's much-praised innovations. They built the Gymnasium, which was located on the starboard side of the Boat Deck next to the second funnel. It was 13 meters long, 5.50 meters wide and about three meters high.

On the brochure of that time, you can read: "*Medical equipment for physical training,*" simply said, that they produced "sports equipment."

The room had eight large windows and was decorated with illuminated color pictures of the TITANIC and a world map showing the *White Star Line's* steamship network.

Passengers could ride, row and cycle on special equipment under the supervision of trainer T. W. McCawley.

A special attraction was the famous "electric camel," of which fortunately, photos are still preserved, as well as numerous photos of the Gymnasium shortly before the departure of TITANIC.

Floor Tiles from Villeroy & Boch

Even the quite well-known German company *Villeroy & Boch* has its part in the TITANIC story. The floor tiles and the wall paneling of the bathrooms and toilets on board the luxury liner were created by *Villeroy & Boch*. Depending on the class, the tiles were of different quality and also had different designs. The tiles for the galleys were fitted with deep grooves to minimize the risk of slipping for kitchen staff when the floor was wet.

The tiles in the bathrooms, which were laid in all three classes of the ship, were also given a rough texture rather than a glossy mat finish. Harland & Wolff then decided on the visually appealing mosaic design on the tiles. For years, historians argued about whether the tiles on board had really been made by *Villeroy & Boch*, but on dives to the wreck of the TITANIC, the last doubts were eliminated, as the diving teams found large quantities of floor tiles with the unmistakable mosaic design from *Villeroy & Boch* on the seabed. Afterwards, there was no doubt that the German company had supplied the tiles.

The "TITANIC-Organ" from Bruchsal

One component which was not installed on the TITANIC is highly controversial among experts: the TITANIC organ from Bruchsal!

The company *M. Welte & Söhne*, from Freiburg in Breisgau, is supposed to have built the self-playing salon instrument for the TITANIC on behalf of the *White Star Line*. Due to various circumstances, the organ was not in

England in time (it is said that one component was not finished in time) and could therefore not be installed. The owner, Karl Bockisch-Welten, was already in Southampton and was invited to the maiden voyage of the TITANIC.

Shortly before departure, Bockisch-Welten received a telegram calling him home because a close family member had fallen seriously ill. So Bockisch-Welten did not board the TITANIC and escaped the disaster. Today, the "TITANIC-Organ" is in the Museum of Mechanical Musical Instruments in Bruchsal Castle near Karlsruhe. In September 2011, Brigitte Heck from the Baden State Museum in Karlsruhe attempted to clarify the history once and for all, tracing the stations of the small organ.

But when the researcher searched archives in Germany and abroad for information and contacted experts and private collectors from Europe, Asia, and the USA, she encountered insoluble problems. As a result of the Second World War, important records, and thus certainties, were irretrievably lost at the Welte Organ Building Institute in Freiburg and at the Harland & Wolff shipyard in Belfast. An order from the shipyard to the organ builder in Freiburg can therefore neither be proven nor excluded.

The Last Voyage of the TITANIC

The Maiden Voyage of the TITANIC Begins

On Tuesday evening, April 2nd, 1912, and under the command of Captain Edward John Smith, the TITANIC left the port of Belfast with the destination Southampton, where they anchored at Berth 44. There the ship was subjected to a further inspection by the government - as required by the Merchant Shipping Act of 1894.

> The regulations had been legally binding for 18 years, which was to have fatal consequences for some aspects. The TITANIC had a tonnage four times larger than the LUCANIA, which was the largest ship in the world at the time the regulations were issued. And the regulations had not been modified. The number of lifeboats, for example, was not based on the number of passengers, but on the tonnage of a ship (and that is still taking 18-year-old figures into account).

> In 1887, the chairman of the House of Commons Committee on Maritime Transport, Lord Charles Beresford, had claimed that it was counterproductive to have so many lifeboats on a ship in which all passengers could be accommodated. In bad weather, the crew would not be able to lower all boats before the ship sank anyway (My goodness, this man had limited faith in the crews of ships). He considered it more sensible to keep the ship afloat by all available resources, for example, by dividing the structure of the hull into several watertight compartments.

Today, absolutely not understandable, but the law at that time was Article 112 of the Merchant Shipping Act which even allowed to go below the legal minimum number of lifeboats if the ship's structure had watertight bulkheads, which seemed to the legislators to be safer than the lifeboats. The lifeboats and folding boats of the TITANIC could have accommodated 1178 passengers, which was almost a quarter more than the legal requirement.

In this now, really, totally outdated and unrealistic law, an ocean liner of over 10,000 tons was considered the largest class of ship. The fact that the OLYMPIC and the TITANIC, with over 45,000 tons, went far beyond that was of course not taken into account. Taking into account its 16 watertight compartments, it would even have had to have room for only 960 passengers in the lifeboats. By today's standards an absurdity, but still the law in 1912.

After her arrival in Southampton, the TITANIC was loaded with cargo and supplies from Thursday, April 4th, to Tuesday, April 9th, 1912. Among other things, 40,000 fresh eggs, 75,000 pounds of fresh meat, 20,000 bottles of beer, 1,500 bottles of wine and much more were brought on board the luxury liner.

Not much would have been missing, and the maiden voyage of the TITANIC would have had to be canceled, because on Thursday, February 29th, 1912, the first coal strike in the history of Great Britain had begun. More than a million miners, who supplied fuel to the country and the ships, united in their claim to a statutory minimum salary. They virtually paralyzed the entire country: the trains remained in the station and the ships in the port. Only on Saturday, April 6th, 1912, four days before the maiden voyage of the TITANIC, the government finally gave in to the miners' demands after tough negotiations.

When the TITANIC set out on her maiden voyage, many ships were still anchored in the port of Southampton, as they had not bunkered enough coal to continue their journey. The TITANIC would also have had problems with the amount of coal if the *White Star Line* had not unceremoniously moved the coal from the anchored ships to the luxury liner.

Another problem was that some potential passengers had been deterred by the strike, and so they did not book a passage on the TITANIC. For the *White Star Line*, an almost empty TITANIC on her maiden voyage would have been a publicity disaster, and so the company management decided to offer passengers from the stranded ships a ticket for the maiden voyage of the TITANIC and thus re-book them on the new ship.

One of these ships was the PHILADELPHIA from which some passengers changed to the TITANIC. Among the original passengers of the PHILADELPHIA was the Hart family. When they were offered a passage on the TITANIC, Benjamin Hart was absolutely thrilled. He thought it was wonderful because the whole world was talking about this ship. His wife Esther, on the other hand, had a strange premonition that was completely unusual for her. She said, "*No, we cannot do this. It would be completely wrong. Something terrible will happen!*"

How right Esther Hart was with her premonition, but she could not, of course, have guessed at this time. But four days later, her premonitions were to become a terrible reality! Her husband Benjamin was killed in the sinking of the TITANIC while she and her daughter survived the disaster. The at that time seven-year-old Eva Hart later became one of the most famous and popular TITANIC survivors.

It nearly seems like a bad omen that the departure of the TITANIC from the port of Southampton was almost a disaster.

This pre-sinking RPPC (real photographic postcard) shows Titanic leaving Southampton © collection of the author

When the huge ship was pulled past quays 38 and 39 by the tugboats HERCULES, NEPTUNE, AJAX, ALBERT EDWARD and VULCAN, the enormous mass of water displaced by the TITANIC created such a strong suction, that the mooring ropes of the 158-meter-long NEW YORK, which was tied up at Berth 38, broke loose. The NEW YORK drifted into the middle of the channel, thus heading amidships on a direct collision course with the TITANIC.

The captain of the tug ship VULCAN reacted with lightning speed. He headed for the stern of the NEW YORK instead of making the futile attempt to pull the ship across the bow to the quay where she was anchored. With this action he was able to prevent the NEW YORK from drifting away. Without damaging the TITANIC, the stern of the NEW YORK slid past the luxury liner.

On the Bridge of the TITANIC, Captain Edward John Smith, together with George William Bowyer, a very experienced pilot with over 30 years of professional experience, had stopped the engines and lowered the starboard anchor to just above the waterline. A serious and expensive collision was very closely avoided. The other tugboats in Southampton supported the successful efforts to bring the NEW YORK back to the quay. Due to this whole action, the departure of the TITANIC was delayed by one hour. For many superstitious passengers, this was a very bad omen...

The 15-year-old South African, Edith Brown, who was on her way to Seattle with her parents, where her father wanted to open a hotel, remembered exactly this incident many years later:

"*It looked as if the New York would collide with the Titanic. My father said: 'This is a bad omen!' After that he said nothing more.*"

Almost inevitably, the term, "unsinkable," comes up when talking about the sinking of the TITANIC. But where did this disastrous term originally come from? The merchant shipping journal, "The Shipbuilder," wrote in 1911 about the watertight bulkheads of the OLYMPIC class of the *White Star Line*:

"Each bulkhead is held in the open position by a suitable friction clutch, which can be released immediately by a powerful electromagnet controlled from the bridge, so that in the event of an accident or at any other time when it seems appropriate, the captain can close all the bulkheads immediately by simply moving an electric switch and make the ship practically unsinkable."

As you can see here, there is talk about "practically unsinkable", but the officials of the *White Star Line* talked about the ship being "unsinkable" until the sinking of the TITANIC.

Also, the crew of the TITANIC, including Captain Smith, assumed that the ship could not sink. An "unsinkable ship" simply made itself better known to the public. Also, most of the passengers fatally believed in it, as the later evacuation of the TITANIC should show.
After a short voyage of 80 miles across the English Channel, the TITANIC reached the port of Cherbourg in France at 6:35 p.m. Since she could not dock there due to her enormous size, the 274 passengers (142 in First, 30 in Second and 102 in Third Class) were brought aboard the TITANIC with the tender ships TRAFFIC and NOMADIC.

The Nomadic just after the turn of the century. © public domain

Among the new passengers of the TITANIC brought on board by the NOMADIC were such illustrious names as John Jacob Astor, who went on board to return to America, accompanied by his 19-year-old wife Madeleine, who was five months pregnant.

Margaret, "Molly" Brown, who later became legendary and a friend of Astor's, as well as mining millionaire, Benjamin Guggenheim and his 24-year-old lover, Ninette Aubart, also boarded the luxury liner.
Most of the passengers in Third Class came from Croatia, Armenia, Syria and other Middle Eastern countries. They were all united by the hope for a better life in America.

The restored Nomadic in Belfast in 2017 © private photo of the author

In Cherbourg, 22 passengers (15 in First Class and seven in Second Class) left the Ship. They had paid one and a half and one-pound sterling, respectively, for the rather short crossing from Southampton to Cherbourg, but were satisfied to have crossed the channel on the TITANIC.

After a short stay, the huge ship left Cherbourg at 8.10 p.m. and set off for her last stop on land - Queenstown (now Cobh) where she was to pick up the remaining passengers. She arrived in about 15 hours. Sometime during this time, probably even earlier, a heavy smoldering fire broke out in a coal bunker in Boiler Room No. 5 on starboard side. Eight to ten men were called away to extinguish the burning coal while the guards were on duty. This smoldering fire is still a recurring theme when writing about the reasons for the sinking of the TITANIC (see chapter "Interesting Conspiracy Theories and Bad Omens").

On the morning of 11th April 1912, the TITANIC was heading west, and Captain Smith carried out some test maneuvers without any problems. When the ship was near Queenstown, the speed was reduced to allow the pilot to get on board.

In Queenstown, a large crowd of people had already gathered, eagerly awaiting the arrival of the TITANIC. As there was no pier in Queenstown where the huge TITANIC could have docked, the *White Star* Liner dropped anchor three kilometers from Roches Point.

The tenders AMERICA and IRELAND brought 113 passengers in Third Class and seven passengers in Second Class on board. In addition, the TITANIC took 1,385 mail bags aboard. After all, the TITANIC did not wrongly bear the designation RMS (Royal Mail Steamer). Moreover, it was a profitable business for the *White Star Line*.

In order to check the number of passengers again, the Immigration Officer E. J. Sharpe boarded TITANIC. A number of traders were allowed on board to trade in their Irish lace and fabrics. Among other things, John Jacob Astor purchased a silk scarf for his wife on this occasion.

Meanwhile, seven passengers left the ship. Among them was 32-year-old Jesuit Priest Francis Browne, to whom we owe some of the last surviving photographs of the TITANIC. One of the showpieces of this collection is undoubtedly the last known photograph of Captain Edward John Smith, which shows him on the starboard side of the Bridge, looking down at the TITANIC. A photograph of Radio Operator Harold Bride at his workplace on board has also been preserved. The Odell family took some remarkable photos as well which are also still preserved.

Before their departure from Queenstown, the American flag was raised on the upper deck, indicating New York as the next port of call. At 1.30 p.m., the TITANIC pulled up her starboard anchor for the last time and began her fateful voyage to New York.

The 29-year-old Irishman, Eugene Daly, had boarded in Queenstown. While the TITANIC slowly left the Irish coast behind, he played the Irish ballad Erin's Lament at the stern of the ship.

For the 708 Third Class passengers, like Eugene Daly, it was very difficult to find their way around the huge ship in the following days. When you consider that even the officers of the TITANIC had some trouble to find their way and still got lost in places, you can easily imagine how difficult it was for the passengers in the steerage.

A further sign of the importance of the passengers in Third Class in the eyes of the *White Star Line* was, for example, the fact that there were only two bathtubs for the many people in the steerage, around which one had to stand in line. What a difference to the luxury in First and Second Class!

However, the accommodation and catering for the Third-Class passengers was downright luxurious compared to other ships of that time. The mere fact that there were several rich meals a day, served to them on top of that, was completely unusual for the majority of the steerage passengers.

Thus, there was a very comprehensive breakfast, a multi-course lunch menu with pre-soup, (most of the time a vegetable soup), a main course (consisting of potatoes, vegetables, and meat, afterwards fruit), a kind of smaller tea-time (simple pastry with a choice of tea, hot milk or hot cacao) and for Third Class Passengers, a sumptuous dinner with a final hot milk or hot cacao.

How extraordinary these rich meals were for the passengers in Third Class is shown by statements of surviving stewards who reported that at lunch, the passengers had to be told that after the pre-soup, the actual main menu would be served. A large part of the passengers believed after eating the soup that this was the end of lunch and that they had to get up...

The *White Star Line* was so clever from a marketing point of view that every menu was designed as a postcard on the back so that, for example, emigrants who wanted to catch up with their families back home could send these cards as proof of the opulent meals on board. The aim of this message was clear: if the meals in Third Class were so good and opulent, the next family should emigrate on a *White Star Line* steamer if possible.

Most of the capacity on board the luxury liner was used for the fewest passengers, as the First-Class Dining

Room on D Deck had room for 600 passengers, while the least capacity was used for the Third-Class passengers. This made it necessary that the Third-Class Passengers could not all take their meals together. So, they had two meal sessions in a row, half an hour apart. Those who missed one session could not eat the same meal half an hour later.

Another anecdote is that almost half of the passengers in steerage had never seen running water or electric light. According to the stewards, the toilets were constantly blocked by children who probably saw a water closet for the first time in their lives. The children were constantly standing there and pulling the chain, because they liked the whirling sound and the flowing water so much.

Lucky Coincidences of Fate

The sinking of the TITANIC on April 15th, 1912, is one of the most famous ship disasters of all times. By a lucky coincidence of fate, some people were not on board the tragic luxury liner despite having a ticket for the maiden voyage. Here are some of their stories:

Reverend J. Stuart Holden

After receiving his ticket, J. Stuart Holden, vicar of St. Paul's Church, Portman Square in London, prepared for his forthcoming trip to America on the TITANIC. In America he was to speak at the six-day Christian Conservation Congress at the famous Carnegie Hall in Manhattan, New York City. Holden was to deliver his speech on Saturday, April 20th, 1912.

But luckily for him, things turned out differently. His wife suddenly fell ill, and since a speedy recovery was not to be expected, Holden postponed his trip on Tuesday, April 9th, 1912, one day before the luxury liner was due to leave port, in order to take care of his sick wife. His boarding pass remained for posterity, and after the sinking of the TITANIC, he had this card framed with the inscription *"He delivers you from death"*.

The card remained in the family after Holden's death in 1934 before it became part of the collection of the Merseyside Maritime Museum in Liverpool.

John Pierpont Morgan

The American financier of the *White Star Line*, John Pierpont Morgan, was also originally supposed to be on board the maiden voyage of the TITANIC, but he canceled his passage for the so-called "Millionaire Suite" B 32 at literally the last minute on the grounds that he did not feel comfortable.

However, on Wednesday 17th April 1912, two days after the ship sank, Morgan, accompanied by his French girlfriend, was found in apparently perfect health in the French spa town of Aix-les-Bains. Whether he really canceled the crossing for health reasons or because he preferred to enjoy himself with his girlfriend is not known...

George Vanderbilt

One of the most famous cancellations is probably that of the extremely rich millionaire, George Vanderbilt, who wanted to travel on the TITANIC together with his wife Edith.

According to tradition, his mother got a bad feeling about the crossing (*"so many things can go wrong on a maiden voyage"*) and urged George Vanderbilt not to travel on the TITANIC so urgently that he canceled the voyage on Monday, April 8th, 1912.

For the TITANIC, the Vanderbilts had booked a First-Class Cabin befitting their status, while for their servant Frederick Wheeler, they booked a comfortable cabin in Second Class. As the cancellation was too short notice, the luggage remained on board the TITANIC, and Frederick Wheeler stayed on board (by the way, he can be seen on a very famous photo from the maiden voyage in which he is walking on the deck of the TITANIC with passengers Ada and Elsie Doling).

Unfortunately, Frederick Wheeler did not survive the sinking of the TITANIC. He went down with the Vanderbilts' luggage. His body was never found.

According to some accounts, Alfred Gwynne Vanderbilt was to have been another Vanderbilt on board the TITANIC. He was the nephew of George Vanderbilt, and according to a report in the New York Times, he boarded the luxury liner in Cherbourg. However, this report turned out to be wrong, because on the day of the sinking of the TITANIC, when the terrible news spread worldwide, he sent a telegram to his mother that he did not go aboard the ship after all and that he was safe in London.

However, this did not save Alfred Vanderbilt from death in a sinking, for three years later, he was killed in the legendary sinking of the *Cunard* liner, LUSITANIA, on Friday, 7th May, 1915.

Family Jensen from Third Class

Some passengers in Third Class also missed their passage on the TITANIC. On the North Sea island of Föhr in the village of Alkersum, the story of the Jensen family, who actually wanted to travel on the TITANIC, is still told today.

The news of the sinking of the TITANIC also spread on the tranquil North Sea island of Föhr. And on Friday, April 19th, 1912, the "Föhrer Zeitung" reported in its headline: *"Terrible ship disaster. 1500 people drowned!"* In her notes, Christina Martens (1902-1982) remembered this day exactly when her father picked up the newspaper as usual after dinner with the family:

"Then a look appeared on his face that we never saw before. He read for a long time without saying a word. We didn't start with our schoolwork either and sat there helplessly, because we were waiting for something and didn't know what it was. Then father said: 'The Titanic has sunk!' At last, we knew what was in the air so eerily. In the night, from 14th to 15th April 1912, the big luxury steamer had hit an iceberg and had dragged people down with it in 1517. What shook me most was that the band had played to the very end."

The evening story time for Christina's little brother was canceled. She kept silent after this news because, *"If the Titanic goes down, you can't tell fairy tales."*

Meanwhile, in the small Frisian village of Alkersum, people remained in fear and prayed for a message from their relatives. It was about Johann Diedrich Jensen, born in 1874, who had emigrated to America in 1890 at the age of 16, where he worked on his uncle's farm and supported many islanders in their new home (there is still a remarkably large community of former Föhrers in America today). One of them was the young Alkersum woman, Inge Margarethe Boyen (born in 1877), called Getje, whom he married in 1901.

Ten years later, John D., as he was called in America, and Getje visited the old Föhrer home together with their four children. It was almost their last visit to the island of their ancestors because Johann Diedrich Jensen wanted to treat his family to something special and had booked a passage on the TITANIC for the entire family.

Shortly before departure on Wednesday, April 10th, 1912, however, all the children fell ill with measles and were not allowed to board the ship with this contagious disease. This saved the lives of the entire Jensen family.

The Ice Warnings

No other part of the sinking of the TITANIC is more controversially discussed than the question why the ship's command around Captain Edward John Smith did not reduce the speed of the luxury liner after numerous warnings of ice from other ships.

It is without a doubt that the TITANIC was enough warned about ice. This is proven by the documents of the other ships and the radio stations which prove that the warnings were received on the TITANIC. Some messages were directly addressed to the great liner, while other ships used the TITANIC as a relay station to transmit the messages.

To this day, it is unclear what happened with the messages on board the luxury liner and if all messages were really reported to Captain Smith and his officers.

Especially on Sunday, 14th April a large number of ice warnings were received quite early by the two Wireless Operators, Jack Phillips and Harold Bride, in the Wireless Room.

At 9.12 a.m. the *Cunard Line* steamship, CARONIA, which was traveling from New York to Liverpool, sent a two-day-old ice message to the TITANIC:

"Captain, 'Titanic.' West-bound steamers report bergs, growlers, and field ice in 42 degrees N., from 49 to 51 W. April 12. Compliments. Barr."

The time information always refers to TITANIC time on board. So, the time which was valid on board of the luxury liner.

This message had been given to Smith, who put it on display in the Chart Room for his officers.

At 11.40 a.m. the Dutch steamship NOORDAM also reported ice in almost the same area as the CARONIA.

The ice warning of the BALTIC (*"From S.S. 'Baltic,' April 14th, to Captain Smith, Titanic, have had mod var [moderate variable] winds and clear fine weather since leaving. Greek steamer Athenai reports passing icebergs and large quantities of field ice today in lat. 41 51 N., long. 49 52 W. Last night we spoke German oil-tank steamer Deutschland, Stettin to Philadelphia, not under control, short of coal, lat. 40 42 N. long. 55 11 W. Wishes to be reported to New York and other steamers. Wish you and Titanic all success. - Commander."*) which arrived at 1.54 p.m., has become famous because of Bruce Ismay (see "The Destroyed Reputation of Bruce Ismay").

From the Wireless Room of the TITANIC, the following answer came at 1.57 p.m.: "*To Commander Baltic. Thank you for your message and good wishes; we've had good weather since departure.*"

According to the sworn statement of the captain of the BALTIC, the BALTIC had sent a second message to the TITANIC, which was noted as sent in the radio logbook of the BALTIC, but the wording of which was not listed:

"*The Baltic sailed from New York to Liverpool on Thursday 11th April. And on Sunday 14th April, messages were received from a number of ships which had passed ice and mountains at positions between 49° 9°` and 50° 20°` West on the southern route to New York. These ice messages were sent in the usual way to all other ships with radio communication, including the TITANIC. The messages were sent just before noon, New York time. Our radio operator received a reply from the TITANIC at 1:00 am the same day (3:00 pm TITANIC time, "author's note")*"

At 5.03 p.m., the German passenger steamer AMERIKA reported to the US Navy's Naval Observatory:

"*Two icebergs at 41°27° N, 50° 8° W on April 14th.*"

The Naval Observatory passed this information on to the *North Atlantic Shipping Company*, and it was received by Jack Phillips on the TITANIC. Phillips allegedly kept this warning to himself, as he was busy with other telegrams. However, Fourth Officer Joseph Groves Boxhall later testified that he was informed about the message...

Around 7.30 p.m., the TITANIC again operated as a relay station, this time for the steamer CALIFORNIAN which sent a message to the TITANIC Radio Room for the ANTILLIAN which was on its way east:

"*To the captain of the Antillian: 18.30 pm ship time; 42° 3`N, 49° 9`W, Three large icebergs 5 miles south. Greetings, Lord.*" This was about 30 kilometers north of the course of the TITANIC, which continued to cross the Atlantic with high speed. According to Harold Bride, he gave this message to an officer on the Bridge, but later he did not know to whom he had given it. At least that was his version after the disaster...

At 9.52 p.m., Jack Phillips was in charge in the Wireless Room when he received a message from the SS MESABA heading west:

"From 'Mesaba' to 'Titanic.' In latitude 42 N. to 41.25, longitude 49 W. to longitude 50.30 W., saw much heavy pack ice and great number large icebergs, also field ice, weather good, clear."

Since 1912 this message has been the subject of much controversy, because Phillips put it aside at first and did not forward it, since now the Cape Race Land Station in Newfoundland was within range of the TITANIC, and he now saw the opportunity to finally send the messages that had accumulated during the day.

But this ice warning was directly addressed to the TITANIC, and he would have been obliged to deliver it to the bridge immediately. That he presumably did not do so was to prove fatal, because this warning roughly indicated the position where the TITANIC later sank...

For Second Officer Ligtholler, this message was the most important one of them all:

"The one vital warning that was sent to us but never reached the bridge came from the Mesaba. This omission was the main reason for the loss of the ship!

However, it is still disputed whether this message really did not reach the Bridge, or whether this is just another claim of protection of the surviving officers of the TITANIC.

Of course, this message would have been more than suitable to reduce the speed of the ship and to operate much more carefully. But the ship's command around Smith did not do this and continued to sail through the night at much too high a speed. Is this an indication that the message was not known? It would have been negligent to ignore the warning, but since the *White Star Line* did everything possible to cover up their own negligence that night, it is not really out of the question that the message was known but the Bridge continued as before. After the disaster it was easier to blame a dead man (Jack Phillips) for not reporting it, than to admit that they knew about it but didn't react to it.

It also seems that the opinion prevailed on the Bridge that every iceberg on the ship's course could be seen in time under such good visibility conditions as that night, and that there was no need to reduce the speed. Smith acted with this in exactly the same way, as it was usual at that time. The ship continued to sail at high speed until an object was identified.

At 11.00 p.m., a very important event took place which probably finally sealed the catastrophe. Phillips was still busy with the radio communication with Cape Race when he was interrupted by a deafening signal from the obviously very close CALIFORNIAN:

"*MGY MGY MGY! Say, old man, we are stopped and surrounded by ice.*"

Annoyed and almost numb by the message in the ether, Phillips called back:

"Shut up, shut up, I am busy; I am working Cape Race"

The position of the CALIFORNIAN could not be communicated to their Wireless Operator Cyril Evans. He waited about 15 minutes for the TITANIC to give him the possibility to give the position, but there was no answer anymore. Since Evans had been on duty all day and was completely exhausted, he went to bed and switched off the transmitter. So even this very important ice warning never reached the officials on the Bridge of the TITANIC!

For Radio Historian Parks Stephenson, the case is clear: The mistake was on the side of Cyril Evans, the Wireless Operator of the CALIFORNIAN, because he did not prefix his report with the abbreviation MSG (Master Service Gramm). This abbreviation indicates that this message is intended for the Bridge of the ship. According to Stephenson, Jack Phillips had the right to ignore this important message.

Be that as it may, Captain Smith and his officers, all of whom had a Captain's Patent, had ample opportunity to respond to the numerous reports. But apart from a slight course correction which Smith made at 5.50 p.m. (the TITANIC slightly changed her course from S 62° W to S 86° W), nothing happened...

The Iceberg Collision

In recent years, intensive research has revealed a different view of the events during and after the collision of the TITANIC with the iceberg, which will now be discussed in more detail.

It is a fact that the TITANIC hit the iceberg at 11:40 p.m., but according to experts, lookouts Frederick Fleet and Reginald Lee are said to have seen the iceberg much earlier.

Frederick Fleet testified before the American Inquiry that he saw the iceberg at 11:30 p.m. However, as is well known, the collision did not take place until 11:40 p.m., ten minutes later. Mrs. Crosby, a First-Class Passenger, made a very interesting statement to the American Inquiry, which throws a slightly different light on the matter:

"*On the Carpathia, passengers said that the lookout who was on watch when the Titanic touched the iceberg said: I know they will blame me for this, but it was not my fault; I warned the officers three or four times that we were near icebergs, but they did not pay attention to my signals.'*"

Though most TITANIC experts assume that Frederick Fleet was mentioned here as the lookout, in front of the two inquiries, Fleet made no reference to this direction - probably in order not to present his employer *White Star Line* in a negative light...

Very interesting as well is the testimony of Able Seaman Joseph Scarrott on Friday, May 3rd, 1912, before the British Inquiry:

Mr. Butler Aspinall: *"How quickly did they feel the shock after hearing the three bells?"*

Joseph Scarrott: *"Since I did not hear the three bells, I can hardly remember. But I think it was five or eight minutes, or at least it seemed that way to me."*

The question here is what bells Scarrott meant. It can hardly have been the all-decisive one if it took five to eight minutes until the ship was shocked by the collision.
That rather allows the assumption that Fleet really did strike the bell several times, but it was the one shortly before the collision that was reacted to on the bridge.

Contrary to the general historiography since the sinking, some experts believe that Captain Smith was probably also on the Bridge during the collision. At least First-Class Passenger George Brayton claims to have seen Smith on the Bridge:

"Some of us enjoyed the fresh air and walked on deck. Captain Smith was on the bridge when the lookout yelled for the first time that there was an iceberg ahead of us. It was about one meter high when I saw it and maybe 200 meters ahead of us. Captain Smith gave some orders... Some of us ran to the bow of the ship. When we saw we had to hit it, we ran to the stern. Then there was a crash, and the passengers panicked."

Whether or not this statement is to be trusted, it remains to be seen...

In the night of April 14th, unique weather conditions prevailed on the course of the TITANIC, because it was starry, windless and there was no moon. This meant that you could see the stars reflected in the water. There was a continuous curtain of stars on the course of the ship, and there was very good visibility.

This lulled the officers of the TITANIC into apparent safety. But then the iceberg appeared at a distance of about 450 meters, which Fleet and Lee initially only perceived as a small black hole and which only slowly began to appear against the star curtain. What really happened in the seconds between Fleet's report of the iceberg and the collision on the bridge of the TITANIC is still a mystery today.

That the TITANIC only hit a single iceberg on her way, which appeared as if from nowhere, as the responsible persons of the *White Star Line* would have us believe, is more than questionable. Just considering how much ice was on the ship's course, it is more likely that the TITANIC was in the middle of a huge ice field and was simply traveling much too fast there!

Some survivors of the crew later testified that command to Helmsman Hichens had read: "*Hard to starboard and full speed astern!*" But that is, according to our present knowledge, highly improbable...

If there was only the "hard to starboard" rudder command, to which Robert Hichens' helmsman attached great importance, then according to the spare helmsman at the stern, the whole side of the ship would have had to be torn open. Thus, for Titanic Historian Susanne Störmer (German Titanic Society), it is a blatant contradiction that the damage was only in the front part of the ship.

If the TITANIC had indeed only followed the rudder command "hard to starboard", the ship would have gone straight on for quite a while, then the bow would have had to move to the left and thus would have passed the iceberg. But since the ship is steered at the stern, it would have sheared off and headed for the iceberg with the rudder, with the fatal result that the TITANIC would have collided with the iceberg with its full broadside and would have suffered great damage from the middle of the ship to the stern. But exactly that did not happen! The damage occurred only in the first 90 meters of the ship, so the command "hard to starboard" is rather improbable...

Rather, conceivable is a so-called "port around maneuver" which is mandatory for ships of this size. The aim is to steer the stern of the ship freely and out of the danger zone. Also, the replacement Rudder Man, George Thomas Rowe, explained to the American Inquiry that there is only one way to avoid an obstacle: To steer the ship first to port and then to starboard, like an S-curve.

Also controversial is the handed-down command, "full speed back," to the Engine Room. Such a command would hardly have been feasible in the time remaining. For the Titanic Historian Günter Bäbler (Titanic Society Switzerland), the case is crystal clear that it would have taken several minutes before it would have been possible to execute this command with the crew available at the time of the collision (two relatively inexperienced engineers) ...

Of the four survivors from the Engine Room who were there at the time of the collision, none of them can remember the command "full reverse power". They all agreed that they received only the order to stop. But what happened in the collision? The maneuver initiated by Murdoch prevented a head-on collision of the TITANIC with the iceberg, and from the point of view of Frederick Fleet and Reginald Lee in the Crow's Nest, it looked as if they had been lucky again, because the ship slid past the iceberg on the starboard side. Or so it seemed...

However, appearances are tedious, because the TITANIC scraped along the iceberg and probably sailed over an underwater spur of the iceberg. The force of the impact pressed the rivets of the ship into place, allowing water to enter the ship through the open seams in at least five different places. Although the damage added up to just 1.2 square meters, it was the death for the TITANIC!

Should Murdoch perhaps have risked driving head-on into the iceberg against the rules to prevent greater damage, as many experts believed after the disaster?

This inevitably raises the question of whether it would have been normal to drive into an obstacle if it was still possible to avoid it. To this day, historians still disagree on how much damage a head-on collision with the high speed of the TITANIC would have caused to the ship. For sure at least two, if not three watertight compartments of the ship would have been flooded immediately, not to mention the devastating damage to the bow that would have resulted. But she would probably have remained afloat, although recent studies also doubt this, citing the very high speed of the TITANIC on impact with the iceberg as the main reason.

But would a head-on collision really have been an option for Murdoch? Probably not, because that would have been the immediate end of his career with the utmost certainty, because he couldn't explain to anybody why he, despite the still existing possibility to avoid the iceberg, simply drove into it. So, this possibility falls out from the beginning, even if it seems to many people interested in TITANIC as a chance to prevent the later sinking.

> **To find out whether the rivets on the ship were not correctly processed, scientists carried out several tests with rivets recovered from the wreck, and the result was quite clear. The rivets used in the construction of the ship were not strong enough to withstand the collision with the iceberg!**
>
> **Some of the rivets had been applied mechanically, others manually. To rivet the ship's hull, the workers of the Harland & Wolff shipyard in Belfast used a huge machine.**
>
> **However, as this machine was too big to be used on the front part of the ship, this part was processed manually.**

Wrought iron rivets were used, as they are easier to process manually. But wrought iron is less durable than steel. The workers were aware of this problem.

To compensate for this weakness, a slag substance was added to the molten iron. By forming tiny glass particles inside the metal, the rivets can be made more durable. But the mixture of iron and slag is questionable. If the dosage is not correct, the opposite effect - namely weakening of the rivets - can be the result!

In the case of the TITANIC, it seems that exactly this effect has occurred, because the riveting of the ship shows clear weaknesses. Unfortunately, the concentration of the slag was so high that it led to weakening of the rivets.

But a point which should not be forgotten is: Back in 1912, the steel used for the Olympic-class liner was the best steel of the time.

Compared with each other, the steel we are using nowadays is better due to the technical progress, but that does not mean that the TITANIC was built out of weak steel. The opposite was the case: The *White Star Line* and Harland & Wolff used the best steel available!

Another very controversial point is that some survivors later reported that the TITANIC had taken up speed again. This decision by the ship's command may have caused much more water to enter the ship, thus considerably accelerating the sinking process. Also, the TITANIC Historian Claes-Göran Wetterholm, who himself has organized several successful TITANIC exhibitions, believes that the TITANIC was still sailing at half speed for about ten minutes after the collision, perhaps because the Bridge was of the opinion that the damage was not that serious?

At least that would solve a mystery that appeared in the late 90s. During some dives to the wreck of the TITANIC in 3,800 meters depth, several machine telegraphs were discovered on the seafloor, which were set in the position "half power ahead". This could not be explained at that time, but if the TITANIC really was still running at half power for about ten minutes after the collision, this would be the logical explanation for the discovery.

But why did the TITANIC, which was also obviously damaged for the ship's management, continue to sail? The granddaughter of Second Officer Charles Herbert Lightoller stated in 2012 that Joseph Bruce Ismay himself had urged the captain to continue after the collision. Whether this is really true, however, cannot be clarified any further.

> In the epilogue to her book, "Good as Gold," the granddaughter of Charles Herbert Lightoller, Louise Patten, admitted that Joseph Bruce Ismay put her grandfather under massive pressure, even before the arrival of the CARPATHIA in New York,
> to protect the shipping company and all the jobs connected with it by making appropriate statements.

Thus, Lightoller is said to have covered up the real cause of the accident in order not to jeopardize the existence of the *White Star Line*. Furthermore, according to Patten, quartermaster Robert Hichens confused port and starboard during the evasive maneuver, which then led to the fact that the decisive seconds for clear steering were missing!

Many passengers perceived the collision with the iceberg completely differently, if they noticed it at all:
"*I didn't feel much, and we thought the ship had lost the rudder or something like that. Someone said, 'Another trip to Belfast.'*"
(James Johnson, a steward in the First-Class Dining Room, busy preparing the dining room for breakfast)

"*Suddenly we felt a loop that somehow seemed to turn the whole room slightly. As far as I could make out, they all rose and some of them hurried quickly through the swinging doors on the port side to the railing behind the mast. I stood there and listened to the gentlemens' speculations. They were wondering what might have happened, and one of them shouted, 'A mountain has passed aft,' but I don't know who shouted that. I have not seen the man since.*"
(Hugh Woolner, a First-Class passenger who played cards with Major Archibald Butt and Clarence Moore in the First-Class Smoking Room)

"*My wife woke me up and said, 'Wake up, you're dreaming!' I was actually dreaming, and when I woke up, I heard a slight bump. I didn't pay attention until I noticed that the machines had stopped. When the machines stopped, I said: 'This is something serious; something is wrong. Let's go up on deck just in case'*".

(Testimony of First-Class passenger Charles E. Stengel on Tuesday, April 30th, 1912, during the American Inquiry)

"My husband woke me up at a quarter to twelve and told me that the ship had rammed something. We got dressed and went up on deck, looked around and couldn't find anything. We noticed this immense cold. In fact, we had already noticed it around eleven o'clock that night. It had been uncomfortably cold in the lungs. We looked all over the deck, walking up and down a couple of times, when one of the stewards (it was probably the steward Alfred Crawford – "author's note") came and smiled at us. He said, 'You can go back down. There's nothing to worry about. We just hit a little piece of ice and drove by.' So, we went back to our cabin and went to bed."

(Testimony given by First Class passenger Mrs. Helen W. Bishop on Tuesday, April 30th, 1912, during the American Inquiry)

"I felt the collision in all its violence. My comrades and I were thrown from our bunks onto the floor. It was a hard, scratching sound. I crashed on deck and saw that the forward corrugated deck was covered with chunks of ice torn out of the iceberg. We went back down and grabbed some clothes. Our boss, William Small, burst in and shouted, 'Everybody down!' But we couldn't go down through the ladder shafts into the boiler room because the water was rising; you could see it clearly. So, we had to climb up to the main deck. Next, the top heater came running up and ordered us to return, put on life jackets and go up to the boat deck. Thus, we go back to the front of the ship, put on our life jackets and climb up to the boat deck. The officer in charge wanted to know 'what the hell' we were doing and sent us back down."

(Fireman John Thompson)

"It sounded like chains clanking along the ship. It happened so fast that I thought there was something wrong with the engines on the starboard side... At the request of my wife, I set out to find out what had happened... I looked to the starboard end of our corridor, from where an iron walkway leads to the quarters of the postal workers and on to the baggage room and, I think, the mail sorting room. At the top of the iron stairs, I found two postal workers, wet to the knees, who had been bringing up straight bags of registered mail from below. Since the door in the bulkhead of the deck below was open, I could look straight into the luggage compartment; there the water was already up to half a meter below the ceiling. We stood there and joked about the soaked luggage and the letters floating on the water.
(First Class passenger Norman C. Chambers who was in cabin E 8)

From these statements one can already see how differently the collision of the TITANIC with the iceberg was perceived by the passengers and crew members.

Absolutely bizarre, however, is how Quartermaster Rowe experienced the collision with the iceberg. At the time of the collision, he was keeping watch on the Docking Bridge. He had seen the iceberg, which was close enough to reflect the ship's bright white lights. After a few seconds, the iceberg had disappeared into the darkness. Rowe assumed that they had managed to avoid the iceberg, and he believed that if anything really important happened, he would be taken off his post, so he kept his watch and did not think about the incident any further.

An hour went by. Rowe saw no one, heard nothing. And then a lifeboat floated down under him on the starboard side. He picked up the phone and called the Bridge.

"*What's wrong?*", asked a nervous voice at the other end.
"*There's a lifeboat off to starboard.*"
"*Who is it?*"

The voice was no longer nervous, but incredulous.
"*Quartermaster Rowe*", he answered, "*I am keeping watch on the aft bridge. Is there anything wrong? Do you know there's a lifeboat in the water?*"
"*Yes. There is something wrong. Come to the bridge immediately and bring distress rockets with you.*"

Rowe climbed down from the Poop Deck, pulled a crate of distress rockets out of the cupboard and ran to the Bridge. He was the last member of the crew to learn that the TITANIC was going down. It was almost 1:00 a.m. in the morning...

The Evacuation of the Ship

Shortly after the collision with the iceberg, Thomas Andrews was commissioned to inspect the damage of the TITANIC.

He was confronted with a terrible situation:

Within a very short time, ice-cold seawater had made its way into the ship, damaging at least five of the 16 watertight compartments to such an extent that the ship could no longer be saved.

The collision with the iceberg had damaged the Forepeak, the Cargo Rooms and Boiler Room No. 6. Under certain circumstances the ship could have withstood water in four compartments, but a fifth (now there is even talk of six damaged compartments) flooded compartment was definitely too much for the TITANIC!

When Andrews returned to the Bridge, he told the shocked captain that, according to his calculations, the ship had at most two hours left before it would sink forever in the icy waters of the North Atlantic. Captain Smith was fully aware that there was only a lifeboat place for about half of the 2,200 people on board - a terrible situation!

The Fourth Officer, Joseph Groves Boxhall, was ordered by Smith to calculate the current position of the TITANIC in order to make a distress call as soon as possible. Boxhall immediately went to the Chart Room and calculated the world-famous coordinates 41°46°`N,

50°14°`W from the data available to him and wrote them on a piece of paper which he then handed over to Smith.

> Since the official discovery of the TITANIC wreck on Sunday, September 1st, 1985, it is clear that Boxhall had miscalculated. The location of the wreck is at 41°43°`N, 49°56°`W, which is 13.2 nautical miles (24.5 kilometers) away from the place Boxhall had calculated on April 15th, 1912!

With the calculated position, E. J. Smith personally went to the Wireless Room, where he instructed the astonished wireless operator, Jack Phillips, to send the international distress code CQD with the given position to other ships to come to the help of the TITANIC.

At 12:15 a.m., Phillips sent the first distress call, which was received by the French ship LA PROVENCE, the Canadian ship MOUNT TEMPLE and the land station Cape Race. At 12:25 a.m., Phillips sent a distress call to all ships:

"*Immediate assistance. Running on iceberg. CQD. Position 41°46°`N, 50°14°`W.* "

This radio message was received at a distance of 58 nautical miles (107 kilometers) by the 21-year-old Wireless Operator Harold Cottam, who was about to go to bed on the *Cunard* steamer CARPATHIA. When he received the CQD message from the TITANIC, Cottam didn't believe his ears. The TITANIC in danger on her maiden voyage? It couldn't be. Or could it? He transmitted back to the TITANIC as soon as he heard the CQD transmission:

"Should I inform my captain? Do you need help?"

The answer from Jack Phillips was clear: *"Yes, come quickly, we are sinking!"*

Cottam immediately rushed into the cabin of his captain, Arthur Henry Rostron. When Cottam told him about the situation of the TITANIC and assured him that it was serious, Rostron immediately mobilized his crew and set the CARPATHIA in motion to the stated position of the TITANIC.

At 12:35 a.m., Cottam transmitted back to the TITANIC:

"Course changed. We're coming in under extreme power!"

On the TITANIC, however, the evacuation of the passengers proceeded very slowly. There was no general ship alarm, and so the stewards knocked respectfully on the cabin doors and asked the perplexed passengers to get up, put on their life jackets and proceed to the Boat Deck. At least that's what happened in First and Second Class, according to tradition. In Third Class, it seems that not all passengers were woken up. Some of the passengers on the steerage were probably woken up by the water flowing into their cabin!

Some of the steerage passengers soon realized that something very bad must have happened - they saw with their own eyes that there was water in the ship.

Third Class passenger Carl Jonsson remembered: *"When I started to get dressed, I noticed that water was coming* towards my feet. It rose slowly at first, but after a while I was up to my ankles in it."

It remains unclear to this day whether, for example, the stewards were informed that the TITANIC would sink. It seems at least that a large part of them did not know...

At least in the initial phase of the evacuation, First and Second-Class passengers were not aware of the danger to their lives. For many, it became too cold on the Boat Deck, and they went back inside the ship. There was really no time to lose...

However, Second Class passenger Lawrence Beesley realized a little faster that something was wrong with the huge luxury liner. The inclination of the TITANIC was hardly noticeable at first, but Lawrence Beesley noticed it:

"When I passed the door to go down, I looked forward, and to my great surprise I recognized a slight inclination from back to front. Just a slight deviation, which I didn't think anyone would have noticed, - which in any case was hardly noticeable."

After the disaster, some experts have suggested that the TITANIC would have sunk much more slowly if the watertight doors had been left open, which would have resulted in a more even distribution of the intruding water. In the 1990s, a model experiment was undertaken to clarify this question. The result was that such a decision would have had fatal consequences for the ship and its passengers. If the doors had been opened, all Boiler and Engine Rooms would have been flooded.

> As a result, the entire power supply would have collapsed, and the passengers would have had to wander through the ship in complete darkness. As a further consequence, the ship would have laid on its side, and by far, not all lifeboats would have been able to be launched. The investigation came to the conclusion that the TITANIC would have sunk a full 33 minutes earlier!

In the lower decks of the TITANIC, people tried to get on the Boat Deck, which was impossible for many of them - they came from all over the world and were mostly not able to speak English, which was very problematic on a completely English-speaking ship. Furthermore, they were faced with the problem that especially in the lower decks the ship was so twisted that many passengers suddenly got stuck in a dead end and could not get further.

When they got further, they would find themselves in front of locked iron gates in some places, which prevented them from leaving the steerage. This was not done maliciously, however, but was common on ships of the time to shield Third Class passengers from the upper decks and to prevent the outbreak of diseases.

Much more obstructive for the Third-Class passengers and their rescue was their "barrier in their heads". Actually, the iron gates were superfluous, because hardly any of the steerage passengers would have seriously considered entering the First-Class area in order to get up to the Boat Deck. Unfortunately, the class principle worked absolutely perfectly on the TITANIC, so most of the Third-Class passengers stayed down in the belly of the ship and waited for someone to tell them what to do. After all, they had been used to it all their lives...

However, it can be assumed that the ship's command simply forgot to give the order to open the gates in the general rush. In some cases, this did not really stop the passengers from getting to the top, according to later traditions - they simply tore down the bars!

21-year-old Daniel Buckley later remembered this:

"Some sailors tried to hold us down. When one of us tried to open the door to the third-class stairwell to the first-class deck, some guy pushed him down and locked the door. So, we kicked it in."

Some of the stewards who had observed this seemed to be more interested in accusing the passengers of damage to *White Star Line* property than in helping them - typical for that time.

Once it was clear that the TITANIC was sinking, Captain Smith instructed his officers to put "women and children first" into the lifeboats. What would happen to the men on board he left unanswered.

On the Boat Deck the crew started to clear the lifeboats under the perplexed looks of some passengers who had noticed that the TITANIC must have collided with an obstacle. Now, however, the canceled lifeboat maneuver had a negative effect, because a large part of the crew had enormous problems with loading and lowering the lifeboats, because they were not sufficiently or not at all familiar with the newly created Wellin-Davits. Actually, a briefing would have been absolutely necessary there as well...

On this night it was of existential importance, especially for the male passengers, on which side of the ship they tried to get into a lifeboat. The reason for that was that on the port side of the ship, Second Officer Lightoller was in command and he interpreted the rule, "women and children first," so strictly that he made it, "women and children only." He preferred to lower the boats half-empty than to fill them up with men!

This behavior led to partly grotesque scenes, because he refused even boys to enter the lifeboats, who were not of full age by far, on the grounds that they were "men". The 13-year-old John Ryerson, for example, owed his survival solely to the courageous intervention of his father, who dissuaded Lightoller from sending his son to a certain death. Arthur Ryerson (he died in the sinking of the ship) literally burst his collar when Lightoller wanted to deny his son access to the lifeboat as well, as he was a "man." He drove at the stunned officer:

"The boy is only thirteen and will stay with his mother!"

Apparently Ligtholler was so impressed by this speech that he actually let John Ryerson into the lifeboat. From today's point of view, the practice used by Lightoller is completely incomprehensible, but in 1912 it was quite normal that boys from the age of twelve were called "men," because child labor was still very widespread at that time, and boys at the age of twelve were already regarded as full-fledged men.

After the disaster it became apparent that Lightoller in particular was responsible for the fact that so few men and boys had survived the disaster. He tried to justify himself by believing that the lifeboats would row back to pick up survivors after the ship had sunk. But unfortunately, this did not happen! Why the experienced officer, who had survived a shipwreck before, speculated on this will probably remain his secret forever. In any case, it would have been better to load the boats fully than to wait to pick up drowning or freezing people from the icy-cold water.

The men were luckier on the starboard side, where First Officer William McMaster Murdoch was in command. He also stuck to "women and children first," but if there were still places left in the boat, he also let men on board. In this way he saved the lives of countless men who, on the port side, would almost certainly have had no chance of surviving the disaster.

The situation was aggravated for Murdoch, Lightoller and the other officers by the fact that many women could not be persuaded to get into the boats. They considered the brightly lit and warm ship, which had hardly sunk noticeably at first, to be safer than a swinging lifeboat. Considering how high the Boat Deck of the TITANIC was, it is understandable that many passengers were afraid of being lowered into the depths, because if you looked down, all you could see was the black night!

Also, some officers were afraid that the boats could break through under the weight of the passengers - in principle they only had to take a look at the boats, because on each lifeboat it was clearly engraved how many people it could take...

Meanwhile, in front of the office of Purser McElroy in the Foyer on C Deck, tumultuous scenes took place. A huge bunch of passengers angrily demanded their jewelry, cash and other valuables from the ship's safe. The passengers had no idea that their valuables would be the least of their problems that night...

The whole time, McElroy tried to make it clear to the passengers that they should hurry and get to the boats, but he only got through to the fewest. He must have been well aware that the TITANIC was lost - he had sailed the oceans with Captain Smith for many years, and it is believed that Smith informed him of the seriousness of the situation.

At 12:45 a.m., the Fourth Officer Boxhall started firing distress rockets on the order of Captain Smith to draw the attention of other ships nearby to himself and the plight of the ship. And indeed, after a short time, the lights of another ship on the port side could be seen!

As he fired the first distress rocket, Boxhall saw the other ship approaching. Shortly afterwards he could see the red port light and the green starboard light with his naked eye.

Boxhall was not the only one who saw the other ship, because some of the passengers also saw it, like the 15-year-old South African Edith Brown:

"I was standing at the railing with my father when we suddenly saw a light in the distance. Another ship!"

Captain Smith ordered Boxhall and Quartermaster Rowe (who was the last of the crew to hear of the situation) to contact the other ship via the Morse Lamp and fire additional distress rockets.

Was this the rescue for the over 2,200 people on board the TITANIC? Unfortunately, not, because after some time the ship disappeared, and with it, every chance for rescue was gone (see also "Stanley Lord and the Californian").

Almost at the same time as the first distress rocket was fired at 12:40 a.m., the first lifeboat was launched on the starboard side under the command of William McMaster Murdoch. It was Boat No. 7, and it was launched with 28 people on board. But there would have been room for 65 people!

However, Murdoch seems to have gained more and more confidence in the boats during the night, because from 1.30 a.m. on, in contrast to Officer Ligtholler on the port side, he occupied the boats almost or - like Boat No. 11 - even beyond the capacity limit!

But at Lifeboat No. 1 he deviated from his direction of march:

The boat under the command of Lookout George Symons had received instructions from Murdoch to wait at a distance of 200 meters and to row back if necessary. This seems to be the reason why Murdoch, contrary to his usual handling, let so few passengers into the boat that night. According to some experts, however, Lifeboat No. 1 was not lowered under the supervision of William McMaster Murdoch, but the Fifth Officer, Harold Lowe, who was presumably in command at that time. However, among the passengers of this very "exclusive" boat were Sir Cosmo and Lady Lucile Duff-Gordon with their secretary Laura Francatelli.

After the sinking of the TITANIC, the Duff-Gordons were reported to have stopped the remaining occupants of the boat from rowing back and taking people out of the water.

Stoker Hendrickson emphasized that it was he who had suggested they return and that he had shouted out: *"It's up to us to return and put whoever else in the boat!"* But he was ignored...

According to Hendrickson, it was Sir Cosmo and the two ladies (Lady Duff-Gordon and her maid Laura Francatelli) who objected and said it was too dangerous to turn back. Also, Stoker Taylor confirmed that someone had suggested turning back, but that a lady whom he believed to be Lady-Duff Gordon (there were only two women on board the lifeboat) was afraid that boat could be stormed and sunk. He also implied that there was another gentleman involved in the discussion who said, *"We will be made to sink when we return. It would be too dangerous!"*

It was later revealed that Sir Cosmo had given five pounds to each of the seven crew members (a lot of crew with only twelve passengers!) which, according to his wife, was intended to replace the lost belongings and equipment of the crew members. But nobody believed her, and to this day, many publications still mention that Sir Cosmo had paid the money for not rowing back to the scene of the accident...

After the rescue, however, souvenir photos of the Duff-Gordons with the crew members became public, which created the impression in the public that these crew members had been a "personal rescue team."
Sir Cosmo's reputation was ruined afterwards...

Further evidence of the firm belief in the "unsinkability" of the TITANIC was observed by Colonel Archibald Gracie shortly before 1:00 a.m.:

Sitting in the First-Class Smoking Room were Major Archibald Butt, Military Adviser to President Howard Taft, 65-year-old painter and writer Frank Millet, Washington-based archaeologist, and globetrotter Clarence Moore, and a fourth person unknown to Colonel Gracie (who for a time was probably Hugh Woolner), calmly playing cards. Later, Gracie reported:

"All four of them seemed completely oblivious to what was going on outside on the decks. It is also impossible to assume that they didn't know about the collision with the iceberg and hadn't noticed that the room they were in had been hurriedly cleared by everyone else. At that time, I had the impression that these men wanted to show their complete equanimity in the face of danger and that I would have been laughed at by them if I had pointed out to them how serious the situation seemed to me."

Even these gentlemen will hardly have been unaware of the TITANIC's increasingly visible inclination, but they remained seated there with their whiskey glasses.

At least Archibald Butt was probably firmly convinced of the "unsinkability" of the TITANIC, because shortly before the ship's departure he said to his friend, the Italian Diplomat Baron Carlo Alotti: "*I'll be back in Washington in time, because I'm lucky to have made a reservation on the new TITANIC. When I go on board the TITANIC, I will feel absolutely safe. You see, she is unsinkable!*"

Around 2.00 a.m., 20 minutes before the sinking, the four gentlemen are reported to have finished their round of cards after all and gone onto the Boat Deck, which was rising steeply out of the water. Whether they finally realized that the TITANIC would sink, and that they would not survive the night is not known, because none of these four gentlemen was supposed to survive the night, just as the well-known Author William T. Stead who also sat most of the night in the Smoking Room and read a book in peace. At 2.15 a.m. Major Butt is said to have been last seen near the Bridge. His body, as well as that of his fellow players, was never found.

No one had to explain to the stokers deep in the belly of the ship how serious the situation looked: They saw it with their own eyes! Like the brave men in the Engine Room that night, they did almost superhuman things. They are the true heroes of the TITANIC!

Engineers Herbert Harvey and Jonathan Shepherd ran the bilge pumps at full power to slow down the rising water. And they had managed to delay the sinking of the ship about an hour after the collision. A tremendous performance! Some firemen could already be dispatched as reinforcements to the lifeboats on the Boat Deck, which undoubtedly saved their lives. The situation was under control for the time being.

Stoker Frederick Barret was also in charge of Boiler Room No. 5, which was located just below the Grand Staircase. However, a quarter of an hour earlier an accident had happened: Because of the clouds of steam that kept escaping from the extinguished boilers, Shepherd had overlooked the hatch left open by Frederick Barret, had fallen over it and broken a leg in the process (the hatch served as a drain for the water in Boiler Room No. 5 down into the ship's hold, from where the bilge pumps carried it back into the North Atlantic). The injured Shepherd was taken to the Pump Room by Barret, Harvey and George Kemish.

Then the disaster happened: Suddenly and unexpectedly they were interrupted by a deafening noise when the bulkhead separating the two rooms broke. Herbert Harvey shouted desperately at Barret to climb the emergency stairs. At the same time, he hurried to the aid of the injured Shepherd, but the water was too fast and swallowed both men in a violent whirlpool. They had no chance!

The fate of the TITANIC was now finally sealed because Boiler Room No. 5 was the last bastion that had to be held as long as possible to slow down the sinking. Now everything was lost!

The ship had now reached exactly the position where the water could enter the sections of the ship that were not damaged by the collision. For the passengers who were inside the TITANIC and were looking for a way to the Boat Deck, the problem arose that the freezing cold water on their escape was now coming towards them. It literally made its way. Whoever was still in the steerage at that time was almost certainly lost...

One consequence of the loss of Boiler Room No. 5 was that shortly afterwards (some witnesses speak of about 1.15 a.m.), the TITANIC started to tilt rather abruptly from starboard to port, which made her increasingly unstable. The deck was now tilting more and more, which made the evacuation of the passengers even more difficult. According to reports from some survivors, Chief Officer Henry Tingle Wilde then gave the order: *"All hands to starboard to get her upright again!"*

The passengers and crew members now went over to starboard, and the TITANIC did indeed straighten up for a short time.

The chaos and panic on board the TITANIC increased more and more. and at Lifeboat No. 11, the crew had reached the point where they would not let any adults into the lifeboats. There were simply too many people on board, but too few lifeboats. The women were faced with the terrible decision of whether or not to part with their children. Some women refused to abandon their children, because they neither wanted to be left alone nor to leave without them. When Lifeboat No. 11 was finally lowered, it was completely overloaded with over 70 people on board, but at least the freezing cold sea was still calm, and everything went smoothly. The boat was submerged up to the gunwale and protruded only a little bit out of the water, so that you only had to reach over to touch the water.

Shortly afterwards, another accident occurred due to the continuing difficulties of the crew in lowering the boats:

Obviously, nobody on the Boat Deck had noticed that Boat No. 13 had not yet left the ship when Boat No. 15 was launched. Both boats had been occupied by Murdoch with 65 people to the limit of their capacity, and now No. 13 was in danger of being crushed by No. 15.

Desperately, the passengers of No. 13 shouted upwards that the lowering should be stopped until they had come away from the ship, but No. 15 was getting closer and closer. Somehow the passengers of No. 13 managed to avert the disaster and escape Boat No. 15, but it was very close.

On the port side, the boats were still not nearly fully loaded under the command of Lightoller – Boat No. 14, for example, had been lowered at 1.25 a.m. with only 42 instead of 65 passengers, because there were no women and children around. When a group of Second- and Third-Class men tried to climb into the boat, they were violently restrained by officers who obviously still preferred the men to die rather than let them into the lifeboats!

In the Wireless Room, Jack Phillips sent his distress calls to other ships without interruption (in the meantime, at

Harold Bride's suggestion, he also sent the relatively newly introduced SOS). At 1.45 a.m. he transmitted to the CARPATHIA:

"Come as fast as you can. The water is already between the boilers."

The answer from Wireless Operator Harold Cottam came promptly:

"Coming with all possible force. Two shifts are working in the engine room. Lifeboats are ready."

This radio message of the CARPATHIA was not confirmed by the TITANIC. It is known that Phillips continued transmitting until about ten minutes before the sinking, but the electricity became weaker and weaker, and therefore, the radio messages arrived only fragmentarily. It was coming to an end!

For many years, a very controversial topic of discussion was whether or not there was a shooting on board the TITANIC. There is enough testimony from survivors that Fifth Officer Harold Lowe at least fired warning shots along the side of the ship when some men tried to storm the boats. But it was denied that passengers were shot by the crew.

After the release of the movie "TITANIC" by James Cameron, a letter was written by 21-year-old Karl Albert Midtsjo from Krakstadt in Norway, who survived the sinking of the TITANIC as a Third-Class passenger, to a relative on Friday, April 19th, 1912:

"You get very serious when you have experienced something so terrible... I feel as if I can still hear the cries for help today. And some of them were shot while trying to board the boats. Karl Albert Midtsjo, April 19, 1912."

Since then, the authenticity of this letter has often been questioned, but years later, Second Officer Charles Herbert Lightoller privately admitted that he, too, had used his gun...

Third Class passenger Eugene Daly also saw passengers on board the TITANIC being shot:

"They put women in the boats. There was a huge crowd of people standing there. The officer in charge pointed to a revolver and waved his hand, saying that if a man tried to enter, he would shoot him on the spot. Two men tried to break through, and he shot them both. I saw him shoot them. I saw them lying there after they were shot. One seemed dead. The other one tried to pull himself up on the side of the deck, but he couldn't. I tried to get to the boat too, but I was afraid I'd be shot, and I stayed behind. After that there was another shot, and I saw the officer himself lying on the deck. They told me he shot himself, but I didn't see it."

Inside the TITANIC, hundreds of passengers were still trying to get up to the Boat Deck, but the freezing cold sea water was just faster in many cases. It shot through the corridors and staircases, which had now become regular shafts, with an unimaginable elemental force and tore the people from their legs who had no chance to escape. It is known from some Third-Class passengers that they recognized the hopelessness of their situation and returned to their cabins where they awaited their deadly fate.

Even the rich passengers on board the TITANIC, like John Jacob Astor IV, realized that they would not survive this night. Even their immense richness could not save them!

Astor helped his pregnant wife Madeleine into a lifeboat and asked Officer Lightoller to accompany her. Of course, he asked the wrong man. As was to be expected, Lightoller refused the request and had this boat lowered only two-thirds full. Astor asked pro forma for the number of his wife's lifeboat (No. 4) so that he would find it later, but then he waved to his wife for the last time and calmly left. It was 1:50 a.m. It seems that Astor was later killed by the falling first funnel, although this is now highly doubted in expert circles.

> A week later Astor's soot-smeared and shattered body was found in the North Atlantic.
> In his shirt, his initials were found in the collar, which clearly identified him. On his body was found a gold watch, a diamond ring with three stones, gold cuff links with diamonds, 225 pounds in English banknotes, $2,440, five pounds in gold, 50 francs and a gold pin.
> The sooty and shattered condition of the body alone suggested that he must have been killed by the falling funnel...

Since the collision, Thomas Andrews had helped to get women and children into the lifeboats. He went through the whole ship, opened many cabin doors and asked the passengers to get into the lifeboats.

Did he think about it, that he couldn't prevail against Bruce Ismay to take more lifeboats on board? Quite possible, but he did everything in his power that night to save as many passengers as possible. To a larger group of dithering women, he shouted:

"Ladies, you must board immediately! There is no time to lose. You can't pack and choose your boat in peace. Do not hesitate. Get on board, get on board!"

As the end approached, he stood completely demoralized and paralyzed in the first-class smoking room, which was directly adjacent to his own cabin. He had his arms crossed in front of his chest and stared at a picture, "The Approach of Plymouth Harbour," hanging over the fireplace. His whole life's work was going down right before his eyes, and he had decided to go down with the ship he had designed and conceived together with Alexander Carlisle. His life jacket was lying on a chart table, and the Steward John Stewart was the last person to see Thomas Andrews alive.

He asked him several times: *"Won't you at least try, Mr. Andrews?"* But Andrews gave no answer to this question, and that was the last we saw of the builder of the TITANIC. His body was never found. However, there are reasonable doubts about this version, as is explained in the book, "On a Sea of Glass" by Tad Fitch, J. Kent Layton and Bill Wormstedt.

The scene at the fireplace did indeed take place, but probably much earlier in the night. Later Andrews was still seen by some passengers when he threw some deck chairs overboard shortly before the sinking so that they could serve as rafts for other passengers.

Since the beginning of the evacuation, the eight musicians around band leader Wallace Hartley had played unwaveringly to calm the passengers.
At 2.10 a.m., the freezing cold water came closer and closer to their location in front of the Gymnasium, and Hartley told his men that they had now fulfilled their duty and could try to save themselves if they wanted to. But none of the eight musicians left their posts! They played one last tune around which a legend was born over the decades - "Nearer, My God, to Thee"!

Wireless Operator Harold Bride believed to have heard the hymn "Autumn" when he was desperately fighting for his life in the water, but this melody was not on the official music list of the *White Star Line* at all. Moreover, a few years earlier, Hartley had replied to the question which piece of music he would play when he was on a sinking ship: "Nearer, My God, to Thee!"

Maybe Bride had meant the waltz "Songe d`Automne", which was very popular at that time and was also only called "Autumn"...

At least survivor Eva Hart, who was seven years old at the time of the sinking, was absolutely sure:

"There's no question that they were playing and there's no question that after we were on the water, they made a version of: Nearer, My God, to Thee. We argued about that so many times. It was the version I heard a few months later when I was visiting my grandmother in church. I was so scared that I

ran out of the church. But some people won't accept that. People say, No, no. It wasn't that. It was just ragtime. But that's not true."

None of the eight musicians survived that night. Only the body of Wallace Hartley, who was later buried in his birthplace of Colne, and the remains of John Law (Jock) Hume and J. F. P. Clarke were found. Hume was buried at Fairview Lawn Cemetery and Clarke at Mount Olivet Cemetery in Halifax.

The monument for the eight musicians in Southampton © private photo of the author

At the end, the TITANIC sank faster and faster, and in this total chaos not all 20 lifeboats could be lowered. The last regular lifeboat was Collapsible D, which was lowered away by Officer Lightoller, and TITANIC with 25 persons (instead of 47 possible). The four collapsible lifeboats were affixed folded up on the officers' cabins, so they took up little stowage space.

100

The crew tried desperately to free Collapsible B shortly before the sinking, but they did not succeed. When the ship sank, it was washed off the deck and floated keel up in the water. Collapsible A was also washed away and was thus half-flooded but remained halfway seaworthy. About half of the people who managed to escape into this boat died of hypothermia, some of them lying in the seawater.

Collapsible B, now upside down in the water, served as a raft for many people fighting for their lives in the freezing cold sea.

On the rescuing Collapsible B, for example, were Officer Lightoller, Wireless Operator Harold Bride, Colonel Archibald Gracie, the then 17-year-old Jack Thayer as well as the famous ship baker Charles Joughin. According to his own statement, he had drunk an entire bottle of whiskey in the face of his imminent death and had climbed up the stern, which was rising higher and higher into the air, to the very end of the stern railing. On the way to the stern, he passed Priests Joseph Byles from England and Joseph Peruschitz from Germany who gave absolution to several hundred passengers on the steeply rising stern. When the ship finally sank, he had put his arm around the flagpole and went down with the ship.

It was said that it felt to him like he was in an elevator. It was said that his hair didn't even get wet. Different sources reported that in the beginning, Wireless Operator Jack Phillips also made it on Collapsible B, but died during the night. His body was never found, and to this day, it is controversial whether he really made it on Collapsible B.

All night long the people on this boat were busy balancing it under the guidance of Officer Lightholler. Lightoller had the men stand up and line up in two rows on each side facing the bow. Whenever the boat swayed back and forth in the swell, he shouted to the men: "*Lean left,*" "*Stand upright,*" "*Lean right,*" depending on what was needed to counteract the movement of the boat.

From time to time, the men in the choir would shout, "*Boat ahoy, boat ahoy!*" But when they didn't get an answer, Lightoller told them to stop and save their strength. As soon as someone on the boat froze to death, they were gently let into the water by the others and another was pulled up. This happened several times that night...

The completely exhausted 53-year-old Colonel Archibald Gracie had experienced the terrible situation as follows:

"*After I sank with the ship, a powerful force seemed to push me through the water. It must have been the underwater explosions, and I remembered stories of people being boiled to death. Again, and again I prayed for rescue, although I was sure I was going to die. I had great difficulty holding my breath under water. I knew that the water would choke me as soon as I inhaled. When I was under water, I pushed to the surface with all my strength. After - it seemed to me - infinite time, I finally got air again. Around me was only the sea, ice and large parts of the wreck. All around me, dying men and women groaned and cried heartbreakingly.*"

"I moved from one part of the wreck to the next and finally reached a cork raft. Soon it was so crowded that anyone else would make it sink, so, we had to keep others from climbing aboard to avoid sinking ourselves. That was the most terrible and awful thing. The terrible cries of the people around us still ring in my ears, and I will not forget them until my death. 'Stay where you are,' we shouted to everyone who wanted to get on board. 'One more and we all sink!' Many of those we did not take aboard answered, in the face of death, ''Good luck. God bless you!'"

After his rescue, Archibald Gracie suffered the consequences of the severe hypothermia he had contracted that night. He also suffered from severe psychological problems, as he was unable to cope with the terrible accident that killed some of his best friends. On Wednesday, December 4th, 1912, he died at the age of 53 years of severe complications due to his diabetes. Before that, he had written one of the most detailed and successful books about the sinking of the TITANIC, "The Truth about the Titanic," which is still published under the title: "Titanic: A Survivor`s Story."

In the freezing cold, -2° degree cold, North Atlantic Ocean, under a starry and moonless sky, people were now drifting in their life jackets, screaming for help - a horrible chorus that sounded to Jack Thayer *"like the high hum of locusts back home in Pennsylvania"*.

But why didn't the lifeboats drifting nearby return to the drowning and freezing people to help them?

To this day, there is controversy over the reasons for the denial of aid. But it is very difficult to judge because every person behaves differently in such an extreme situation (and the sinking of the TITANIC was definitely one of them). But one thing seems to have been not really clear to all the people who made it into a lifeboat: How long does a person survive in freezing cold seawater before he dies, and how much strength can he even develop?

A person cannot survive for very long in such cold water, and after a very short time, he is no longer able to make great efforts. So how should people fighting for their lives in the water, to whom one first had to row over, manage to, "*capsize the boats and pull all the inmates in them into the deep,*" as some survivors said after the disaster?

In fact, this seems to be just a protective claim of the survivors to appease their own conscience. But can you really blame them for that? Well, here again, you were not there yourself that night, and of course you must not ignore what the people in the lifeboats had just experienced or were experiencing: The largest and supposedly safest (unsinkable) ship in the world had just sunk before their incredulous and horrified eyes! This was unbelievable, and the people were certainly paralyzed with horror. Then the passengers heard loudly (even if some passengers vehemently denied it) the cries for help of the people floating in the water. The fear of being dragged into the freezing cold and deadly water is not unnatural for most of the passengers, but it is not less bad. The survival instinct was probably stronger there. And in many cases, it was the women who did not want it to be reversed. For some ladies, the shipwrecked were just "*hysterical steerage passengers who slept through the sinking!*".

Some of the women seemed not to have realized that, in many cases, their husbands were also among these people struggling in the water.

Meanwhile, the icy sea was the scene of indescribable dramas that many of the surviving passengers and crew members should not forget the rest of their lives. The story is told of two men who shared a deck chair in the icy water. One of the two was forced to comment on the gruesome scene around him in the face of his imminent death. He is said to have said over and over again: *"What a night! What a night!"* Shortly afterwards he collapsed dead and sank into the icy sea. The other man survived the disaster and so this story survived too.

During the night, Fifth Officer Harold Lowe could no longer bear the cries of the people who were dying and returned with Lifeboat No. 14 to save more lives. So many corpses were already floating in the icy sea, that Lowe and his men could hardly row through them. He saved at least a few more lives in the freezing cold water, including Chinese passenger Fang Lang, who was tied to a door with his face to the front. As the sea water was already sloshing over him, Lowe thought he was dead and so he just said, *"It's no use. He's probably dead, and if not, there are others who deserve to be rescued more than a Jap!"*

When Lowe finally pulled him into the boat after all, it soon became clear that the young Welsh man was not only mistaken about the nationality of Fang Lang, but also about his resilience and will to survive. Once in the boat, Fang Lang quickly regained consciousness and began rowing with all his might, whereupon the completely perplexed Lowe suddenly changed his mind about the brave passenger:

"*My God, I'm ashamed of what I said about that little guy!*" He admitted that he "*would save the little guy six more times if I had the chance!*

In his home country China, however, Fang Lang was not held in such high esteem after his return. His fate was similar to that of the only rescued Japanese passenger Masabumi Hosono: he was condemned for not going down with the TITANIC and dying!

A total of five boats were moored together by Lowe, then he put up mast and sails in Boat No. 14 to get to the CARPATHIA faster. In between he picked up survivors from the water, including the 43-year-old William F. Hoyt, a New York importer of lace. He was the first man to be pulled into Boat No. 14. Since Hoyt was a rather large and heavy man, it took the men some effort to get him into the boat. When the crew found him, he was bleeding heavily from nose and mouth, indicating internal injuries. Unfortunately, William F. Hoyt succumbed to his internal injuries shortly after he was pulled under water with the sinking TITANIC (in some publications he was confused with Frederick Maxfield Hoyt, who survived the sinking of the luxury liner; author's note).

Collapsible A was also rescued by Lowe - more than 30 centimeters of water had already penetrated there. The ten passengers still alive (nine men and one woman, Rosa Abbott) were hoisted aboard Lowe's boat, while the three dead were left in the boat that drifted off into the night.

In mid-May 1912, Collapsible A with the three dead on board was recovered from the Oceanic more than 200 kilometers from the wreck site of the Titanic.

The area at the wreck site was full of chairs and pieces of wood that had been thrown into the water by passengers at the last minute, possibly to serve as rafts.

Contrary to popular belief, Lifeboat No. 4 returned to the dying people in the water and was able to pull some people out of the freezing water, as Emily Ryerson remembered: "*Then we turned around to pick up some of them in the water. Some of the women protested, but others insisted, and we pulled out six or seven men. The men rescued were mostly stokers, stewards, sailors, etc., and were so chilled and frozen that they could hardly move.*"

Even before the TITANIC sank, a total of four people were pulled out of the ice-cold water into the boat. Among them was Lamp Trimmer Hemming, who had jumped death-defyingly from the ship and swam to Boat No. 4.

It took until 4.00 a.m. in the morning of April 15th until CARPATHIA, which had rushed to the rescue, finally arrived at the scene of the accident and was able to see the first boat of the TITANIC, Lifeboat   No. 2. From 3.00 a.m., Captain Arthur Rostron had ordered rockets to be fired every 15 minutes so that the survivors knew that help was close.

Contrary to the hopes of the crew of the CARPATHIA, nothing more could be seen of the TITANIC. Captain Rostron had brought the CARPATHIA to the never reached speed of 17.5 knots (the actual top speed was 14.5 knots) - but it was in vain. He had not made it in time for the sinking TITANIC.

Now he could only take care of the rescue of the survivors in the lifeboats.

At 4.10 a.m. the first survivors of the TITANIC began to climb aboard the CARPATHIA under the leadership of Fourth Officer Joseph Groves Boxhall. Ladders and nets were thrown over the side for the men, while the women were hoisted in slings and the children in linen bags, as Eva Hart later remembered.

"Then in the morning we were taken up by this little ship, the Carpathia. Rescuing shipwrecked people from lifeboats in the middle of the sea is a pretty frightening undertaking. Our little boats went alongside what seemed to be a huge ship. In fact, the Carpathia was quite a small ship. But from down there she looked big. And as for coming aboard, there was no gangway like there is when you are on land. And so a kind of, I don't know if this is the right word, a hatch opened in the side of the ship through which the luggage was loaded. And they threw out rope ladders, and people like my mother and other adults, had to climb up a swinging rope ladder in the middle of the sea, which, she said, was very frightening."

"But what should the children do? We could not climb the rope ladder, so they fetched these large luggage nets. And the meshes are very big, the children would have slipped through them. In any case, our legs and feet would have slipped

through, so they put each kid in a bag. And I remember being so scared that I almost died when I was put into that sack. And that was pulled together, and the sacks with these children were put into these huge nets and then naturally hoisted aboard without any risk. But it was really quite frightening. When I was on board, I couldn't find my mother. It was hours before I found her, but finally, I found her. It must have been shocking how these poor women, like my mother, went through the ship the next day looking for the husband they had been separated from."

Miss Elizabeth Allen was asked by Purser Brown what had happened to the TITANIC and she replied that the ship had sunk.
Captain Rostron asked Joseph Groves Boxhall directly:

"The TITANIC has sunk?"

"Yes. She went down at about 2.30 a.m."

"Were there many people still on board when she sank?"

"Many hundreds. Maybe a thousand. Maybe more. My God, sir, they all went down with her. They couldn't survive in those cold waters. We had room in my boat for another dozen people, but after the ship went down, it was dark. We couldn't take on any swimmers. I set off flares. I believe that people were pulled into the depths by the undertow. The other boats are somewhere around here."

The captain nodded briefly and sent the completely broken and heavily crying officer down to the First-Class Dining Room.

In the following four hours, the survivors of the TITANIC were taken in by the CARPATHIA. Under the leadership of Charles Herbert Lightoller, Boat No. 12 with over 70 people on board was the last to be picked up. Due to the weight of the many people, this boat laid so deep in the water that Lightoller was afraid it could be overlooked, and he had to draw attention to himself several times with his sailor's whistle. Most of the passengers of the boat, also Lightholler himself, had been on the overturned Collapsible B, where they had experienced hell on earth, and were then taken over by Boat No. 12

Around 8.30 a.m. his call for help was finally heard, and six hours after the sinking of the TITANIC, the small and completely overloaded boat moored next to the CARPATHIA. As the last of the survivors of the TITANIC, Lightoller climbed over the ladder on board the rescue ship.

Later the CARPATHIA returned to the scene of the accident to see if anyone had survived, but only a single body was found floating in the water.

Before the CARPATHIA left for New York with her own passengers and the survivors of the TITANIC, Captain Rostron had a service held in memory of the victims of the tragedy. The passengers of the CARPATHIA, themselves terribly shocked by the tragedy that had befallen the TITANIC and her passengers, selflessly helped out with all sorts of things. They lent their clothes and sewed coats for the children out of blankets.

By order of Captain Arthur Rostron, the passengers of the TITANIC were counted, and the number of survivors was 705. The *White Star Line* named 757 survivors on its list published on Saturday, April 20th, 1912, (where this completely wrong number came from is still a mystery), while the British Inquiry named the number 712 which is to be regarded as generally valid.

A detailed, careful investigation carried out by historians in the late 1990s showed that the actual number of victims was not over 1500, but that it was lower than generally assumed. The new figure, called "solid" by some historians, is presumably 1496 fatalities. There is probably only doubt about whether restaurant employee Lazar Sartori was really on the TITANIC. In the crew list of the TITANIC, he is considered as "not appeared," while the *White Star Line* later declared him as a victim at the British Board of Trade. So, if he really did not go on board, the number of dead is 1495.

In Samuel Halpern's book, "Report into the Loss of the SS Titanic: A Centennial Reappraisal", published in 2012, the author presents the updated figures, which irrefutably show that 712 survivors disembarked in New York, despite a count of 705 on board the rescue ship CARPATHIA.

The Carpathia saved 712 passengers of the TITANIC © public domain

The CARPATHIA arrived in New York in the evening hours on Thursday, April 18th, 1912. By this time, the world press had recognized the enormous extent of the disaster, and the offices of the *White Star Line* in New York and Southampton were literally stormed. There was almost a state of emergency.

However, many of the names that were given from the CARPATHIA were inaccurate or false and bore very little resemblance to the people on board. Friends and relatives of the survivors only believed that their relatives were still alive when they were faced with them in person.

More than 40,000 people had gathered in Battery Park in New York to witness the arrival of the CARPATHIA, which almost ceremoniously stopped at *White Star* Pier 59 to unload the lifeboats of the TITANIC. Tears were in the eyes of almost everyone present. Afterwards the ship drove to Pier 54 and let the survivors of the TITANIC off board.

When the exhausted and traumatized survivors fell into the arms of their relatives on the pier, the different classes of the TITANIC went their separate ways again. The First-Class passengers, such as the widows of Charles M. Hays, George Widener and the Thayer's, left on private trains while others stayed in the best hotels in the city.

The New York Herald also reported about the incredible tragedy of the TITANIC. © Library of Congress

The Third-Class survivors, many of whom had lost all their belongings in the disaster, sneaked ashore and did not know where to spend the night.

The *White Star Line* then provided them with accommodation for some time.

The cable ship MACKAY-BENNET was given the sad task to recover the bodies of the TITANIC. With tons of ice, more than a hundred coffins, 40 embalmers and an Anglican priest on board, the ship left Halifax, Nova Scotia on Wednesday, April 17th, 1912. The ship arrived at the wreck site at 8 p.m. on Saturday, April 20th, 1912.

Three other Canadian ships participated in the search: the cable ship MINIA, the lighthouse supply ship MONTMAGNY and the sealing ship ALGERINE.

After more than five days in the icy water, many bodies were disfigured. The MACKAY-BENNET recovered a large number of bodies - 166 of them were buried at sea immediately.

From the sinking area, which was still full of wreckage and corpses, 334 dead were recovered, 328 of them from the MACKAY-BENNET and five more by passing steamships on the North Atlantic route. In total, 337 bodies were recovered, including those recovered by the OCEANIC from Collapsible A. All those that still had recognizable features or characteristics were embalmed and brought to Halifax for identification.

The German liner SS BREMEN also passed the bodies as the First-Class passenger Johanna Stunke remembered on Saturday, April 20th, 1912:

"We saw one woman in her night dress, with a baby clasped closely to her breast. Several women passengers screamed and left the rail in a fainting condition. There was another woman, fully dressed, with her arms tight around a body of a shaggy dog."

Upon returning to Halifax, 59 identified bodies were returned to their relatives' respective homes. The remaining 150 victims were buried in three cemeteries in Halifax. At Fairview Cemetery, also known as the "TITANIC Cemetery", 121 victims of the disaster are buried, 44 of whom could not be identified.

Gravestones of Titanic victims at the Fairview Cemetery in Halifax © private photo of the author

This Happened when the TITANIC Sank

Since the tragic night of April 14th, 1912, the question has been asked what really happened when the TITANIC sank. Why and in what way did the ship split in two? Only in recent years, new research on the wreck, computer simulations and model tests have finally brought light into the dark. This chapter describes the scientific state of affairs as it will be in 2018, 106 years after the disaster.

Until the official discovery of the wreck of the TITANIC on Sunday, 1st September 1985, the thesis was valid that the TITANIC was slashed open by a 91-meter-long crack on the starboard side almost like a tin can. As it came to an end, the stern straightened up at a 90-degree angle and the TITANIC sank to the seabed in one piece. So, by 1985, the state of knowledge...

> A very curious aspect of the official discovery of the wreck of the TITANIC by Dr. Robert Ballard and Jean Louis Michel is without any doubt that the British newspaper, "The Observer," reported to the world public even before the official notification of the research vessel, that the world-famous ship was found in two large parts and in countless pieces of debris, broken but standing upright on the seabed. How could "The Observer" know about this, if the TITANIC had not yet been found at all, especially since until 1985 it was assumed that the TITANIC sank in 1912 in one piece and intact, and there was no talk of the ship breaking apart when it sank?

This was already strange at that time, but it was cleverly not discussed any further, because the world public was too busy to be fascinated about the discovery of the wreck after 73 years. This strange "little thing" was quickly forgotten.

How Ballard knitted on his legend already at that time was shown in the famous video recordings of the "discovery" of the TITANIC. Since Ballard was sleeping in his cabin at the time of the "discovery," it was decided without further ado to re-enact the discovery of the wreck for posterity, this time with Robert Ballard. So, the famous exclamations of the crew of the research ship, "A boiler, this is a boiler!" with the celebrating Ballard are only an illusion for posterity.

Twenty years later, Paul-Henri Nargeolet, who was co-leader of a total of five expeditions to the TITANIC, dropped the bomb in an open letter in the Titanic Historical Society (THS) newspaper: The wreck of the TITANIC was not discovered by Robert Ballard, but eight years earlier by the British Navy!

Therefore, the Franco-American expedition knew exactly where to look because the HMS HECATE, a ship of the British Navy, is said to have discovered a large shipwreck in two parts already in 1977 during a secret weapons test near the last known position of the TITANIC. Because of the secret weapons test, the discovery could not be made public. The details of the 1977 mission are expected to be made available to the public in 2027. It should be interesting to see if the history books will have to be rewritten then...

More than 30 years later, the entire sinking process looks completely different. From the moment the TITANIC struck the iceberg on her starboard side, the forward half of the luxury liner filled with seawater continuously for two hours and forty minutes. The perfectly functioning watertight compartments kept the ship on the surface for much longer than Thomas Andrews had assumed in his damage evaluation. He had given the TITANIC a maximum of two hours before she would sink in the North Atlantic...

For the passengers and crew members on board, it looked for a very long time as if the ship would be able to stay on the surface for a longer time, as it sank almost gracefully slowly. This also contributed to the fact that a large part of the lifeboats were far from being used to full capacity.

It was only when the passengers in the boats were on the water and rowing away from the TITANIC, that they saw the ship must have been in serious trouble.

Ten minutes before the final sinking, around 2.10 a.m. board time, things moved very quickly: the water now flowed through windows, doors and corridors into the non-watertight decks and also down the stairwells. Due to the increasing water pressure, the anchors of the funnels cracked. First the front funnel hit the water and the people swimming in it, and shortly afterwards number two fell over as well.

In his book "Mission TITANIC," movie director James Cameron solved the mystery of the overturned funnels. Until now, it was assumed that the funnels had tilted forward when the TITANIC tilted forward and sank over the bow.

However, there is a serious problem with this obvious theory: When the TITANIC's funnels fell, the ship was tilted about ten degrees forward with the bow down. But the funnels were fixed in such a way that they were inclined slightly more than nine degrees backwards. So, at this point they were in an almost upright position. They should have been in a stable position, but that's when they fell!

So, the previous assumption that the funnels fell because the ship was tilting forward is not true. The funnels were also braced with wire ropes that could withstand inclinations of up to 45 degrees in a storm.

Cameron tried to find out by model tests how the two collapsible boats could have been lowered into the water in the officers' quarters if the stays (the wire ropes that held the funnels upright in the longitudinal direction) had still been in place.

Just before the deck was flooded, the crew on the sinking TITANIC had managed to get the boats down from the deckhouse and hooked them into the davits. On the film set for "TITANIC," it became clear that the lifeboats would have fallen into the stays and been pulled underwater with the sinking ship. This is exactly what happened when the film set was sunk.

According to Cameron's conclusion, they would have had to cut through and remove the tensioning parts fixing the stays to free the boats. Several survivors had reported officers screaming for knives, which they then borrowed from passengers. Apparently, they wanted to cut through these stays with the knives. As soon as the funnels came loose from their moorings, they were also torn away from the pipes and all the other fixtures below. These 18-meter-long pipes were no longer held in place by anything at the foundations, and they were probably only blocked on one side because the stays on the other side had already been cut.

Exactly in this moment they finally buckled...

The ice-cold seawater then plunged into the openings created by the lack of funnels.

Below these were the boiler shafts, which consisted essentially of long vertical shafts cutting through the horizontal decks.

Now the sinking speed of the front half of the ship increased rapidly. At this point, the bow of the TITANIC was already on the verge of sinking to the bottom. However, it was still held on the surface by the stern of the ship, which was not flooded. In this very fragile connection between the already flooded bow and the still floating stern, the ship swung, and the stern rose into the air.

Due to the unbelievably strong material tension in the middle of the ship, the luxury liner began to break apart. The crack began at the upper corner on starboard and continued very quickly to port, then straight through to the double bottom. The crack stopped briefly at the more robust construction of the keel. The tension under which the two halves of the ship were standing was suddenly released and the severed bow with its almost 140 meters length came free and swung downwards until it hung almost vertically. Meanwhile, the stern, which was now no longer held by the bow, fell back to the water surface.

However, the bow was still held by the connection at the double bottom of the keel plate and still did not sink to the sea floor. This area, about 20 meters long, had been broken off by a so-called "greenwood fracture."

> **James Cameron demonstrated this situation very vividly in the documentary "TITANIC, Analysis of a Tragedy," using a banana that you break through in the middle and where the skin still holds the two halves together.**

After a short time, the bow broke off and fell down almost like a bomb without any buoyancy, because it was completely flooded and had hardly any trapped air inside.

For a short moment the people in the lifeboats around the sinking TITANIC had the impression that the stern might continue to drift on the surface. But that was just wishful thinking, because the stern now began to fill with water very quickly via the crack. When the double bottom of the ship was demolished, Boiler Room No. 1 had been exposed and the Engine Room became freely accessible to the seawater.

Sometime before the rupture, the luxury liner had already tilted clearly to port with an estimated heel of ten degrees. After the rupture, the stern heeled to port many times more violently. Hundreds of people, who had now realized that they would probably not survive the night, tried to climb towards the stern to safety…a short reprieve, because there was no more safety or even a rescue. It only delayed the inevitable a little bit longer!

During their desperate climbing attempts, many people were hurled against the port railing and then crashed into the ice-cold North Atlantic from a great height while other passengers slid over the increasingly steep Boat Deck into the sea and almost certain death. After the TITANIC was torn apart in in the middle, the five single ended boilers from Boiler Room No. 1, which were kept in operation until then to supply the emergency generators, broke out of their moorings and fell into the sea.

Now the ice-cold seawater rushed into the gaping front end of the stern, which began to tilt and slide down. Faster and faster, it filled with water until it finally stood at right angles in the water and held this position until it disappeared below the surface.

Depending on the angle of view of the passengers in the lifeboats, the tilting movement of the stern over 30, then 50 and then 80 degrees may have caused passengers of a lifeboat directly behind the stern to perceive the sinking stern as standing upright. Other eyewitnesses spoke from 30 degrees to absolutely vertical. According to the latest findings presented by Cameron, all passengers are probably right and have not lied, as has been claimed many times in recent years.

Second Class passenger Lawrence Beesley watched the final moments of the TITANIC from Lifeboat No. 13:

"And then, as we stared in awe, she slowly straightened up, apparently turning around her centre of gravity a little further back than the middle, until she reached an almost vertical position; this is how she remained - motionless! As she swung up, her lights suddenly went out. Those that had shone all night without flickering only flashed again briefly. At that moment there was a noise that many people, I think erroneously, described as an explosion. To me it always looked like it was nothing more than the machinery crashing out of its beds, crashing through the compartments, and smashing everything in its path. Partly it was a tube, partly a groan, partly a rustle and partly a crash, but it was not a sudden bursting, as happens in an explosion. It lasted for several seconds, maybe fifteen or twenty, when the heavy machines fell, down into the depths of the ship. I suppose they went through the hull and sank first, before the ship. But it was a sound that no one had ever heard before, and no one will ever wish to hear it again."

Also, the fact that many people did not see the breakup of the TITANIC is in principle quite simple to explain. Until shortly before the sinking the lights of the ship were burning. Almost at the same time as the ship broke apart, it suddenly went out and it was pitch black night. The human eye is hardly able to react so quickly to the new light conditions and before the people in the lifeboats knew it, the stern was already vertical. That many passengers assumed that the TITANIC had sunk in one piece is therefore absolutely understandable.

Lawrence Beesley was one of the passengers who thought that the TITANIC did not break apart when she sank, because he describes the sinking as follows:

" When the crash was over, the Titanic stood upright like a comma. We could only see her as a stern section, and about 150 feet of hull stood as an indistinct patch in the darkness against a starry sky, and she remained in that position for a few minutes - I think about five minutes, but it could have been less. Then, sinking a little deeper at the back at first, I suppose she slowly slid down and dived diagonally downwards. The sea closed over her, and we had seen the last of the wonderful ship we embarked on four days ago in Southampton."

17-year-old First Class passenger Jack Thayer swam for his life in the -2° degree cold North Atlantic. From there he watched the final sinking of the TITANIC:

"Her deck was turned a little to us. We could see groups of the almost one thousand five hundred people on board, clinging together in bunches or bundles like swarming bees; only to fall in masses, pairs or individually, as the bulk of the ship, two hundred and fifty feet from it, rose up into the sky until it reached a sixty-five- or seventy-degree angle. Then, it seemed, it took a pause, which lasted a few minutes. Gradually it turned its deck away from us to hide the terrible spectacle from us. I looked up - we were under the three huge propellers. For a moment I thought they were coming down safely on us. Then, with the dulled sound of the last of their bulkheads cracking, she slid quietly away from us into the sea."

First Class passenger Hugh Woolner made the following statement to the American inquiry:

"When the lights went out, you couldn't see your hand in front of your face. The whole stern had been brightly lit, and suddenly the lights went out, and our eyes hadn't yet adjusted *to the darkness, so that you couldn't see anything, only hear sounds."*

Reading these survivors' statements, one thing is for sure: The last moments of the TITANIC were pure horror!

TITANIC DESTINIES

The Tragedy of the Allison Family

A particularly tragic fate befell the wealthy Allison family that night. The married couple Hudson Allison (born on Friday, December 9th, 1881) and Bess Allison (born on Sunday, November 14th, 1886) had met on a train in 1907 and then married on Hudson's 21st birthday on Monday, December 9th, 1907. The couple boarded the luxury liner together with their daughter Lorraine, born on Saturday 5th June 1909, and their son Trevor, born on Sunday 7th May 1911. In addition, four domestic servants had also gone on board.

The 30-year-old Hudson Allison was a member of the board of the British Lumber Corporation and had attended an important directors' meeting in England. The family of four made a detour to the Scottish Highlands where Hudson Allison bought two dozen Clydesdales and Hackney stallions for his cattle farm in Canada. On top of that he bought furniture and hired domestic help for their two residences - George Swane was hired as chauffeur, Mildred Brown as cook, Alice Cleaver as nanny for Trevor and Sarah Daniels as chambermaid for his 25-year-old wife Bess.

The Allisons paid 151 pounds and 16 shillings for three cabins on C Deck (C 22, 24, 26, ticket number 113781).

The Allison couple occupied their own cabin, Sarah Daniels and Lorraine traveled in the second cabin and Alice Cleaver and Trevor occupied the third cabin. The other domestic workers traveled in Second Class.

On the night of the sinking, chaos broke out over the Allisons as well. After the TITANIC had struck the iceberg, Alice Cleaver grabbed little Trevor and took him into Lifeboat No. 11, taking her and the baby to safety. Unfortunately, this information did not reach the parents desperately searching for their little son.

There is great disagreement among experts about the last moments of Bess Allison. Some sources say that Bess was packed into a lifeboat with Lorraine when she realized in the boat that neither Alice Cleaver, nor her little son were on the boat. So, she and Lorraine got out of the lifeboat and went in search of Alice and Trevor. Shortly after, a sailor is said to have tried to bring little Lorraine to safety by calling her to him, but Bess Allison herself practically prevented the rescue of her child by calling Lorraine back, because she did not want to be separated from her second child. This version is considered by some to be pure fiction.

The rescued First-Class passenger Major Arthur Peuchen later told the Montreal Daily Star of his encounter with Bess and Lorraine Allison: "*Mrs. Allison could be in perfect safety, but someone told her Mr. Allison was in a boat on the other side of the deck, and then she ran away from the boat with her little daughter. When she got to the other side, she found out that Mr. Allison was not there. Meanwhile, our boat was lowered. She went to the deck without her husband and was sent to the other side of the boat by an officer. She couldn't find Mr. Allison and was quickly forced into one of the collapsibles.*"

What happened to Lorraine Allison and her mother after that cannot be said, but the sad fact is that Lorraine Allison was the only First-Class child that died in the sinking of the TITANIC. Also, her mother Bess and her father Hudson, whose body was found a few days later and shortly after buried in the Allisons' family grave on Maple Ridge Cemetery in Winchester, Ontario, Canada, died in the sinking of the luxury liner.

The other employees of the Allisons had a different fate. The chauffeur George Swane had knocked on the cabin door of his colleagues after the collision and warned them to get dressed as soon as possible. His colleague Mildred Brown had been reluctant to leave her warm bed and only after endless discussion with her cabin mate Selina Cooks, she could be persuaded to finally get up, get dressed, put on a life jacket and go to the Boat Deck.

Like Alice Cleaver, she climbed into Lifeboat No. 11 and survived the disaster of which she told her mother in a letter on Friday, April 19th, 1912:

"My dear Mother,

At last, I have made myself sit down to write. I don't know how the time has gone since the wreck, but I can`t help thinking how lucky I was to be amongst the rescued. There were 2,000 people, about that, on board and only about 700 were rescued. It happened at 11:30 Sunday night. Our boat ran into an iceberg, and within 1 ½ hours, the vessel had sunk. I couldn't believe that it was serious and would not get up until Swain came and made me. That was the last I saw of him, poor fellow. No sooner was I on deck than I was bustled to the first-class deck and pushed into one of the boats, and I found Nurse (Alice Cleaver) and the baby (Trevor Allison) were there. It was awful to put the lifebelt on. It seemed as if you really were gone.

Then came the lowering of the boats. I shut my eyes in hopes I should wake up and find it a dream. Then came the awful suspense of waiting till a vessel happened to pass our way. The wireless telegraphy had been used, and this vessel that was southward bound came miles out of its way to pick us up. By the time we had got out of reach of the suction, we stopped to watch her go down, and you could watch her go too. It went in the front until I was standing like this, then all the lights went out. Shortly after, we heard the engines explode and then the cries of the people for help. Never shall I forget it as long as I live. I don't let myself think of it. We were on the water from 12 till 6 in this small boat. Thank goodness it was a calm clear night, or I don`t know what would have happened. We were nearly frozen as there were icebergs all round us.

Ever since I have been on here, I have felt in a stupor. Everything seems too much trouble, and I don't care what happens to me. I found Sallie (Sarah Daniels) had got on alright but, poor girl, she keeps worrying about her things. Of course, we have lost everything bar what we stand up in. I had my watch on my arm. in fact, it hasn't left it since we sailed, and my money was in my pocket. I have not seen Mr. and Mrs. Allison. I suppose they have gone under, but there is just the hope that they may have been picked up by another boat. But still, I am not going to worry about that as they have several friends on board. And then there are the partners of the firm. We have been offered a home until they can find us a place suitable. This vessel has turned back to New York with us. I have slept on the Dining Room floor both nights. We had a most awful thunderstorm last night and today, it's that *foggy. I shall be glad to be on terra firma again. We had a bad start. The New York broke adrift and ran into us at Southampton Harbour.*

Well, I wo't write any more now. Will you let Neil read this and Aunt Em or anyone that you think, as I do't feel like going over it again. Do'nt worry about me as I shall be well looked after, and I have made several well-to-do-friends.

Lots of love to all

From your ever-loving daughter

Millie"

Mrs. Allison's maid, Sarah Daniels, was grabbed by the arm of a sailor and pulled to Boat No. 8 just as she arrived on deck. She had tried desperately to convince Mr. Allison of the seriousness of the situation and had therefore returned to the Allison's cabin on C Deck. In gratitude for her efforts, she was only scolded for disturbing the family for the second time...

When the sailor helped her into the boat, she protested vigorously and said that she had to take care of her employer's family. When the man finally assured her that he would personally take care of the Allisons' safety, she climbed into the boat.

The already mentioned chauffeur, George Swane, did not survive the sinking of the TITANIC, as Millie Brown had already feared in her letter to her mother. His body was later found and buried at the Fairview Cemetary in Halifax, Nova Scotia, on Monday, May 6th, 1912.

The gravestone of George Swane at the Fairview Cemetery in Halifax © private photo of the author

But this story is far from over, because the rescued Trevor Allison died under very mysterious circumstances on Wednesday, August 7th, 1929, at the age of 18 years, by a meat poisoning. Afterwards, there were many speculations about poisoning in order to get the big family fortune of the Allisons'. But this has remained pure speculation until today.

In the 1940s the history of the Allisons took up again enormous speed, because a certain Helen Lorraine Kramer appeared in the family and claimed to be Lorraine Allison!

She reported on the radio, she was taken to one of the few lifeboats by her father at the last minute and was saved. After the sinking, a Mr. Hyde, who she thought was her father, would have taken care of her. Only shortly before his death, the man would have revealed the truth to her that he was not her real father, and more importantly, had kept his true identity a secret. He was in fact Thomas Andrews, the designer of the TITANIC!

Of course, the Allison family was not very enthusiastic about this story and of course they did not believe it. If the whole thing had turned out to be true, it would have cost the family dearly, because then the heiress would have been entitled to a large part of the family money.

The dispute between Helen Lorraine Kramer and the Allison family over the inheritance of her alleged parents continued until Helen Lorraine Kramer's death in 1992. But even after that it continued, because Kramer's granddaughter Debrina Woods fought from Florida for the rights of her deceased grandmother. She created a website about her alleged story and planned to publish a book about it. She also presented a piece of evidence to the public in the form of a suitcase full of documents to support her claims.

The Allison family obtained a restraining order to stop Woods from making their demands. One of the demands was that her grandmother's ashes should be laid to rest in the Allison family grave. Naturally, this request was denied.

With the help of Forensic Scientist Professor Tracy Oost from Laurentian University in Canada, the mystery of identity was finally solved. She asked both sides of the dispute for DNA samples. While a member of the Allison family immediately agreed to the test, Debrina Woods refused a scientific verification. However, her half-sister agreed to a test.

The test came to the clear conclusion that there is no genetic link between Kramer and Woods on the one hand and the Allison family on the other. Therefore, Helen Lorraine Kramer was not Lorraine Allison.

Professor Oost commented: *"It is good to finally have clarity, but we must not forget that this is one of the more tragic stories of the TITANIC. The only mystery left in this case is, 'Who is Helen Kramer?'"*

Her granddaughter, Debrina Woods, however, still maintains her demands. She did not want to comment on the DNA investigations. Instead, she wanted to present her own results and then publish them in a book.

How she refutes clear DNA evidence remains her secret...

The Legendary Straus Couple

Whenever the sinking of the TITANIC and the tragic fates of her passengers are discussed or written about, one story must not be missed: The story of Isidor and Ida Straus!

Isidor Straus was born on 24th March 1845 in Otterberg near Kaiserslautern, Germany, as the son of the Jewish businessman Lazarus Straus and his wife Sara. When he was eight years old, his family emigrated to the USA and settled in Talbotton, Georgia, where Lazarus Straus opened a shop. In 1874 Lazarus Straus came into possession of the tableware department of the R.H. Macy department store in New York. Together with his brother Nathan, Isidor Straus became a partner of the department store in 1888.

Isidor Straus was also not inactive politically, because from 1894 to 1895 he was represented for the Democratic Party in United States House of Representatives.

In 1871 he had married his great love Rosalie Ida Blun (called Ida), whom he had known and loved since childhood. Like him, the four years younger Ida originally came from Germany. Together they had seven children (one of the sons unfortunately died in infancy):

- Jesse Isidor Straus (1872-1936), married Irma Nathan (1877-1970)

- Clarence Elias Straus (1874-1876), died as an infant
- Percy Selden Straus (1876-1944), married Edith Abraham (1882-1957)
- Sara Straus (1878-1960), married Dr. Alfred Fabian Hess (1875-1933)
- Minnie Straus (1880-1940), married Richard Weil (1876-1918)
- Herbert Nathan Straus (1881-1933), married Therese Kuhn (1884-1977)
- Vivian Straus (1886-1974), married Dr. Herbert Adolph Scheftel (1875-1914) and George Dixon, Jr.

On 10th April 1912, the Straus couple and two employees (John Farthing as Isidor's servant and Ellen Bird as Ida's maid) boarded the TITANIC as First-Class passengers. Originally Ida Straus had been looking for a French maid, but she could not find one, so she hired an English maid in the form of Ellen Bird. On the ship Isidor and Ida lived in cabin C 55-57 which was in the immediate vicinity of the suite of John Jacob Astor and his young wife Madeleine. Because of their attachment to their old home country Germany, the couple had so far mostly chosen German shipping companies for ship voyages, but the new TITANIC fascinated Isidor so much that he booked a passage on the new ship.

After the collision with the iceberg, the two of them went onto the Boat Deck, and when Lifeboat No. 8 was to be lowered around 1.10 a.m., Ida Straus was asked to get into the boat.

But she refused her place in the lifeboat because she did not want to leave Isidor. She said to Isidor: *"We have lived together for many years. Where you go, I go."*

When a fellow passenger remarked that no one would deny an older gentleman like Mr. Straus a place in the lifeboat, he replied:

"No. I do not want any preferential treatment."

But he tried desperately to get his wife to get into the lifeboat. The New York Post reported that he had said to her: *"Please, please, my dear. Get in the boat!"*

But she was not willing to leave him, and both remained aboard the TITANIC, bravely facing their fate after watching the departure of Mrs. Straus' maid Ellen Bird, who, with tears in her eyes, had accepted her employer's fur stole as a farewell gift. Finally, both were seen sitting, hand-holding on a deck chair on the Boat Deck, while others apparently claim to have seen them on their way to their cabin.

When the news of the sinking of the TITANIC shook the world, the children of Isidor and Ida set off for New York to obtain information about their parents' whereabouts. Meanwhile, the body of Isidor Straus was recovered as No. 96 by the MACKAY-BENNET from the North Atlantic. Unfortunately, the body of Ida Straus was never found.

Isidor was buried in a mausoleum in New York. Even today, a park near their former residence in New York reminds us of the famous couple.

Some sources report that in Ida's honor the Straus family took water from Titanic's wreck site, poured it into an urn and buried the urn next to Isidor. This story sounds great but has been proven as wrong by the Straus Historical Society.

A memorial plaque at the Macys department store still reminds us of the legendary Straus couple © private photo of the author

The Elegant Sinking of Benjamin Guggenheim

One of the most famous personalities on board the TITANIC was without a doubt the mining millionaire Benjamin Guggenheim, whose fortune at that time was estimated at $380 - a fabulous fortune especially by the standards of the time!

At the beginning of the last century, the Guggenheim family controlled a large part of the world's copper production. When Benjamin Guggenheim returned to the USA in 1903 after a two-year stay in Europe, he built a factory for mining machinery in Milwaukee. Three years later he became Chairman of the Board of the International Steam Pump Company, in which the family held large shares. Another three years later he became president of the company, which operated seven plants in the USA and one in England and employed almost 10,000 people.

As contemporaries reported, Benjamin Guggenheim was a "bon vivant" and had numerous affairs with mostly much younger women. His marriage to Florette Guggenheim, née Seligman, whom he married on Wednesday, October 24th, 1894, and from whom three daughters emerged, actually existed only on paper.

The Guggenheims' middle daughter was the famous "Peggy" Guggenheim, who later became a world-

famous patron of the arts, a collector and gallery owner of 20th century art.

Ben Guggenheim boarded the TITANIC together with his 24-year-old French mistress Ninette Aubart, his valet Victor Giglio and the Swiss Emma Sägesser, who served his lover as a chambermaid.

On board the ship, there was of course a lot of whispering about the couple, but the upper class was already used to Benjamin Guggenheim's stories about women...

After the TITANIC had the fateful collision with the iceberg, he made sure that Ninette Aubart and her maid got a place in Lifeboat No. 9. Then he retired to his cabin B 84 together with his valet, put on his best evening clothes and went down "like a gentleman" together with Victor Giglio!

Legend has it that the two men smoked cigars and drank brandy while waiting to die. Guggenheim told Steward Howard Etches:

"I think there are serious doubts about the men getting away. I am prepared to stay and play the men's game if there are not enough boats for anyone other than women and children. I will not die here like an animal. Tell my wife that I have played this game consistently to the end. No woman should be left aboard this ship just because Ben Guggenheim is a coward. We put on our best clothes, and we're prepared to die like gentlemen. Tell my wife I did my duty."

The elegant Benjamin Guggenheim © public domain

There is not much information about his mistress Leontine Pauline (better known as "Ninette") Aubart. She was born in Paris on Friday, 20th May 1887. She was a professional singer and lived at 17 rue Le Sueur in Paris.

During her time as a singer, she met Benjamin Guggenheim, 22 years her senior, whose marriage to Florette Guggenheim had broken up, and became his lover.

On the evening of April 10th, 1912, she boarded the luxury liner in Cherbourg with her Swiss maid Emma Sägesser, where she occupied cabin B 35 (ticket number PC 17477).

After her rescue she wrote a short telegram to Paris on Thursday, April 18th 1912: *"I am saved, but Ben is lost!"*

Some sources claim that she received a lot of money by Benjamin Guggenheim's widow Florette after her arrival in New York in order to avoid a social scandal.

Not much is known about her further life, except that she is said to have organized some lavish parties in the twenties, which even had to be stopped by the police. She died on Thursday, October 29th, 1964, at the age of 77.

The Wedding Ring of Gerda Lindell

In the icy North Atlantic on the night of April 14th, 1912, three Swedish friends were desperately fighting for their lives. They were the young married Gerda (30 years), her six years older husband Edvard Lindell as well as the 27-year-old August Wennerström, who had left his home country of Sweden as a political refugee to start a new life in America.

The Lindell couple wanted to emigrate to Hartford, Connecticut and had received the long-awaited permission from America to enter the country on Tuesday, April 4th, 1912. The original plan of the Lindell's was that Edvard should travel to Hartford alone and his wife would join him later. But Gerda did not want to separate from her husband and decided to go with him on the TITANIC.

In Southampton Gerda wrote one last postcard to her brother in Helsingborg:

"Tomorrow, we will go aboard the Titanic. We were already in the harbor to see the colossus. You should see how huge it is. Greetings from Gerda."

Thus, on Wednesday, April 10th, 1912, the couple boarded the new luxury liner in Southampton under ticket number 349910. They paid 15 pounds and 11 shillings for the ticket.

During the crossing they had met their countryman, August Wennerström and made friends with him. They loved their home country Sweden very much but saw the need to leave the old Europe for a better future and to seek their fortune in the new world. When the ship struck the iceberg, they felt the impact much more intensely deep down in Third Class. After the collision, like most steerage passengers, they were left to their own devices and tried to find their own way out of the obviously doomed ship. When they were still on their way to the lifeboats, the stern of the TITANIC already began to lift herself out of the water as August Wennerström later remembered: *"The water was rising faster now than before, and people were trying not to slip on the deck, which was rising steeper and steeper."*

As the stern rose ever steeper into the air, the friendly Swedes plunged into the freezing cold water. The two Lindell`s reached Collapsible A, but it capsized, and they fell helplessly back into the icy sea.

Wennerström and Edvard Lindell made it back into the now leaking boat. Gerda Lindell was nowhere to be found at first, then Wennerström saw her in the water and took her hand. Weakened by the icy cold, he could unfortunately not help her.

"I don't know how long I was off the boat. When I reached it again, it was full of water. My friend, Mr. Lindell, had climbed in, too. I saw Mrs. Lindell in the water and grabbed her hand, but I didn't have the strength to pull her into the boat. Mr. Lindell looked straight ahead. He did not move and said not a word.

He was frozen to death. After half an hour, my strength weakened, and I watched Mrs. Lindell go down."

The bodies of the Lindell couple were never found. Edvard's body was probably lowered overboard to make the unstable boat lighter. The wedding ring of Gerda Lindell was found by the crew of the OCEANIC on Monday, May 13th, 1912, when they found Collapsible A, which was not taken by the CARPATHIA. According to Wennerström, Edvard Lindell had his wife's ring in his hand when he died, then it seems to have fallen back into the boat when he was hoisted out of it. While his friends were dying, August Wennerström survived and spent most of the rest of his life in America, where he finally died.

Although the boat had been drifting around for a month, the ring miraculously could still be found in it. It was taken to New York, where *White Star Line* employees began to identify it. It was discovered that the ring "belonged to a Mrs. Gerda Lindell," so it was sent to the Swedish Consulate in New York. However, the passenger list showed a passenger by the name of "Elin Lindell," but it was not possible to recognize that there was actually an Elin Gerda Lindell on the TITANIC:

"And therefore, we ask you to help us by allowing us to give you this ring, provided that you agree to investigate this matter, and if the ownership claims are to be determined, to locate the rightful owner and hand over her property to Mrs. Lindell via her branch in Sweden."

The letter was dated Friday, 7th June 1912, and the *White Star Line* stationery (it still had both the OLYMPIC and the TITANIC on its letterhead) contained the ring. In fact, they were two rings forged into each other with the engraving on the inside. A few weeks later the letter arrived in Stockholm with the appeal of the Ministry of Foreign Affairs to find the owner by publishing it in some newspapers. Gerda's brother, Nils Nilsson, was employed by the Swedish National Railways and commuted between Malmö and Gothenburg. One day when he was in Gothenburg, he noticed the call in a newspaper. He became aware and showed the article to his parents. In July 1912. Gerda's father Nils Persson received the ring in Gantorfa as his next of kin. It was all that was left for him and his wife from their daughter, and her death overshadowed the rest of her life.

For many years, no one in the family knew where the ring had gone, and only by coincidence did it become known that it was still in the family's possession. The ring was inherited by Gerda to the daughter of her brother, who later, when her own wedding ring did not fit anymore, used it for this purpose. Today this ring is shown in various exhibitions.

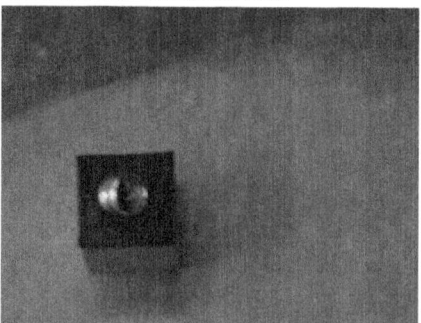

The wedding ring of Gerda Lindell was presented during the Titanic Exhibition 2010 in Wiesbaden © private photo of the author

The Tragic Story of the Goodwin Family (The "Unknown Child")

A particularly tragic TITANIC story is without a doubt that of the British Goodwin family. The family of eight had originally booked a passage on the NEW YORK, but like some other passengers, the Goodwin family was transferred to the TITANIC in Southampton where they boarded the luxury liner as Third-Class passengers. The head of the extended family was Frederick Joseph Goodwin who wanted to start a new life in America with his wife Augusta and his six children Lillian, Charles, William, Jessie, Harold, and the small, 19-month-old Sidney Lesley.

Frederick's brother Thomas had emigrated to America some time before and lived in Niagara Falls, New York State. He wrote to his brother that a power plant would be opening in the immediate vicinity and that manpower was needed there. Probably this power plant was the famous Schoellkopf hydroelectric power station (Station A) which was opened in 1912. Frederick Goodwin, an electrical engineer by profession, did not hesitate for long, sold his house in Fulham, lived temporarily in Marcham and set off for America with his wife and six children.

The Goodwin family. From left to right: William, Frederick, Charles, Lillian, Augusta, Jessie. In the middle is Harold. Sidney is not in this photograph. © public domain

There is not much known about the activities of the Goodwins on board the TITANIC. They were accommodated in opposite areas of the ship - Frederick and his elder sons had their cabin in the bow, while Augusta with the girls and little Sidney were accommodated in the stern of the ship. However, it is known that Harold Goodwin spent some time with the later survivor Frank Goldsmith, as Goldsmith later reported.

After the collision with the iceberg, the Goodwin family had to get together first, which took endless time. Time, which they unfortunately did not have as passengers in Third Class.

When they finally reached the Boat Deck, all lifeboats had been lowered and there was no hope of rescue. The entire Goodwin family of eight lost their lives when the TITANIC sank on April 15th, 1912. Their bodies were never found.

It was thought for almost a century...

Flashback: On Sunday, April 21st, 1912, six days after the tragic sinking of the TITANIC, the crew of the cable ship MACKAY-BENNET, chartered by the *White Star Line* for the recovery of the victims, finds the body of a little boy amidst wreckage. For the hard-boiled crew of the recovery ship, the sight of the boy is a hard test. The Morning Chronicle newspaper from Halifax reported on Wednesday, May 1st, 1912, about the recovery: "*The body floated along the boat, tenderly taken on board by the rescuers. The sight of the face-up drifting boy brought tears to the eyes of many of the tough sailors.*"

The boy is the fourth dead man to be taken on board. The coroner noted the sad find: "*NO. 4 - male - estimated age 2 - blond hair. Clothing: grey coat, fur on collar and sleeves, brown frock coat, petticoat, flannel clothing, pink wool undershirt, brown shoes and knee socks. No other signs, probably third class.*"

The crew of the MACKAY-BENNET decided that if no one would make a claim on the child, they would take care of the burial.

And so, it was done. The crew bought a beautiful coffin and donated a tombstone with the words, "*Erected to the memory of an unknown child whose remains were recovered after the disaster to the Titanic April 15, 1912,"* and appeared in a united front at the funeral on Saturday, May 4th, 1912, at Fairview Lawn Cemetery in Halifax, which created a real crowd.

In 2001, Marine Geologist Alan Ruffman attempted to uncover the identity of the unknown child, and together with Ryan Parr of Lakehead University in Ontario, obtained a special permit to open several Titanic graves to find the names of unidentified victims. The grave of the unknown child was among them. At first, they found nothing but mud - the decomposition was already too far advanced.

But the two researchers were able to recover a six-centimeter-long bone fragment of a forearm and three teeth for DNA analysis.

After initial investigations, six victims known to the two scientists were shortlisted as the "unknown boy". The shortlisted included: the five-month-old Gosta Leonard Paulson from Sweden, the 19-month-old Sidney Leslie Goodwin from England, the two-year-old Eugene Rice from Ireland and the 13-month-old Eino Viljami Panula from Finland.

In order to get DNA samples from relatives and descendants, Ruffman set off on a journey through Europe. Together with other experts, Ruffman discovered very well-preserved mitochondrial DNA (mtDNA) in the unearthed teeth of the unknown boy. Investigations revealed the following picture: The genetic material sequences contained in the teeth were duplicated with those that the researchers had discovered in the DNA samples of the descendants of the Finnish boy. This was announced by Ruffman and Parr on Wednesday, November 6th, 2002: The unknown child is Eino Viljami Panula from Ylihärma in Finland.

But unfortunately, this message was not correct!

According to Ruffman, the researchers did not take into account what the research had found out in the meantime, because many male Northern Europeans show the discovered match within the mtDNA. So, the chance of having identified the child correctly was only 50%. And so the search began again...

The researchers were helped in clarifying the identity by chance, because in the same year a pair of weathered brown leather shoes appeared, which increased the doubts. In 1912 the belongings of the found TITANIC victims were burned to get rid of souvenir hunters. This operation was monitored by the police, but Clarence Northover, a sergeant, did not have the heart to let the small shoes burn.

In July 2002, the Sergeant's grandson donated the pair of shoes to the Maritime Museum of the Atlantic in Halifax. After three years of examination, it was then certain that the shoes were those mentioned by the coroner of body No. 4 in 1912.

This put Ruffman and Parr in a dilemma, because if the museum experts' findings were true, Eino Viljami Panula would have worn shoes that were far too big for a child of only 13 months, so the scientists started a new attempt to clarify the identity.

Together with American experts, who identify fallen soldiers of the Second World War, the decisive breakthrough was actually achieved: The "unknown child" can only be Sidney Leslie Goodwin, born on Friday, September 9th, 1910, who died at the age of 19 months in the sinking of the TITANIC!

His shoes would have fit him, too. So the identity of the child, known for almost one hundred years as "unknown child", was finally clarified on Wednesday, July 30th, 2008! The original gravestone, under which the remains of little Sidney rest, still stands in the cemetery. A gravestone with the imprint of Sidney Leslie Goodwin now stands in the immediate vicinity.

The gravestone of Sidney Leslie Goodwin © private photo of the author

Thomas Millar and the Story of the Two Pennies

To this day, the sad and very emotional story of crew member Thomas Millar is told by his descendants:

On a sunny Sunday morning in 1911, Thomas Millar, born on Monday 11th August 1879 in Carrickfergus near Belfast in Northern Ireland, organized a special gift for his two little sons, Ruddick (four years old), and Tommy Jr. (ten years old): a sightseeing tour of the Harland & Wolff shipyard in Belfast.

He wanted to show his sons the ship he was working on. His younger son Ruddick remembered this day many years later, and that he had been disappointed with the TITANIC, because in Ruddick's mind a "boat" was something you could see at a glance. The TITANIC, on the other hand, was a high metal mountain that seemed to float above him, blocking the light, and making him really scared. To his father he tried to hide his true feelings, because he knew what it meant to him to build these huge engines that would drive this giant through the water.

For the 32-year-old Thomas Millar, working on the TITANIC and previously on the OLYMPIC was the reward for many years of hard work. Since he was determined to make something of his life, Thomas spent many nights learning and improving his skills. This was in stark contrast to many of his colleagues who preferred to work in a family environment. Thomas, on the other hand, was very ambitious and had no qualms about going anywhere if it helped him in his career and there was a chance to learn something.

This quest for improvement brought Thomas from the Belfast shipyard, Workman, Clark & CO, to the Vickers of Barrow shipyard in Furness, Cumbria. As new positions were filled at Harland & Wolff, Thomas took the opportunity to return to Belfast to work for an advanced shipyard at the forefront of new advances in shipbuilding. However, he had to cope with the disadvantage of not having any family members working in the shipyard to explain to him what was going on.

He worked in the shipyard during the day, and at night, he learned to expand his knowledge of the trade.

Later, Thomas was eager to travel to Canada or America, because as a trained engineer, he knew that there would always be a need for men with his skills. His dream seemed to come true when he heard that the prestigious *White Star Line* was looking for experienced engineers for their ships. On top of that, *White Star* offered very good pay and the opportunity to work overseas.

On Thursday, 18th January 1912, the family was struck by a heavy blow of fate when Thomas' wife Jeannie died at the age of 32, leaving him behind with his two young sons.

Thomas decided that his future would not be in Ireland but in America. He joined the *White Star Line* as an Assistant Deck Engineer. After an introductory training on the ship, which engines he had built and installed, he signed his contract with *White Star* in Belfast on Tuesday, 2nd April 1912. On the same day he arranged a goodbye for his two little boys, who were staying with their aunt during his absence. In New York he wanted to take the opportunity to look for a place to stay for himself and his two sons.

As a farewell present, he gave each of them two new pennies from 1912 with the request: *"Don't spend them until I see you again!"* Unfortunately, this was never to happen, because Thomas Millar was lost in the sinking of the TITANIC. Some survivors later reported that he had rushed to the Engine Room to help. That was the last time he was seen alive.

Many years later, Ruddick told his family he was playing by a stream on Tuesday, April 16th, 1912, where he put folded boats into the water.

His cousin Isabel had heard the news of the sinking of the TITANIC and tried to explain to him that within three months he had lost first his mother and now his father.

When the paper shuttle collided with a rock in the creek and slowly filled with water, and the paper could no longer give the construction a hold, she found the right words to tell Ruddick about the tragedy. He didn't say anything for quite a while before suddenly asking: *"What happened to Daddy's gold watch?"*

The two pennies have remained in family possession to this day and are shown as items in various Titanic exhibitions.

The story of the two pennies was first presented to the public by Millar's great-granddaughter Susan (Susie) Millar, who became president of the Belfast Titanic Society in 2017 and published a book about the story years before.

The Sad Death of Frederick Fleet

When Frederick Fleet from Liverpool and his experienced, 42-year-old colleague, Reginald Lee, started their shift in the Crow's Nest of the TITANIC on April 14th, 1912 at 10 p.m., he had no idea how much his life would change. Prior to this, both men had been instructed by the officers and their other colleagues in the lookout, Archie Jewell and George Symons, to pay particular attention to ice on the ship's course.

It was freezing cold that night, starlit and there was a new moon which did not make the work of the two men any easier. Also, the binoculars that were normally required in the Crow's Nest had not been found since Southampton (David Blair, who was originally intended to be the Second Officer for the TITANIC, is said to have locked them in a cupboard on the bridge and taken the key with him). Although binoculars were not necessarily of help in the weather conditions of that night, they are very helpful when an obstacle is seen.

Frederick Fleet was only 24 years old, but an "old stager" when it came to shipping. At the age of 12 he had already started his training on a training ship, which he left at 16 before he went to sea as a cabin boy in 1903. Before he joined the TITANIC, Fleet had already worked as a lookout on the *White Star* liner RMS OCEANIC for four years. As a lookout, he can be described as experienced.

So far, the maiden voyage of the TITANIC had been uneventful, but that was to change abruptly. Contrary to the long-standing opinion that only one single iceberg was sighted by Fleet and Lee, the opposite was probably the case. Frederick Fleet later said that he had sighted icebergs much earlier than 11:40 p.m. and reported them to the Bridge. But there they had not been disturbed by this and had simply continued their journey. Fleet claims to have seen and reported the unfortunate iceberg ten minutes before the collision. Fleet later said: "*I warned those on the bridge three times, and they did nothing. Now they're gonna pin the whole thing on me!*"

In the official version, at 11:40 p.m., Fleet rang the four-inch brass bell that was in the Crow's Nest, picked up the phone and called the Bridge. There the Sixth Officer James Moody reported, who would not survive the disaster. Fleet told the officer: "*Iceberg right ahead!*" To which Moody replied, "*Thank you.*"

After the TITANIC had stopped her journey, Fleet and Lee were pulled out of the Crow's Nest around midnight. During the course of the night, Fleet was ordered by Officer Ligtholler to fill and board Lifeboat No. 6.

At about 12:55 a.m., the lifeboat, led by Quartermaster Robert Hichens, left the sinking TITANIC. The legendary "unsinkable" Molly Brown also sat in this boat and is said to have had a heated debate during the night with Quartermaster Hichens, who presumably did not want to row back to the dying people in the water. In the meantime, experts are debating whether this battle of words really existed or is just another legend of the TITANIC.

After the terrible disaster of the TITANIC, Frederick Fleet was summoned to both inquiries of the TITANIC tragedy as a witness. Fleet did not cut a particularly good figure in either inquiry. His clumsy statements ("*How high was the iceberg?*" - "*As high as these two tables here!*" or "*I have no idea about distances and sizes, sir!*") caused disbelieving head shaking.

Also interesting is his statement in response to the following question from Senator William Alden Smith on Tuesday, April 23rd, 1912:
"*Can you somehow indicate the time that elapsed between your telephone message and the bell signal to the bridge and the collision of the ship with the iceberg?*"

Fleet said, "*I cannot say.*"

Senator Smith: "*You can't say it?*"

Fleet: "*No*"

Senator Smith couldn't believe it and asked, "*You can't tell if it was five minutes or an hour?*"

Fleet said, "*I can't tell.*"

Of course, that didn't make a very good impression on Frederick Fleet in public. But Fleet became quite unpopular with his superiors with his statement about the missing binoculars in the Titanic's Crow's Nest. Fleet testified that they would have discovered the iceberg earlier if they would have had binoculars in the lookout, as was usual and intended.

Senator Smith: "*Suppose you had glasses like those on Oceanic or like those between Belfast and Southampton. Could you have seen this black object at a greater distance?*"

Fleet: "*We could have seen it a little earlier.*"

Senator Smith: "*How much earlier?*"

Fleet: "*Well, soon enough to make our move!*"

It's obvious that these statements were not well received by the *White Star Line*.

Fleet continued to work for the *White Star Line* as a lookout and full seaman on the OLYMPIC, of all ships, but he had a hard time with *White Star* because of his unfortunate statements before the investigating committees, so he later changed to the *Union Castle Line* to work on their ships.

Fleet ended his career at sea at the age of almost 50 and worked during the Second World War as a shipbuilder for Harland & Wolff and later as a watchman for Union Castle. As he grew older, Frederick Fleet became increasingly impoverished and was forced to sell newspapers on a street corner in Southampton.

His life ended tragically, because shortly after the death of his wife, who died on Monday, 28th December 1964, he was forced to evict by his brother-in-law, with whom the Fleet couple had lived in a house. Out of sheer desperation, Fleet then took his own life on Sunday, 10th January 1965 by hanging himself in the garden.

He was then buried in a paupers' grave in Southampton. It was not until 1993, thanks to donations from the Titanic Historical Society (THS), that a gravestone was erected on which the TITANIC and the name of Frederick Fleet are engraved.

His colleague in the lookout at the time of the collision, Reginald Lee, died on Wednesday, August 6th, 1913, almost one and a half years after the sinking of the TITANIC, of heart failure after pneumonia, which had just been overcome.

Even Archie Jewell, the third lookout of the TITANIC, did not survive the tragedy for too long. He died on Tuesday, April 17th, 1917 as a soldier in World War I when his ship, Donegal, was sunk by a German submarine. The body of Archie Jewell was never recovered.

Interesting detail: Together with Violet Jessop (former stewardess) and John Priest (former fireman) Archie Jewell survived the sinking of the Britannic, the sister ship of the TITANIC, on Tuesday, November 21st, 1916.

The fourth lookout in the group, George Symons, died on Wednesday, December 6, 1950 at the age of 62.

The Destroyed Honor of Masabumi Hosono

From today's point of view, the fate of the only Japanese on board the TITANIC, Masabumi Hosono, is almost unbelievable. He was born in Tokyo on Tuesday, November 8th, 1870, and graduated from school in 1886 at the age of 16.

Since 1910, Hosono worked for the Japanese Ministry of Transport. In order to continue his education alongside his job, he took Russian language courses, which would soon enable him to travel to what was then still Tsarist Russia on behalf of his employer. One of these trips took him from Russia via London and from there to Southampton, where he finally boarded the TITANIC as a Second-Class passenger under ticket number 237798.

When he was woken by one of the stewardesses on the night of the accident, he first thought of a test alarm. Although it was at an unusual hour, he had no idea that it would become bitterly serious.

On his way to the Boat Deck, however, he was quickly prevented by a crew member from getting into a lifeboat as he thought he was a Third-Class passenger.
Only by incredible luck, Masabumi Hosono reached the Boat Deck to realize that the number of boats would never be enough for all passengers on board.

When he looked over to Lifeboat No. 10, he could hear one of the officers shouting that there were two seats left in the lifeboat. After a short hesitation, he seized the chance and jumped into the boat. This changed his future life tragically...

Masabumi Hosono before his departure with the TITANIC © public domain

On board the CARPATHIA he wrote a letter to his wife telling her about his rescue:

"All the while flares signaling emergency were being shot into the air ceaselessly, and hideous blus flashes and noises were simply terrifying. Somehow, I could in no way dispel the feeling of utter dread and desolation," he wrote.

"I tried to prepare myself for the last moment with no agitation, making up my mind not to leave anything disgraceful as a Japanese. But still I found myself looking for and waiting for any possible chance for survival."

Hosono saw his chance for rescue when an officer shouted" *Room for two more*" and a man jumped in.

"I, myself, was deep in desolate thought that I would no more be able to see my beloved wife and children, since there was no alternative for me than to share the same destiny as the Titanic. But the example of the first man making a jump led me to take this last chance.

After the ship sank there came back again frightful shrills and cries of those drowning in the water. Our lifeboat, too, was filled with sobbing, weeping children and women worried about the safety of their husbands and fathers. And I, too, was as much depressed and miserable as they were, not knowing what would become of myself in the long run."

After his return to Japan, Masabumi Hosono experienced that his fears for the future were more than justified. In his home country, he was reviled and attacked because he had saved himself while so many other people died.

The hostility even went so far that he was denounced by the Japanese press as a coward who must have pretended to be a woman on the ship, under false pretences, to get into a lifeboat. He had disgraced the country and its government and betrayed the self-sacrifice in the spirit of the Samurai.

In Japanese textbooks his survival on the TITANIC was described as a model of shameful behavior, and an ethics professor called him immoral and unethical. The Ministry of Transport dismissed him because they did not want to employ a dishonorable man. Other sources reported that the ministry "only" demoted him, but be that as it may, he no longer worked in his previous senior position.

Until his death on Tuesday, March 14th, 1939 as an impoverished and broken man, Masabumi Hosono and his entire family were considered a disgrace to the country. And until his death, Hosono never spoke again about the events of that night that destroyed his entire life, although he was actually one of the 712 lucky survivors of the disaster. However, he wrote down his experiences and left the memoirs to his wife.

In 1997, when James Cameron's blockbuster "TITANIC" was a great success in Japan, the Hosono family decided to donate the estate to a museum. A few years later, Masabumi Hosono was honored posthumously in the Yokohama Minato Museum with a small exhibition and thus subsequently received back the honor his own nation had taken away from him.

Scandinavian Destinies

The fate of the wealthy passengers of the TITANIC has been reported much more than that of the countless immigrants who boarded the ocean liner to start a better life in the New World. Especially from Scandinavia, many emigrants had boarded the ship. The tragic story of two friends from Sweden is told here:

The 43-year-old carpenter and qualified skipper John Fredrick Alexander Holm (born on Saturday, February 20th, 1869) wanted to earn enough money in America to build up his own life, together with his fiancée, the shipowner's daughter, Emmy Tanngren. He already had a job in America at a sailing club just behind Coney Island in Brooklyn, New York. He wanted to send everything that could be saved through an agent to his home country, Sweden, or sew it into his vest for his return journey.

> **Sewing the money into the vest or the belt was a common habit on long journies at that time. After the sinking of the TITANIC, the money was found in the vests or belts of many dead bodies.**

He hoped that he would be able to raise enough money to move into a small apartment with his great love Emmy after his return to Sweden. He had great love sickness during the whole journey because he would be separated from his fiancée for so long. The two letters he had already sent home to Emmy Tanngren from England bear witness to this.

His 30-year-old friend Mauritz Adahl (born on Wednesday, June 15th, 1881 in Asarum, Smaland) was greatly amused by the heartache of his 13-years-older friend. During the long journey by train from Karlshamn via Malmö, Copenhagen, Esbjerg and Harwich, he had tried in vain to distract his buddy. Then Mauritz wrote to his wife that John was not in the right place: "*foreheaded as a klockarkatt.*" John behaved like a house cat that had been thrown out of the door, but that would probably soon pass.

Mauritz Adahl had already gone to America in 1903. Only three years later, he was allowed to have his wife Emilie from Stockholm to join him. He had worked in a large cabinet maker's shop in New York and had earned very reasonable money there. The two daughters of the couple, Vera and Georgia, were very small, straw-blonde New Yorkers. But his wife just didn't feel at home in the big city. She wanted to go back to the quiet Asarum in southern Sweden, and so she and her two daughters went back to their Swedish home. In autumn 1911, Mauritz followed his family. He was able to buy his family a nice piece of land for his earned money, but unfortunately, he could not buy a fine white wooden house as he had hoped. After night-long discussions, he finally decided to return to America to get the necessary money for a house.

On the tracks in Karlshamn and Malmö, the two carpenters had a conversation with Aurora Adelia Landergren (born on Wednesday 19th June 1889 in Karlshamn). The 22-year-old intended to board a small steamer of the Danish Scandinavian-American Linjen in Copenhagen.

This would take her north around the British Isles to the States after a short stay in Christiania (now Oslo).

She was very happy to have Mauritz and John, two trustworthy men from her home country, who were also in firm hands, with her for the long and dangerous journey, and she let herself be persuaded to leave Southampton. Also, because she felt safer then because the ports of England were teeming with pickpockets at that time. The emigrants were also a popular and lucrative victim, because at the American Immigration Office on Ellis Island, every immigrant had to present a large cash deposit as security - usually double the fare of the just passed Third Class passage to be allowed to enter American soil. The Swedish emigrants preferred to travel in small groups so that they could take better care of each other.

As fate would have it, none of the three would have originally sailed on the TITANIC, but the famous coal strike by Welsh miners had crippled all the American Line ships Mauritz and John had originally intended to travel on. But as she also belonged to the *IMM* (*International Mercantile Marine*) of John Pierpont Morgan, they were transferred to the TITANIC.

Six days after their arrival in Harwich on the English North Sea coast, Aurora Adelia Landergren (ticket number 7077), Mauritz Adahl (ticket number 7076) and John Fredrick Alexander Holm (ticket number 7075) boarded the TITANIC together with the six-member Stockholm Skoog family and more than one hundred other Scandinavian emigrants. They had each paid seven pounds sterling and five shillings for their ticket.

For the price of a ticket alone, a whole family could have lived in Sweden for a whole year in a very reasonable way!

On board the TITANIC, Miss Landergren missed the usual company of her two new friends, so they regularly arranged to meet on the rear Well Deck where they could get some fresh air. The Swedes were pleasantly surprised by the food on board the ocean liner. Although the roast pork was not prepared there a la francaise like in First Class, but only warmed up, a rich meal was offered on board also for the Third Class. It is known that many passengers on the steerage were told by the stewards that after the preliminary soup, lunch was not yet finished, but that there would be a warm main course - for many an unusual luxury.

Speaking of luxury: When Aurora Landergren heard that First Class had its own swimming pool, she blushed slightly and wondered why the rich passengers needed their own pool as well...

John Holm's longing for his beloved Emmy was also huge on board the TITANIC, so he wrote his bride another card and handed it in at the on-board post office just in time for the emptying in Queenstown.

Shortly after the sinking of the TITANIC, his beloved Emmy had received the two letters from John in England which were mentioned in the beginning. She was overjoyed to read something from her lover.

She wrote to him in New York: "*I spent the best time of my life with you.*" She hoped very much that he had a good crossing, since he had not traveled on the Titanic. This huge ship had never really been her best friend!

The letter was left in the orphanage of John Holm's workplace for several weeks before the sleeping quarters were vacated for a new tenant. The letter ended up in the archives of the Swedish Consulate in New York. For more than 70 years, the letter was completely forgotten until the Swedish TITANIC expert Claes-Göran Wetterholm began to research the fate of the Scandinavian TITANIC passengers and came across this letter.

A few days after receiving the two letters from England, Emmy Tanngren again received a letter from John Holm. Her initial joy turned into sheer horror when she read that the card had come aboard the TITANIC and had been posted in Queenstown. Her dream of a life together with John Holm had been destroyed on April 15th, 1912, together with the TITANIC.

> After John Holm's death, the Swedish Consulate attempted to investigate his estate and found that all bank accounts had been emptied before his trip to Sweden in 1911. When consulate staff entered his apartment, they found very little furniture, dirty laundry and "unsaleable rubbish". A rumor that he had another apartment in Miami, Florida, turned out to be false. His fiancée Emmy Tanngren never moved into the apartment that she and John had prepared in Sweden, and the furniture was sold at auction. Emmy never remarried and continued to live with her parents. A really sad story!

About the last moments of Mauritz Adahl and John Holm on board the sinking TITANIC, we can report that shortly before the sinking of the ship, they were wandering around on the stern deck together with Aurora Adele Landergren and the Skoog family with their four children. Aurora decided to give all her money to John Holm. She believed that the savings on the ship were best kept by the men. What a fallacy!

Somehow, she ended up in one of the last lifeboats. Days later the body of Mauritz Adahl was identified by his watch; the large hand had stopped 14 ½ minutes after the sinking!

In 1915, Aurora Adelia Landergren returned to Sweden from the USA, on the occasion of her father's death. She visited the widowed Emilie Dahl, gave her husband's last greetings from the deck of the TITANIC, and gave her the watch.

Margaret Rice and Her Five Children

The 39-year-old widow Margaret Rice boarded the TITANIC in Queenstown on Thursday, 11th April 1912, together with her five small children, Albert (10), George (8), Eric (7), Arthur (4) and Francis (2 ½). She had managed to obtain a ticket for Third Class (ticket number 382652) for her family and was on her way to Spokane in Washington. However, she was not the typical Irish immigrant, because for her and her children it was a return to a familiar environment.

Margaret Rice was born on Sunday, 6th October 1872 in Athlone, Ireland. Her mother Mary died of tuberculosis on Tuesday, 13th January 1885. On Saturday, 18th June 1898, Margaret married the soldier William Rice in her hometown.

> Some sources report that Margaret Rice went to Canada with her family as a child and settled there and later met her husband William there. Only after that she is said to have returned to Ireland with William and then married him in Ireland.

The couple lived on North Gate Street in Athlone, where on Thursday, April 13th, 1899, their first child was born, William James. Tragically, the baby lived for less than two months, as little William died on Wednesday 31st May 1899. He had swallowed his pacifier four days earlier and never recovered from it. After a series of convulsions, he died quite agonizingly in front of his helpless parents.

The grieving parents could not stand it in Ireland any longer and moved to London, where Albert was born in 1902. At the beginning of 1903, the family of three moved back to Canada and settled in Montreal where their son George was born on Monday, November 30th, 1903.

The couple moved further west and settled in Ontario, where William worked first as an employee at Carleton Place and later in Toronto. There were also born their two sons Eric (born Thursday, August 24th, 1905) and Arthur (born Sunday, August 18th, 1907).

Two years after the birth of Arthur, the family moved from Canada to the USA and lived in Spokane, Washington where their youngest child Francis was born on Monday, September 13th, 1909.

Only three months later, on Monday 24th January 1910, William Rice, who was now working for the Great Northern Railway at Hilyard, was killed in an industrial accident when he was smashed by an engine. He was buried at Fairmount Cemetery in Spokane.

Margaret received a compensation of $300 from an insurance company of the Great Northern Railway, and she bought a house in Spokane and a gravestone for William. She had her husband's body buried at Fairmount Cemetery on Friday, April 15th, 1910 in a more expensive plot of land in the cemetery. As she stood there at her husband's new grave, she could not have known that she and her five children would be dead the same day two years later!

The grieving widow felt very lonely in Spokane with her five sons and decided to return to Athlone in Ireland for a while after William's second funeral. There she lived for two years in a rented flat in Castle Street until she decided in early 1912 that it was time to return to the USA with her children. She convinced four others from the Athlone area to take the step to America with the TITANIC: Eugene Daly, Bridget Mulvihill, Margaret Daly, and Bridget Henry.

After the TITANIC hit the iceberg, Margaret Rice and her five children tried to fight their way to the lifeboats. She was last seen by Bridget Mulvihill:

"Next to me was a family named Rice, consisting of father, mother and six children. The father was not allowed to leave the ship, but the mother and her six children could leave if they wanted to. The mother cried and wept. She did not want to go into the lifeboat and leave her husband to die. 'I cannot go and leave my husband behind,' she cried to the officers, 'Let him come with me, oh, please let him come with me,' she begged. 'I don't want to live if he can't come with me. Then there will be no one to earn the bread for my little children,' she cried. But the officers did not let the man go. 'Then I will stay with my husband,' cried the woman. I saw her clinging to her husband and children when I left the ship. That was the last I saw of her. The whole family went down together."

In this statement by Bridget Mulvihill, however, it is striking that she apparently confused the Goodwin family (father, mother and six children) with Margaret Rice and her five children.

Nevertheless, it is abundantly clear how insane it was that night to do "women and children first" so strictly. Only the body of Margaret Rice was later recovered by the MACKAY-BENNET. Margaret's body was given the number 12 and was taken to Halifax in Canada where the identification process began. A box of pills was found with her body, which contained the information that they were purchased in a pharmacy in Church Street, Athlone, Ireland, on Tuesday 9th April 1912. However, there was no name on the box. Margaret's shoes also gave the name of the shop where they were bought, Parsons in Athlone.

On Friday, May 3rd, 1912, Margaret Rice was buried at Mount Olivet Catholic Cemetery in Halifax Nova Scotia, Canada. However, it was not until Wednesday, September 25th, 1912 that body No. 12 was finally identified as Margaret Rice.

Of the 113 Irish passengers who boarded the TITANIC in Queenstown together with Margaret Rice and her five boys, only 44 survived the journey.

In 1998, a memorial stone was unveiled in Queenstown, now Cobh, in memory of all those passengers who left the Irish port on Thursday 11th April 1912 and died on the TITANIC. The bronze image on the stone shows some of the Irish immigrants on the two small tenders when they were transported to the TITANIC. Margaret Rice and her five young sons are also immortalized on the monument.

On Wednesday, April 15th, 2009, the 97th anniversary of the disaster, a monument was erected at the cemetery in

Spokane, Washington in the Fairmount Memorial Garden.

This memorial was erected to commemorate the death of Margaret Rice and her five young sons, as well as the death of three other Spokane residents who also went down with the TITANIC. The monument was erected behind the grave of William Rice and on the front of the monument, engraved in granite, the connection to the city and the sinking of the TITANIC is explained.

The Fate of the TITANIC Officers

If the RMS TITANIC had not sunk on April 15th, 1912, no one would probably be interested in the officers on board the luxury liner.

Here the fate of the officers of the legendary ocean liner is to be presented:

Captain Edward John Smith (27th January1850 – 15th April 1912)

Of course, the captain of the TITANIC is the most famous of the officers. Edward John Smith was born in Hanley, Staffordshire on Sunday, 27th January 1850 as son of Edward Smith and his wife Catherine Hancock Marsh. He left school at the age of 13 and became an apprentice in the merchant fleet at Gibson & Company in Liverpool. After long and hard apprenticeship years, Smith got a job with the *White Star Line* in 1880. There he made a remarkably steep career, rising from ship's mate to captain over the years. During the following 25 years, Smith commanded 17 ships of the shipping company. On Tuesday, 12th July 1887, he married the eleven years younger Sarah Eleanor Pennington (17th June 1861- 28th April 1931) with whom he had a daughter, Helen Melville Smith (1898-1973). The two led a very happy and harmonious marriage.

Edward John Smith also served in the South African War, better known as the "Boer War" (1899-1902). He commanded ships that transported British troops to the theatre of war. His leadership earned him several honors and the rank of Captain in the Royal British Naval Volunteer Reserve (R.N.V.R.). After the Boer War he returned to the Merchant Navy. In 1904 Smith was given command of the then flagship of the *White Star Line* BALTIC. In the following eight years Smith was in command of every other flagship, be it the ADRIATIC, the OLYMPIC or the TITANIC.

When Smith commanded the ADRIATIC in 1907, he gave an interview to a New York journalist, the wording of which is almost tragic in view of the later fate of Smith and the ship he commanded: "*I cannot imagine what problem could cause one of these recently built ships to sink. Nor can I think of any damage that would be irreparable. Modern shipbuilding has finally put these kinds of contingencies behind it!*"

This short interview also shows how much one was convinced of the safety of modern ships, and so a dangerous carelessness crept in which should have terrible consequences especially for the TITANIC.

When the TITANIC sank, Smith stayed on board the sinking ship until the bitter end and went down with it.

Shortly before his death, Smith stepped into the Wireless Room and asked his two Wireless Operators, Jack Phillips and Harold Bride*: "Help women and children and look to yourselves. You've done your duty!*"

Smith was last seen near the Bridge supervising the desperate evacuation of the TITANIC.

Chief Officer Henry Tingle Wilde (21st September 1872-15th April 1912)

Henry Tingle Wilde, born on Saturday, September 21, 1872 in Liverpool (England), grew up in the Grey Road, in the suburbs of the large port city. He was very ambitious and completed his training on the sailing ships of *Messrs*, James Chambers & Co in Liverpool. When he obtained his Second Mate`s Certificate, he was offered a position with the *Maranhan Steamship Company* as Second Officer.

Shortly after, he received his Master's Certificate, Wilde joined the prestigious *White Star Line* in 1897 as a Junior Officer.

There Wilde worked on the ARABIC (June to October 1905), the CELTIC (December 1905 to April 1906), the MEDIC (September 1906 to April 1908), and the CYMRIC (June to September 1908).

Privately, Henry Tingle Wilde had to endure terrible blows of fate in 1910, for on Christmas Eve 1910 his wife died shortly after his two twin sons had died, probably of scarlet fever, in childhood. This loss hit him infinitely hard. He had to take care of his four other children, Jane, Harry, Arnold, and Nancy, by himself (after Wilde`s death they were raised by his sister-in-law Annie).

In 1911 Wilde came to OLYMPIC as a Senior Officer under the command of Edward John Smith.

Henry Tingle Wilde was not actually intended for the TITANIC, as he was supposed to serve on the OLYMPIC under the command of Captain Herbert James Haddock as Chief Officer, but Edward John Smith requested him for the TITANIC on the *White Star Line*. This is how Henry Tingle Wilde came to the TITANIC. It seemed that he did not like the new ship, because in a short letter to his sister he wrote: "*I still do not like this ship. I have a strange feeling about it.*" Tragically, Wilde didn't seem to have been able to resist that "strange feeling."

Sadly, neither did Henry Tingle Wilde survive the disaster. Not much is known about his final hours aboard the TITANIC. When the ship collided with the iceberg, he was off duty. He was one of the first to insist that the lifeboats be lowered. He was busy lowering the lifeboats until the ship sank. He refused to get into a boat and remained on board until the end. He was last seen trying to lower Collapsibles A and B. His body was never found.

First Officer William McMaster Murdoch (28th February 1873 – 15th April 1912)

William McMaster Murdoch was born on Friday 28th February 1873 in Dalbeattie, Scotland, as the fourth son of Samuel Murdoch and Jane "Jeannie" Murhead. He came from a family with a very long maritime tradition, so it was only logical that he also took this career path. Initially William served on a number of sailing ships before joining the *White Star Line* in 1900, serving on the MEDIC and RUNIC, among others, which sailed in Australian waters.

On one of these voyages, he met the teacher Ada Florence Banks from New Zealand and married her four years later. By this time, he had already been transferred to the Atlantic liners. These ships included the ARABIC, CELTIC, GERMANIC, OCEANIC, CEDRIC, ADRIATIC, OLYMPIC and finally the TITANIC.

On the maiden voyage of the TITANIC, Murdoch was initially supposed to hold the post of Chief Officer, but shortly before the maiden voyage, Henry Tingle Wilde was preferred to him as Chief Officer, and he was downgraded to the rank of First Officer. He probably would not have been very enthusiastic about this, especially since it meant a loss of earnings of about seven pounds per month for him...

William McMaster Murdoch will probably be remembered forever as the one who steered the TITANIC against the iceberg, although he only tried to avoid the iceberg. During the evacuation, a large part of the men rescued owed him their lives, because when there were not enough women around to fill the lifeboats, he filled them up with men and did not let them go half-empty like his colleague Lightoller.

Especially since James Cameron's "TITANIC", there is a fierce argument about his end, because there it is portrayed that Murdoch shot himself shortly before the sinking, and before that, he accepted a bribe from a rich passenger (which he gave back, though). After a huge controversy, Cameron apologized to Murdoch's relatives, but the scene remained in the movie.

It is assumed that a higher-ranking officer of the TITANIC shot himself shortly before his sinking. Saloon Steward Thomas Whitely claimed to have seen, "*Murdoch first shot a man, then himself.*" Later Whitely admitted, "*I didn't see that myself. I heard it from three others who were there!*"

Now, whether that's very trustworthy is debatable...

Carl Jensen, a passenger in Third Class, also assured that, "*when looking back at the bridge, he saw the chief officer put a revolver in his mouth and shot himself. Then his body fell overboard.*" However, Chief Officer Jensen's talking should have been about Henry Wilde, not Murdoch.

In his hometown of Dalbeattie, Scotland, his memory is still highly revered today. The Dalbeattie Museum also remembers the town's famous son.

In April 2012 it became known that the salvage company, RMS Titanic, Inc., has recovered some of Murdoch's belongings from the wreck of the TITANIC. Among other things, a toiletry item, a spare *White Star Line* button, a razor, a shoeshine boy, a pipe, and a pair of long underpants.

William M. Murdoch Memorial in Dalbeattie © private photo of the author

Second Officer Charles Herbert Lightoller (30th March 1874 – 8th December 1952)

Charles Herbert Lightoller was born on Monday 30th March 1874 in Chorley (Lancashire, England) as the son of Frederick James and Sarah Jane Lightoller. His family was quite wealthy and owned a cotton mill in Chorley.

His mother died shortly after his birth and his two siblings, Richard Aston and Caroline May, also died of scarlet fever in early childhood.
At an early age Charles developed a fondness for the sea, so at the age of 13 he began a four-year nautical training on Primrose Hill. He experienced his first shipwreck on HOLT HILL when the ship was caught in a devastating storm and stranded on the uninhabited island of St. Paul. The crew of the HOLT HILL was then rescued by the Coorong and brought to Adelaide (Australia). From there the crew returned to England on the DUKE OF ABERCOM.

At the age of 21 he switched from sailing ships to steamships. After three years in the service of the *African Royal Mail Service* he fell seriously ill with malaria. After his recovery he retired from seafaring for the time being. He then unsuccessfully participated in the gold rush on the Klondike River and tried his hand at being a cowboy in Alberta, Canada, where he finally decided to return to England.

In order to finance the return journey home, he worked as a migrant worker. In the year 1899 he finally reached his homeland on a cattle freighter, completely destitute.

In 1900, after his trip to the new world had not been very successful, he finally remembered his old skills and started his career, at the age of 26, with the *White Star Line*, where he was first hired as Fourth Officer on the MEDIC. Afterwards he changed to the MAJESTIC under the command of Edward John Smith, the later captain of the TITANIC.

In 1903, when he sailed from England to Australia on the SUEVIC, he met his future wife Sylvia Hawley-Wilson, whom he married shortly afterwards.
When he was promoted to Third Officer, he switched from the MAJESTIC to the RMS OCEANIC, which was the absolute flagship of the *White Star Line* at that time, where he served as First Officer before he transferred to TITANIC. Due to the sudden installation of Henry Tingle Wilde as Chief Officer, he was graded one rank like William Murdoch and was therefore only Second Officer.

This was actually quite an affront to Charles Herbert Lightoller, because unlike Wilde and Murdoch, he not only held the captain's certificate but also an additional qualification. Therefore, he was more qualified than his higher-ranking colleagues, which is really remarkable.

He was the highest-ranking officer of the TITANIC who survived the sinking.

In the two inquiries of the Titanic disaster, he got entangled in rather blatant contradictions, which lead to the conclusion that he did not take the truth too seriously in order to save his employer, *White Star Line*, from an existence-threatening compensation for the victims and their relatives.

In World War I he served as a lieutenant in the Royal Navy. After the war he returned to the *White Star Line*, where he soon realized that he had no chance for promotion as a former crew member of the TITANIC. After 20 years he quit his job at *White Star*. In the '30s he wrote his autobiography,"Titanic and Other Ships," which after some initial difficulties had a considerable success. After the threat of a lawsuit by the Marconi Company against Ligtholler, the book had to be taken out of circulation. In his book he had been very critical about the role of the two TITANIC Wireless Operators, Phillips and Bride, which the Marconi Company was very displeased with.

After he and his wife had achieved considerable wealth through Happy Land speculation, he purchased the SUNDOWNER as his private yacht. With this ship he participated together with his son Roger in "Operation Dynamo" during the Second World War. The two of them helped to evacuate the allied soldiers who were encircled by the Germans in Dünnkirchen to Great Britain.

Lightoller lost two of his sons in the Second World War. The youngest son, Brian, died as a Royal Air Force pilot in the bombing of Wilhelmshaven on the first night after Britain entered the war. His oldest son Roger died as a soldier in the Royal Navy in Granville, France, shortly before the end of the war. The other three children, Richard, Mavis, and Doreen survived the war. In the post-war period he ran a small shipyard called Richmond Slipways in London, which built motorboats for the police.

On Monday, December 8th, 1952, Charles Herbert Lightoller died of a heart attack at Twickenham at the age of 78. He found his last resting place in Richmond near London.

Third Officer Herbert John Pitman (20th November 1877 – 7th December 1961)

As the third child of Henry Pitman and his wife Sahra Marchet, Herbert John Pitman was born on Tuesday, 20th November 1877 in Sutton Morris, Somerset in England. When he was three years old, his father Henry died, and his mother married Charles Candy sometime later. At a young age he followed in the footsteps of his dead fathe, and some other family members and began his seafaring career by joining the Merchant Navy in 1895.

At the age of 20 he became an officer and served on sailing ships for over ten years before he was recruited by the *White Star Line* in 1907. Before that, he sailed for the *Blue Anchor Line* and the *Shire Line*, which at that time sailed the routes from Great Britain to Australia and China. On the *White Star Line*, Herbert John Pitman served on the MAJESTIC and the OCEANIC before he came on the TITANIC. There he had an important task in mooring and casting off the lines, assisting First Officer William McMaster Murdoch and keeping the Bridge informed of all-important events on the ship.

When the TITANIC collided with the iceberg, Pitman was off duty and was only informed of the accident by Fourth Officer Joseph Boxhall, in his cabin. Thereupon he helped to clear the lifeboats on the Boat Deck. Together with William Murdoch, he ordered the evacuation on the starboard side.

At about 12.50 a.m., Murdoch gave him the order to fill Boat No. 5 and to board as crew. When the TITANIC sank, he looked at his watch and announced the exact time of the sinking at 2.20 a.m. Pitman actually wanted to return to the sinking site to search for survivors but was told not to do so by the passengers, who were afraid their lifeboat might capsize.

According to his testimony to the Inquiry Committee, he served as Third Officer on the OCEANIC from July 10th, 1912, and sometime later, as his eyesight had deteriorated considerably, as purser on the OLYMPIC. In the early 1920s he finally left the *White Star Line* and joined *Shaw, Savill and Albion Company Ltd.* In 1922.

At the age of 45, he married the New Zealander, Mildred Kalman. During the Second World War, he served as a purser on board the SS MATAROA. In March 1946, shortly before leaving the Merchant Navy, he was awarded the Order of the British Empire for "his long and meritorious service at sea and in dangerous waters during the war".

For over 20 years, Pitman worked as a purser for *Shaw, Savill and Albion Company*. He spent his well-earned retirement with a niece in Pitcombe, Somerset, where he died of a stroke on Thursday, 7th December 1961 at the age of 84. He found his final resting place in the parish churchyard of Pitcombe, Somerset.

A more than curious but true story is the story of Max Dittmar-Pittmann, who toured Germany in the 1930s and claimed to have been an officer on the TITANIC.

However, it is noticeable here that the original Pitman writes himself with only one N in his surname and not with two like Pittmann, but nobody seemed to be really interested in that at that time. In his autobiography he also reported about his experiences on the TITANIC. He even made it into the well-known novel "Titanic. Die Tragödie eines Ozeanriesen," by Josef Pelz von Felinau, in which he initially appeared as an officer. After his exposure as an impostor, Felinau's novel from Pittmann eventually became Petersen, who was also Danish in later editions of the book. But in the GermanTITANIC movie of 1943 Petersen was still a German officer on the British ship.

Fourth Officer Joseph Groves Boxhall (23rd March 1884 – 25th April 1967)

Joseph Groves Boxhall, Jr., was born in Hull, England on Sunday, 23rd March 1884 as the second child of Miriam and Captain Joseph Boxhall, Sr. His further path as a sailor was practically predetermined, for his grandfather was a sailor, and his father was the head of the *Wilson Line* in Hull. On Friday, 2nd June 1899, at the age of 15, he set out on his first voyage on a sailing ship of the *William Thomas Line* from Liverpool.

After he left the ship four years later, he worked for his father on the *Wilson Line*. In November 1907, shortly after he had acquired the captain's certificate and the master's certificate, which was specifically designed for service on the modern liners, he was recruited by *White Star Line*. From then on, he served on the ships OCEANIC and ARABIC.

On Tuesday, 26th March 1912, he was called to the *White Star Line* office at 9 a.m., like the other young officers of the TITANIC. The following day he sailed to Belfast to board the luxury liner. After the departure of the TITANIC in Southampton, he performed his duties, which included assisting passengers or crew and navigating the ship. When Captain Edward John Smith was on the Bridge, he was responsible for giving his orders. It was also his responsibility to record all manoeuvres of the ship in the logbook.

When the TITANIC had her fatal collision with the iceberg, Boxhall was on duty and heard the ringing of the bell in the crow's nest and then went to the Bridge. He arrived there shortly after the collision. Captain Smith ordered him to make a check of the forecastle. Boxhall set off but could not find any damage. When he told Smith about it, he sent him off to get the ship's carpenter to make a closer inspection of the TITANIC. Shortly after leaving the Bridge, the carpenter came to meet him and reported that the front compartments of the ship were already filling with water.

Boxhall was then ordered by Smith to call the Second Officer Lightoller and the Third Officer Pitman. Afterwards he should go to the Chart Room and calculate the position of the TITANIC.

From 12.45 a.m. ship time, he started to fire distress rockets, together with Quartermaster Arthur Rowe. During a last conversation with Captain Smith, Boxhall asked if the situation was really serious, whereupon Smith replied that the TITANIC would sink into the sea in about one to one-and-a-half hours.

At 1.45 a.m. he was launched as commander in Lifeboat No. 2. After the ship sank, he asked the women on board if they should go back to pull survivors out of the water, but the women did not want to do so, although there was still enough room in the lifeboat.

Like the other officers, Joseph Groves Boxhall also testified before the Inquiry Committees. However, his whereabouts during the collision are subject to different statements.

He himself testified that he was on his way to the Bridge, either on the Boat Deck or coming from the Chart Room, but his statements varied on this point. During the interrogation it was Boxhall, who for the first time spoke of another ship nearby that did not respond to the distress code of the TITANIC.

After the disaster, he suffered from chronic pleurisy, which was presumably caused and aggravated by the physical strain of lowering the lifeboats. After his return home he became Fourth Officer on the ADRIATIC.

Before the outbreak of World War I, he joined the Royal Naval Reserve (RNR) and was promoted to lieutenant in 1915. He served on cruisers, a torpedo boat, and a coastal base.

After the war, he was promoted to the rank of Lieutenant Commander. On Tuesday, 25th March 1919, two days after his 35th birthday, he married Marjory Beddels, the daughter of a Yorkshire industrialist, near her home in Sharrow, Sheffield. Although the marriage remained childless, it is said to have been very happy.

Two months later, Boxhall returned to the Merchant Navy and in the following years, he served on other *White Star Line* ships, sailing to the USA, Canada, and Australia. After the merger of the *White Star Line* and *the Cunard Line* in 1934, he worked in a senior position as First and later as Chief Officer of ships such as the AQUITANIA, AUSONIA and FRANCONIA. Like all surviving officers of the TITANIC, he never received a command of his own over a ship, despite sufficient qualifications, and retired from service in 1940.

In 1958, Boxhall was asked to act as technical advisor to the TITANIC film "A Night to Remember." As he had serious health problems, he asked his friend, Grattidge, to work with him on the project, which surprised his family very much, as Boxhall had always been very reluctant to talk about TITANIC. The film, which Boxhall was involved in promoting, was a huge success and is considered in professional circles, even before the blockbuster "TITANIC" by James Cameron in 1997, to be the best and most accurate film about the sinking of the legendary luxury liner. He was one of the guests of honor at the premiere of the film at the Odeon Theatre on Leicester Square in London.

In the years after "A Night to Remember," he talked to some researchers and historians about the TITANIC disaster and also gave an interview to the BBC in 1962 on this subject.

His state of health deteriorated very badly in the 1960s, which led to very frequent hospital stays. On April 25th, 1967, he died at the age of 83 years and he was the last survivor of TITANIC's deck officers.

His mortal remains were cremated, and according to his wishes, his ashes were scattered over the last position of the TITANIC (41°46°`N, 50°14°`W) which he calculated on April 15th, 1912.

Fifth Officer Harold Godfrey Lowe (21st November 1882 – 12th May 1944)

Harold Godfrey Lowe was born on Friday, 21st November 1882 in Llanrhos (Wales) as son of George and Harriet Lowe. At the age of 14 he rebelled against his father, whom he had previously followed very reluctantly to Liverpool to work as an office worker. But although he could have made a career there, office work was absolutely not his talent. Harold, rather, went to sea, so he left home and signed on board a schooner with unknown destination.

After some years of training in the Merchant Navy, he finally joined the *White Star Line* in 1911 where he signed on as Third Officer on the BELGIC and then on the TROPIC. During his 14 years at sea, he had become acquainted with all types of ships, from the smallest schooners to square-sailed vessels, with the destination West Africa.

The voyage with the TITANIC was his first crossing over the North Atlantic. During the collision he was off duty and was fast asleep in his cabin. Only when he heard loud voices outside his cabin did he wake up and go on deck. During the evacuation of the ship, he assisted Murdoch and Pitman in manning the boats.

There he had a loud dispute with Joseph Bruce Ismay who frantically tried to hurry him to lower Lifeboat No. 7. The young and impulsive Welshman Lowe did not seem to know his actual employer personally, as he ordered Ismay in a rather crude tone of voice not to interfere in his affairs:

"You want me to get the boat out quickly? Then they will all drown!"

Without another word, Ismay stole away after this harsh rebuke.

After the sinking of the ship Lowe wanted to return to the scene of the disaster immediately, but he feared that the people in the water could cause the lifeboat to capsize. Therefore, he organized a congregation of five boats on the open sea, where he had the passengers transfer from his own to the other boats to empty his boat. Then he returned to the wreck site as one of only two boats. However, the whole procedure took too much time so that he could only rescue four survivors from the water, one of whom died during the night (see also "The Evacuation of the Ship").

Not much is known about the later life of Fifth Officer Harold Godfrey Lowe. He also testified before both Inquiry Committees, where he attracted attention with some very questionable statements. Among other things, he used "Italian" as a synonym for "coward" before the US Inquiry and had to apologize to the Italian ambassador to the USA, quite rightly. He also admitted to having fired a pistol that night, but only along the side of the ship, to prevent male passengers ("Italians") from storming the lifeboats.

After his return from New York to his hometown Barmouth, 1300 people attended a reception in his honor at the Picture Pavilion. There he received a gold commemorative watch with the inscription: *"For Harold Godfrey Lowe, the fifth officer of the RMS TITANIC from his friends in Barmouth and elsewhere in recognition of his chivalrous service in the sinking of the TITANIC on 15 April 1912."*

In September 1913 he married Ellen Marion Whitehouse and they had two children, Florence Josephine Edge Lowe, and Harold William George Lowe. He remained true to seafaring, but he never took command of a merchant ship.

During the First World War he was appointed commander of the Royal Naval Reserve, where Joseph Groves Boxhall also served.

After the war he retired to his home in North Wales with his wife Marion.

On Friday, 12th May 1944, Harold Godfrey Lowe died at the age of 61 years of high blood pressure and was buried in the Llandrillo-yn- Rhos cemetery in Rhos-on-Sea in North Wales.

Sixth Officer James Paul Moody (21st August 1887- 15th April 1912)

The youngest of the seven deck officers was James Paul Moody, the Sixth Officer. He was born in Scarborough, New Yorkshire (England) on Sunday, August 21st, 1887, as the child of John Henry and Evelyn Louise Moody. His family was among the most influential in Scarborough. Moody's grandfather was a city official, and his father was a member of the City Council. His family was also well known in Grimsby, where one of his ancestors, Charles Bartholomew Moody, was the town's first forensic doctor.

Moody attended the King Edward VII Nautical School in London where he successfully passed his officer examinations in April 1911 and received his patent.

James Paul Moody had also sailed on sailing ships before he got a job on the OCEANIC with the *White Star Line*. The work on the TITANIC did not mean an advancement in rank or salary for him; the conditions were the same as on the OCEANIC.

Thanks to the extensive space on the new liner, he got at least his own-if tiny-cabin. On the other hand, the sheer size of the ship alienated him. During his stay in Belfast, where the last preparations were made, he wrote to his family that he spent most of his time walking the endless corridors and the countless stairs, cabins, and lounges to get used to the new environment.

During the evacuation, Moody is said to have set an example by launching Lifeboat Nos 12, 14 and 16. The last two were manned by him and the Fifth Officer, Harold Godfrey Lowe. Since one of the two boats was to be commanded by an officer, the two young officers discussed who of them was to board the lifeboat. Normally, with Moody, the younger officer would have been preferred, but Moody suggested that Lowe should take Boat No. 14 while he himself looked for another boat. The last time Moody was seen was shortly before the sinking when he and Second Officer Charles Herbert Lightoller tried to get one of the collapsibles afloat which was moored on the roof of the Officers' Cabins. His body was never found.

In Moody's hometown Scarborough, a plaque in the church of St. Martin still reminds us of the Sixth Officer. It bears the line: *"Be thou faithful unto death, and I will give to thee the crown of life!"*

At Woodland Cemetery in Scarborough, Moody's family erected a tombstone with an inscription that reflects the role of the then 24-year-old in the evacuation of the TITANIC: *"Greater love hath no man than this, that a man lay down his life for his friends."*

The Oldest Survivors of the TITANIC

For all survivors of the TITANIC disaster, April 15th, 1912. remained the day when their whole life changed forever. The TITANIC remained a part of their biography, whether they wanted it or not. Eleven years ago (2009), Elizabeth Gladys "Millvina" Dean died, the last survivor of the sinking of the TITANIC. In 1990 there were still 21 survivors of the tragedy. Many of them reached an almost "biblical age" and thus became legends.

Last Survivors of the RMS TITANIC Disaster

2000 to 2009

- Elizabeth Gladys "Millvina "Dean (1912-2009)
- Barbara Joyce Dainton (born West) (1911-2007)
- Lillian Gertrud Asplund (1906-2006)
- Winifried van Tongerloo (née Quick) (1904-2002)
- Michel Marcel Navratil (1908-2001)

1995 to 1999

- Eleanor Shuman (née Johnson) (1910-1998)
- Loise Laroche (1910-1998)
- Edith Haisman (née Brown) (1896-1997)
- Eva Hart (1905-1996)
- Beatrice Sandström (1910-1995)

1990 to 1994

- Robertha Watt (1899-1993)
- Ellen Shine (1891-1993)
- Marjorie Newell Robb (1889-1992)
- Louise Kink (1908-1992)
- Bertram Dean (1910-1992)
- Alden Caldwell (1911-1992)
- Michael Joseph (1907-1991)
- Frank "Phillip" Aks (1911-1991)
- George Touma (1904-1991)
- Anna "Annie" McGowan (1897-1990)
- Ruth Becker (1899-1990)

Among the surviving female passengers, some even made it into the "Hundred Year Club":

104 years: Mary Wilburn (née Davies) (17th May 1883 – 29th July 1987)

Mary Wilburn (née Davies) was the longest living survivor. She was born on Thursday, May 17th, 1883 in Southwark, England.

She was 28 years old at that time and boarded the TITANIC in Southampton as a Second-Class passenger to visit her sister Elsie F. Langford on Staten Island in New York.

When the collision with the iceberg happened, she was already sleeping in her cabin. She was awakened by a steward who assured her that there was no danger. She then returned to bed but was awakened shortly afterwards and asked to go to the Boat Deck. She quickly dressed and then helped Lucy Ridsdale, her cabinmate, who was in the lower bed and was afflicted with a clubfoot. When the two women were dressed, they went up to the Boat Beck together. Two men helped her getting into Lifeboat No. 13, which was lowered shortly afterwards.

It was a moonless night, and the water was calm. The beautiful bright stars seemed to illuminate the sea around the sinking ship. She later remembered that there was hardly any suction when the TITANIC sank in the icy waters. When the CARPATHIA came into sight early in the morning, she was paralyzed from the waist down and practically unconscious from exhaustion and cold.
She returned to England a few months after the disaster when the *White Star Line* offered her a free return trip home. In 1913 she returned to the USA where she worked as a cook. Two years later she married John A. Wilburn, with whom she had a son, Carl. Her husband John died in 1972 and her son Carl in 1994.

Mary Wilburn died on Wednesday, July 29th, 1987 in Syracuse, New York, at the age of 104 years and 73 days. This made her the longest living TITANIC survivor and one of only about 30 still alive when the TITANIC wreck was officially discovered in 1985.

103 years: Marjorie Newell Robb (12th February 1889 – 11th June 1992)

Marjorie Newell Robb was one of the last two survivors (next to Ellen Shine) who was an adult at the time of the disaster - she was 23 when she boarded TITANIC. She was the daughter of Arthur Webster Newell and Mary Emma Greeley and was born in Lexington, Massachusetts (USA) on Tuesday 12th February 1889.

Together with her father and her sister Madeleine Newell (10th October 1880 - 25th April 1969), she returned from a trip to the Middle East and boarded the ship in Cherbourg as a First-Class passenger.

After the TITANIC had collided with the iceberg, Arthur Newell woke his two daughters and implored them to dress. Shortly afterwards, they went up to the Boat Deck where Arthur reluctantly put his daughters in Lifeboat No. 6. Arthur Newell died in the sinking of the ship, and his body was later recovered by the MACKAY-BENNET. His two adult daughters, however, survived the tragedy.

Marjorie married Floyd Newton Robb (1887-1957) in 1917 and they had four children. Her only son was named Arthur Newell Robb in honor of her father.

Marjorie was musically very talented and gave violin and piano lessons in South Orange, New Jersey, and became one of the founders of the New Jersey Symphony Orchestra.

She spent the last years of her life in Fall River, Massachusetts. During this time, she began to talk about her experiences on the TITANIC. She attended several congresses of the Titanic International Society and the Titanic Historical Society where she told her story.

On Thursday, June 11th, 1992, she died in her sleep at the age of 103 years. She was the second longest survivor of the TITANIC after Mary Wilburn. She was buried at Mount Auburn Cemetery in Cambridge, Massachusetts.

101 years: Ellen Shine (30th December 1891 – 5th March 1993)

Ellen Shine was born on Wednesday, 30th December 1891 in Lisrobin, Newmarket, Cork (Ireland) as the daughter of Timothy Shine (born about 1844), a farmer, and Mary Fitzgerald (born about 1851). She was the youngest of nine children.

In the 1901 census, the family appears in House 4 in West Lisrobin, and at the time of the 1911 census, they lived in House 8 in the same place. Ellen Shine had no profession at that time, but her mother and brothers ran the farm. Her father had died of heart failure on Wednesday, 30th June 1909. Shortly after, Ellen decided to leave Ireland and join some of her siblings in New York.

Her brother William had already emigrated to America at the turn of the century and moved to New York, where he died on Saturday, February 6th, 1904. Another brother, Jeremiah, had also lived in America for some time, so she decided to follow her brothers and emigrate to America as well.

Like most Irish emigrants, she boarded TITANIC on April 11th in Queenstown as a Third-Class passenger (ticket number 330968). After her arrival on the CARPATHIA in New York (she was possibly rescued in Lifeboat No. 13), she was taken to a hospital with other Irish survivors and was interviewed by a New York newspaper.

This interview was published in the New York Times on Saturday, 20th April 1912. There she stated that after the collision she wanted to get on the Boat Deck together with other steerage passengers. Some crew members obviously wanted to prevent this and tried to force her back to the steerage. But the women rushed past the crew members and finally reached the deck. When they realized that the TITANIC would sink, most of the women fell on their knees and started to pray. When Ellen saw a lifeboat that was to be lowered, she did not hesitate for long and got in. Before that, four men had been taken out of this boat by force and thus sentenced to certain death.

After her arrival in New York on board the CARPATHIA, Ellen was described as a 16-year-old servant and was finally reunited with her waiting siblings. Her destination address was 205, 8th Avenue, New York, the home of her brother Jeremiah. She remained in New York for the rest of her life and became known in her new home as Helen. In 1921 she married John Callaghan (born September 23rd, 1896), a New York firefighter who had emigrated from Ireland in 1914.

Ellen and John settled in New York City, where they had two daughters, Julia (born Tuesday, November 15th, 1921) and Mary (born Sunday, January 30th, 1927).

During her life, Ellen spoke very rarely about the TITANIC, and her own daughters supposedly did not know that their mother was on the famous ship until the subject came up at school and they discovered her mother's name on a passenger list!

After the death of her husband on Tuesday, March 23rd, 1976, Ellen moved to Glen Cove, Long Island, New York, to be closer to her family. She had the sad fate of surviving her two daughters - daughter Mary, who was married to Lawrence Quinn and had two children, died of breast cancer on Tuesday, December 21st, 1982, at the age of 55, and Ellen was placed in the Glen Cove nursing home at the age of 90. Her unmarried daughter Julia died on Saturday, November 4th, 1989, at the age of 67.

In the last years of her long life, Ellen suffered from dementia which meant that she, who had spoken very little about the TITANIC throughout her life, now spoke about it almost incessantly, much to the annoyance of those around her. Ellen's 101st birthday was celebrated in December 1992 in the nursing home. She died a few months later, on March 5th, 1993, at the age of 101 years, two months, and three days in hospital. She was the last living TITANIC passenger from Ireland, and she died just one day after the TITANIC survivor Bertha Watt from Vancouver, Canada.

Ellen was buried in the family grave with her husband and daughters in St. Charles Cemetery in East Farmingdale, New York.

> Some sources give Ellen Shine a date of birth of 1894 instead of 1891, also, that she was born on Saturday, December 15th, 1894. When she went on TITANIC, she claimed that she was 18 years old, and when she landed in New York, she suddenly stated that she was 16 years old. The censuses of 1901 and 1911 perpetuated the myth that she was under 7 years old. But in the meantime, it is considered certain that she was born on Wednesday, December 30th, 1891.

100 years: Edwina Celia Troutt (8th June 1884 – 3rd December 1984)

Edwina, "Winnie" Celia Troutt, was born on Sunday, June 8th, 1884 in Bath (England). She was the daughter of Edwin Charles Troutt (brewer and part-time cabinetmaker) and Elizabeth Ellen Troutt (née Gay). The family lived at 40 Claverton Street. Winnie was the sister of Edwin, Edgar, Elsie, Louisa L, Emmeline, Harry E and Herbert W.

She made her first Atlantic crossing in 1907, having worked as a preschool teacher and clerk in her brother-in-law's tobacco store.

She spent nearly five years in America, where she worked first as a waitress in New Jersey and later as a domestic worker in Auburndale, Massachusetts. In 1911 she returned to her family's home in Bath.

Her sister, at that time, Mrs. Elsie Scholz, lived in Auburndale. And as her pregnancy was nearing its end in early 1912, Winnie decided to be with her sister at the birth. Originally, she was supposed to travel with the OCEANIC to America, but the coal strike changed her to the TITANIC. In Southampton, she boarded the ship as a Second-Class passenger (ticket number 34218).

She shared Cabin 101 on E Deck with Susan Webber from North Tamerton in Cornwall, and Nora A. Keane from Limerick in Ireland.

When the ship collided with the iceberg, she left her cabin to investigate. When she heard that the ship had hit an iceberg, she went up on deck, and there she saw that the lifeboats were uncovered and prepared for loading. She went back to inform her cabin neighbors.

On the way to her cabin, she met two of her table mates, Jacob Milling and Edgar Andrew.

"What is the trouble, Miss Troutt?" asked Milling," What does it all mean?"
"A very sad parting of all of us!" she replied. "This ship is going to sink."

Trying to comfort her, Milling said, *"Don't worry. I am sorry such a thing has happened, but I sent a wireless today. We are in communication with several vessels, and we will all be saved, though parted. But I won't go back home on so big a ship."*

When Winnie arrived in her cabin shortly after, Susie Webber had already left. The other one, Nora Keane, was still dressing. After she had replaced her robe with a warmer one, Winnie took care of the nervous woman. When Nora insisted on putting on a corset, Winnie tore it from her hand and threw it down the narrow corridor leading to her porthole.

Both women finally reached the Boat Deck and while Nora Keane disembarked in Lifeboat No. 10, Winnie was (probably) rescued in Lifeboat No. 16. Winnie later remembered that the ship band played "Nearer My God To Thee" in the last moments of the ship.

On Sunday, May 26th, 1912, a short note from her appeared in the Boston Herald:

"'In my boat,' she said, 'there were 20 women, not less than a dozen babies, and five members of the crew in charge of Master-at-Arms Bailey. One of these women was Mrs. Harry Faunthorpe, a bride. She was an Englishwoman who had been married in January. With her husband, she was making a pleasure trip to California. Her husband bade her good-bye with a smile and a pat of encouragement and placed her in the boat. As she stepped in, I called to her husband and asked him to take my seat, but he merely laughed and replied: Remember. I am an Englishman…'"

Winnie has been suggested as the woman that rescued Assad Thomas. As she waited for her boat to be lowered, a Lebanese passenger, Charles Thomas, came past with his nephew. He begged for the child to be saved and Winnie took the child into the boat with her. As the boat was lowered, she clutched a toothbrush, a prayer book, and the five-month-old child.

On board the CARPATHIA she slept on a table at first, but when a storm broke out the third night, she became hysterical and was given a bed and some brandy. It took several months before she fully recovered emotionally.

Later she filed a lawsuit against the *White Star Line* for the loss of a jam machine worth eight sterling.

In 1916 she moved from Massachusetts to Southern California, where she joined the Army Corps as an apricot collector. In California she married her first husband, Alfred Thorvald Peterson, in 1918. The two ran a bakery together in Beverley Hills until his death in 1944. In her second marriage she married a Mr. James Corrigan. At the age of 79, Winnie married a third time in 1964. She married James Mackenzie. She spent her retirement in Hermosa Beach, California.

On her 90th birthday in 1974, she received a letter from Richard Nixon, the then President of The United States. At the age of 99, she crossed the Atlantic for the last time, which she had crossed at least ten times before. Winnie was a welcome guest at Titanic events and congresses, even when she was in her late 90s.

On Monday, December 3rd, 1984, she died in Redondo Beach, California, at the age of 100, one of five centenarians of the TITANIC.

100 years: Edith Haisman (née Brown) (27th October 1896 – 22nd January1997)

Edith Brown was born in Cape Town (South Africa) on Tuesday, 27th October 1896, as the second child of Thomas and Elisabeth Brown. Thomas, who was married to Elisabeth in his second marriage, owned a number of hotels, shops and houses in South Africa. But when real estate prices in South Africa fell dramatically, the family decided to say goodbye to their homeland and emigrate to Seattle, where Thomas wanted to open a hotel. After a long sea voyage, the Browns arrived in England in the spring of 1912, where they spent some time getting dressed and making further arrangements for the future.

On Wednesday, 10th April 1912, they took the train from London to Southampton to board the TITANIC as Second-Class passengers under ticket number 29750. Before the family left, Thomas had a terrible nightmare which he never told his wife Elisabeth. He only told this to his 15-year-old daughter Edith. Even when they went on board the TITANIC, he was not at ease, because he hesitated before he went on board, although it was not his first trip.

On Sunday, 14th April 1912, Edith went to bed at about 10.30 p.m. board time, and fell asleep quite quickly, when she was woken by a sudden vibration and immediately jumped out of her bed. She opened the porthole in her cabin and could see glittering ice crystals and even chunks of ice in the absolutely calm water. Shortly afterwards, she was surprised to discover that the ship's engines had stopped. Her mother woke up and asked her what was wrong. At that moment, Thomas Brown knocked on the door and said: " *It is rumoured that the ship has run on ice, but there is no danger!"*

Then Thomas went back to the Second-Class Smoking Room, where he discussed the situation with the other gentlemen over a cigar. When Edith looked out of the porthole once more, she saw no more ice. Her cabin was on the port side of the TITANIC on the E Deck. The collision with the iceberg, however, took place on the starboard side of the ship and so all you could see on port side was the black sea and the twinkling stars, but nothing else.

After about ten minutes, Thomas Brown returned to the cabin and said: *"Put on warm clothes. We're going to the boat deck!"*

Unlike her mother, who was beginning to feel frightened, Edith was not frightened at all. Her father insisted they put on their life jackets, but he himself did not put on a lifebelt. He then led his wife and daughter up to the Boat Deck. As they climbed up the stairs, Edith already noticed a noticeable slanting of the ship.

When they arrived on the Boat Deck, they were met by passengers who wanted to return to their cabins to put on something warmer, as it was much too cold for them on the drafty deck. Suddenly there was a deafening noise, which some passengers at first thought was an explosion. The reason for the noise was that in the Engine Room, they had started to let the excess steam out of the boilers to prevent a devastating boiler explosion.

Just as the first distress rockets were fired by Officer Boxhall, Edith and her father, like some other passengers, saw another ship nearby and thought it was coming to rescue the TITANIC. But unfortunately, this hope was not to be fulfilled...

On deck it was complete chaos, as none of the passengers knew which boat to go to, and in the boats, there was the problem that there were too few crew members who were able to row.

Edith and her mother were placed in Lifeboat No. 14 by Thomas, which was commanded by Fifth Officer Harold Lowe, who fired his pistol into the air several times when the boat was almost stormed. As the boat was lowered, Thomas Brown said goodbye to his family with the words: "*I'll see you in New York!*"

Desperately Elisabeth Brown called to her husband: "*Go to the other side and try to get into a boat!*" But Thomas Brown just stood there, smoking a cigar. And judging by his infinitely sad expression, he knew exactly that he was not going anywhere...

Edith's mother later assumed that her husband later went to the Purser's Office to get his valuables, which were stored in a heavy box. He had sewn the money into his clothes, as was not uncommon at the time, to protect them from theft. Edith, by the way, had left a gold necklace, which her father had brought for her from

London as a present, in her cabin and instead had taken her diary.

From their lifeboat, Edith and her mother Elisabeth saw the TITANIC finally sink. When the huge luxury liner had already disappeared under water, the people in their lifeboat clearly heard the implosion of the stern. Afterwards the sea was very agitated as Edith remembered for the rest of her life.

Edith never forgot the cries of the people in the freezing cold North Atlantic for the rest of her life. After about 15 minutes, the great silence came - most people were frozen to death. Now, after a transfer from one lifeboat to the next, her boat rowed back to the wreck site to rescue any survivors. There was no discussion at all about whether to row back, as Officer Lowe had immediately insisted on it and did not tolerate any objections. The boat rowed back and picked up three more passengers from the icy water (see also "Evacuating the Ship").

However, Lifeboat No. 14 had a serious problem: It was leaking, as were several other lifeboats. A total of six leaks were counted in Boat No. 14! The occupants of the boat were busy half the night scooping the incoming water out of the boat. Many of the passengers, including Edith and Elisabeth Brown, had severely cold feet afterwards. Additionally, Edith ruined her expensive, brand-new shoes because of the salt water.

As dawn slowly came, the boats had to row through a huge number of dead bodies, still floating upright in their life jackets in the water, looking as if they were sleeping. Edith never forgot this horrible sight for the rest of her entire life. When she went aboard the CARPATHIA with her mother, her cold feet made it difficult for her to climb the rope ladder to get on board the rescue ship.

After their arrival in New York, Elisabeth and Edith searched all the hospitals in the city for Thomas for another four days, but he had gone down with the TITANIC. For a short time, mother and daughter stayed with relatives in America, but then they decided to return to South Africa. After weeks of traveling by train and ship they finally reached Cape Town.

On the fifth anniversary of the disaster, Edith met the Englishman, Frederick Haisman, at the Wemmer Sailing Club in Johannesburg. He became the great love of her life. And only six weeks later, on Saturday 30th June 1917, the two got married, and shortly after that, Edith was pregnant.

With her mother Elisabeth, Edith unfortunately got over it, as she could not come to terms with her mother's new husband, who in her opinion only wanted her mother's money.

In 1920, Edith and Frederick Haisman sold all their possessions in Johannesburg and built a new life for themselves in Southampton, in the very city from which the TITANIC began her maiden voyage and where her life had changed forever. Their mother was never to see them again, although they remained in correspondence. Elisabeth Brown died on Tuesday, 29th June 1926, at the age of 53. in a hospital in Salisbury in former Rhodesia (now Zimbabwe). During the Second World War, the ever-growing Haisman family returned to South Africa for several years, as Frederick, who worked in shipbuilding, was stationed there.

In 1948 the family returned to Southampton, where they stayed until 1965 before emigrating to Australia, where large parts of the Haisman family are still based today. Five years later, Frederick expressed the wish to return to England to spend his retirement there, so, Edith and Frederick Haisman moved back to Southampton.

In 1977 the two celebrated their diamond wedding anniversary (60 years) and looked back on a long and happy marriage in which they had ten children together and had traveled the whole world. A few months later, on Saturday 26th November 1977, Frederick Haisman died at the age of 83, which broke Edith's heart.

Almost 84 years after the sinking of the TITANIC, Edith, now wheelchair-bound, returned to the TITANIC wreck site, together with her daughter Dorothy, at the invitation of the president of RMS Titanic, Inc., George Tulloch and laid a wreath in the sea for her deceased father.

On Wednesday, 22nd January 1997, only a few months after her voyage, Edith Haisman died in Southampton at the age of 100. She left behind four sons, two daughters and 40 grandchildren. Her youngest son, David Haisman, still keeps the memory of his beloved mother alive and has published two books about his mother's life and her experiences on the TITANIC.

Didn't quite make it into the so-called "Hundred Year Club":

99 years: Lillian Gertrud Asplund (21st October 1906 – 6th May 2006)

Lillian Gertrud Asplund was one of the last three survivors of the TITANIC, and she was also the last survivor with real memories of the disaster. She was the daughter of Carl and Selma Asplund, both from Sweden, and was born on Sunday, October 21st, 1906, in Worcester, Massachusetts. She had a twin brother, Carl, and two older brothers, Fililp (born 1898) and Clarence (born 1902).

In 1907 the family received the news that Lillian's paternal grandfather had died in Sweden. As her father was the executor of the estate, the family made arrangements to return to Sweden to look after the family estate, which was located near the village of Alseda in Smaland. The family sailed on board the IVERNIA of the *Cunard Line* from Boston and arrived in Liverpool on Thursday, 4th July 1907. From there they sailed to Gothenburg before finally arriving in the remote Alseda.

The family remained there for four and a half years to take care of the farm and Lillian's grandmother. During this time, Selma gave birth to another son, Felix, in March 1909. In early 1912, the family decided to return to America, and Lillian's father booked a passage for his family on the TITANIC.

On Wednesday, 10th April 1912, the whole Asplund family boarded the TITANIC in Southampton as Third-Class passengers. Lillian was five years old at the time and remembered that the ship *"was very large and was just being painted. I remember not liking the smell of fresh paint!"*

When the TITANIC hit the iceberg, Lillian's father woke his sleeping family and then put all the important papers, including cash, in his pocket. Lillian, her mother, and her little brother Felix were loaded into Lifeboat No. 15. Lillian later remembered: *"My mother said she would rather stay with him (my father) and go down with the ship, but he said the children should not be alone. My mother had Felix in her lap, and she had me between her knees. She thought she could keep me a little warmer that way."*

She later described the sinking of the Titanic *"like the sinking of a great building falling down."* Throughout her life, Lillian was haunted by the memory of her father and brothers' faces at the railing as the lifeboat was lowered.

Lillian and her little brother Felix were later loaded into linen bags and hoisted onto the CARPATHIA. Arrived on board, Lillian remembered later:

"A woman undressed me. My clothes had become very dirty and wet in the lifeboat. My mother tried to find me. She said, 'I have a daughter!' Well, she found me. And finally, my clothes were dry, and I put them back on. They took us, the children, to the place where they bring sick people. Well, not sick, but people who needed a little more attention. The people of Carpathia have been very good to us."

After the CARPATHIA arrived in New York, Lillian's mother took her and her brother to Worcester. Lillian's father, and her brothers, Filip, Clarence, and Carl, had not survived the sinking. In the chaos following the disaster, a newspaper in Worcester reported, that both Mr. and Mrs. Asplund had been rescued, along with Clarence, Lillian and Felix, and that Filip and Carl had drowned. A later report said that Selma and "her two babies" had been taken to a local hospital and that Mr. Asplund and Clarence were apparently in another place.

A final report finally confirmed that neither Carl Sr, Filip, Clarence nor Carl Jr were among the survivors. The body of Lillian's father was later recovered by the MACKAY-BENNET and later buried in the All-Faiths Cemetery in Worcester. Since the family's savings and possessions had been lost in the disaster, the City of Worcester held a charity fundraiser that raised $2,000.

Lillian's mother never recovered from the loss of her husband and three eldest sons and refused to talk to anyone about the disaster, saying it was simply wrong to do so. Lillian agreed with her and hardly spoke about the tragedy for the rest of her life. According to her lawyer, she refused interview requests, even if money was offered. Her reasoning was always: *"Why do I want money from the TITANIC? Look what I have lost. A father and three brothers!"*

She worked as a secretary in the Worcester area and retired early to look after her mother. Selma Asplund died on Wednesday, 15th April 1964, the 52nd anniversary of the sinking at the age of 90. Her brother Felix, who never married and lived with Lillian, died of pneumonia on Tuesday, 15th March 1983 at the age of 73.

Lillian Asplund died on Saturday, May 6th, 2006, five months before her 100th birthday, at the age of 99 in her home in Shrewsbury, Massachusetts.

She was buried at the old Swedish cemetery in Worcester, next to her father, mother, and brother. After her death, her ticket from the TITANIC, which she had owned for many years, was sold at auction in 2009. It was a part of documents and objects found in a locker after her death and related to the disaster, for example, her father's pocket watch which had stopped at 2.19 a.m.

98 years: Winnifried van Tongerloo (née Quick) (23rd January 1904 – 4th July 2002)

Winnifried van Tongerloo (née Quick) was one of the last four survivors of the TITANIC and was born in Plymouth, England. She was born on Saturday, January 23rd, 1904, as the daughter of Frederick Charles Quick, a plasterer, and his wife Jane Richards Quick. Her sister Phyllis May was born on Tuesday, July 27th, 1909.

In 1910, Winnifried's father decided to emigrate from England to Detroit, Michigan, to give his family a better life. At first, he emigrated alone and left his family, which he later wanted to catch up with, with Jane's mother in Plymouth. At the beginning of 1912, Frederick had established a secure existence in America, and now the family was to follow.

Shortly after Jane had booked a passage for herself, Winnifried and Phyllis (probably on the Philadelphia, author's note), she was informed that her ship would not sail due to the coal strike, and they were transferred to the TITANIC instead.

Together with her mother Jane and her younger sister Phyllis, Winnifried boarded the TITANIC in Southampton as a Second-Class passenger. Despite the calm sea, she was seriously seasick most of the time on board the ship. On April 14th, Winnifried and her family went to bed shortly after 9.30 p.m. Neither she nor Jane nor Phyllis noticed the collision with the iceberg - they were fast asleep. Only when another passenger knocked on their cabin door and told them there had been an accident, did they realize that something was wrong.

Jane, however, did not believe that the ship had been badly damaged. A steward looked in the cabin after a while and saw how slowly Jane was getting ready. He more than urged her to put on her life jacket, as the ship had hit an iceberg and was sinking. Shocked by this news, Jane woke up her two daughters and dressed them as quickly as she could, and then went up to the Boat Deck. Once there, an unknown man helped Winnifried, who cried hysterically, and her sister Phyllis to put on their life jackets.

Jane put her two daughters in Lifeboat No. 11 - she herself was initially refused entry because the officer in charge only wanted to take children. According to reports, Jane said to him: "*Either we go together, or we stay together!*" Finally, the officer agreed and let Jane get into the lifeboat. She was the last passenger to be let into the boat which, according to Jane, had about 50 people in it. In the lifeboat, Winnifried cried incessantly until someone noticed that her shoes had fallen off, and her feet were stuck in the freezing cold water. No wonder she was crying...

Winnifried finally fell asleep during the night, and only woke up when the people around her cheered loudly as the CARPATHIA appeared on the horizon. Like most children, Winnifried and Phyllis were put into a sack and pulled aboard the rescue ship. She remembered later that she had seen many survivors crying, and even watched the burial of several passengers who had died in the lifeboats. A traumatic experience for an eight-year-old child!

Her shocked father heard the news of the sinking of the TITANIC but received a telegram with the news that his family was safe. When the CARPATHIA arrived in New York on Thursday, April 18th, he was there and happily welcomed the rest of his family. They spent the night as guests of the Hebrew Sheltering and Immigrant Aid Society. The next morning, they left New York City and arrived in Detroit on Saturday, April 20th.

Winnifried left school after finishing eighth grade and worked in the production of sweets and as a saleswoman in a department store, among other things. In 1918 she met the master carpenter Alois van Tongerloo (1899-1987) and married him in 1923. The couple had five children: Bob, Jack, Jim, Jeanette, and Gloria.

The life of their younger sister Phyllis ended tragically; she shot herself in the head when she was only 44 years old. This tragic event took place on Monday, March 15th, 1954. Her mother Jane died on Wednesday, February 24th, 1965 at the age of 84.

In 1966, Alois retired from professional life and from then on, he traveled the USA with Winnifried and reportedly visited all states except Hawaii. When she was once asked if she would ever make a return trip to England, she replied: *"No! I do not like big ships! I like to go up to my neck in water, but not on the water above my head!"*

She did not mind talking about her experiences on the TITANIC, but she never attended an organized gathering of TITANIC survivors.

On July 2nd, 2002, Winnifried died in East Lansing, Michigan at the age of 98 and was one of the last five survivors of the TITANIC at that time. She left behind her three remaining children Jack, Jeanette, and Gloria, nine grandchildren, 16 great-grandchildren and five great-great-grandchildren.

And last, but not least:

97 years: Elizabeth Gladys "Millvina" Dean (2nd February 1912 – 31st May 2009)

Of course, the last survivor of the TITANIC, Elizabeth Gladys Dean, affectionately called "Millvina" by the whole world, should not be missed.
Millvina was born on Friday, February 2nd, 1912, in Hampshire, England. When she boarded the TITANIC in Southampton, with her family, as a Third-Class passenger (father Bertram senior, mother Georgette, and her two-year-old brother Bertram junior) under ticket number 2315, she was just nine weeks old.

Of course, she had no memories of her own of the sinking of the luxury liner, but her stories are nevertheless very exciting:

"We traveled on the TITANIC because we wanted to emigrate to Kansas City where my father wanted to open a tobacco shop. We already had a house there, and he was thrilled to go on the Titanic, and so was my mother. But of course, only the third class was possible for us, because we were emigrants. Everyone was so full of hope, especially the emigrants, to start a new life in America. They were looking forward to it so much that simply everything had to go wrong. Nobody thought of the slightest danger, because the Titanic was considered unsinkable and with such a beautiful ship, nobody thought of danger."

The collision with the iceberg was noticed by the Deans in Third Class a little bit earlier than by the other passengers of the TITANIC:

"All I know is that my father went up on deck to see what had happened. He said that the ship had apparently run onto an iceberg and that you had to get the children out of bed and bring them on deck, and that's what they did. But now, we were passengers in third class, many of whom were not allowed to go up at all. But I think because my mother had a baby and a small child, we were allowed to continue. And therefore, we got a place on one of the boats. It was number thirteen. And my father said that he hopefully would be joining us soon. And I was put in a sack, and my brother. My mother couldn't see him anywhere, but she couldn't do anything."

"The people who were left on the boat started to panic. "All those left on Titanic screamed in fear. "The passengers had no idea there weren't enough lifeboats on Titanic. No one would have thought so."

On board the CARPATHIA the family was reunited, with the exception of the drowned father, Bertram Dean.

"When we boarded the Carpathia, one of the Titanic passengers was waiting there with my brother. When my mother saw my brother, she was terribly relieved. We had lost everything. We had relatives in Kansas City, but we had lost absolutely everything. We had no money, no clothes, we had nothing, so my mother thought the best thing to do was to go back home."

Only when she was already eight years old did Millvina learn from her mother, who later remarried and died on Sunday 16th September 1979, that she had been on board the legendary RMS TITANIC and had lost her father there. She was not particularly interested in the TITANIC for most of her life, unlike her brother Bertram, who met TITANIC's Stoker, George Beauchamps by chance while working in a shipyard in Southampton. He learned a great deal about the ship and the terrible night they both survived.

His wife Dorothy, to whom Bertram was to be married for 60 years, brought her own TITANIC story into the marriage, so to speak, because her father had acquired a music shop in Southampton from the estate of Henry Price Hodges, who died as a Second-Class passenger on the TITANIC...

Bertram Dean died on Tuesday, 14th April 1992, the 80th anniversary of TITANIC hitting the iceberg, at the age of 82.

His little sister Millvina, on the other hand, never married and worked as a cartographer for the British Government during the Second World War and later worked in the purchasing department of a mechanical engineering company.

It was only very late that Millvina began to become aware of her own TITANIC history. But since then, she had been a welcome guest of honor at various talk shows and exhibitions, including the legendary TITANIC Exhibition in Hamburg in 1997.

In the last years of her life, things became noticeably quieter around Millvina, who developed quite a few health problems, after which she had to move to a nursing home in Southampton.

A few months, before her death, she had to sell some of her memorabilia of the Titanic to finance her continued stay in the nursing home. Even Leonardo DiCaprio and Kate Winslet, as well as James Cameron, who became world famous with the blockbuster "TITANIC," donated money for Millvina Dean so that she could stay. Shortly afterwards, however, she died completely unexpectedly on Sunday, 31st May 2009, at the age of 97. Her ashes were scattered in Southampton. This was the death of the last survivor of the TITANIC.

The German press also reported the death of Millvina Dean © collection of the author

The Millvina Dean Memorial Garden in Southampton ©
private photo of the author

Naturally, the male survivors of the TITANIC did not live as long as the female survivors, but some of them reached a rather high age:

97 years: Frederick Dent Ray (20th June 1879 – 15th January1977)

Mr. Frederick Dent Ray (Saloon Steward, First Class) was born on Friday, 20th June, 1879 in Soutwark, London, England. He was the son of Charles Adolphus Hopson Ray (1847-1913), a cooper, and Sarah Newport (1848-1919), both born in London, who had married in Shoreditch on Saturday, November 7th, 1874.

He was married to Annies Beatrice Burt (born in 1885) in Berkshire in late 1908 and later settled in Reading, where he was registered as a resident of 56 Palmer Park Avenue in 1912. Their marriage remained childless.

On Thursday, April 4th, 1912 he registered on the TITANIC and named the OLYMPIC as his previous ship. As a Salon Steward, he could count on a monthly salary of £ 3.15. Among his charges in the salon were: Major Archibald Butt, Clarence Moore, Frank Millet and Mr. and Mrs. Walter Miller Clark.

On Sunday, April 14th, Ray was on duty in the First-Class Dining Room until 9 p.m. He waited for Clarence Moore and Frank Millet, who were dining together from about 7:30 p.m. to 8:15 p.m. Major Butt was absent because he had been dining with the Widener family at the restaurant that evening, Ray recalled. While he remembered seeing Captain Smith at many meals during the trip, he could not recall seeing him there that evening.

Ray was asleep on E Deck midships in Room 3 - the aft-most saloon waiters which housed 28 stewards - at the time of the collision and was awakened by the impact. At first, he thought that something had gone wrong in the Engine Rooms and did not think it was an accident. While waiting for a while, he began to fall asleep again when Saloon Steward William Moss, followed by Second Steward George Dodd, came in to tell them to get dressed and go to the lifeboats.

Ray got dressed and took his time to put on a lifebelt. He left his quarters and walked aft along Scotland Road to a "back stairwell" with about 20 others and climbed up to C Deck where he met Second Steward Dodd again. Dodd asked him to get him a lifebelt, and Ray searched five empty cabins before returning to Dodd with the required item. Ray then headed to the Boat Deck and recalled seeing Clarence Moore leaving the smoking room with a crowd of others he could not identify.

Ray went to Boat No. 9, the boat assigned to him, which was swung out and prepared at that time. There was a small group of men around the boat, a few male passengers and four sailors, working to swing the boat out, and a few other crew members, but he did not see any women. Looking out over the side, he saw Lifeboat No. 7 being launched further forward, and when he noticed how cold it was, he returned downstairs to his quarters, which were empty at the time. He was fetching a coat when he noticed that E Deck at the front was now under water and just managed to get through the door to the First-Class Cabins on the starboard side. When he quickly examined this area and noticed a similar flooding, he began to climb up the forward First-Class Stairwell, passing only a few people.

Arriving on C Deck, he witnessed the pursers and the clerks in their office busying themselves by removing items from the safe and placing them in bags. While he was here, Mr. Rothschild left his cabin, and Ray stayed behind to assist him. He recognized him from the fact that he had previously waited for him aboard the OLYMPIC. Rothschild had just seen his wife away in a lifeboat and told Ray how serious the situation was. Ray dismissed all danger and went with Rothschild up the stairs to A Deck, where the aft starboard boats were filled. He assisted with Boat Nos 9 and 11, which he saw rowing safely away before going aft to Boat No. 13, which was then half filled with women and children.

As he watched Dr. Washington Dodge nearby, Dodge asked him about his wife and child. He replied that they left on an earlier boat. Ray then told him, "*You better get in here...*" and pushed him to and into the boat, with Ray following him. While he was in the boat, Ray remembered a tall lady crying and making a scene as she was being loaded and said, "*Don't put me in the boat. I don't want to go in the boat. I've never been in an open boat in my life. Don't let me stay in the boat.*"

Ray replied, "*You have to go, and you may as well keep quiet.*"

Shortly after that scene, a small child wrapped in a blanket was thrown into the boat. Ray caught the small bundle and saw the mother climbing into the boat shortly after. The boat then began to be lowered, and Ray observed a group of three or four men left behind at the rail who moved aft and got into Boat No. 15.

But the difficulties were far from over. Before Ray and other crew members landed on the water, they noticed the large water outlet on the side of the ship, which he estimated as 2 feet wide by 1 foot deep. Fearing that they would be flooded, they shouted to stop lowering the boat. The crew on deck immediately stopped. Meanwhile, the crew in Boat No. 13 broke out the oars to push the lifeboat away from the side of the ship.

The boat managed to touch the water safely, but Ray remembered that an apparently inexperienced crew had difficulty releasing the falls. In conjunction with this, the outflow from the ship, Boat No. 13 was under Lifeboat No. 15, which was now beginning a hasty descent. Due to this and the list of the sinking ship, Boat No. 15 was in danger of falling from above directly on No. 13.

With calls and cries for knives to free the boat from its bondage, Lifeboat No. 15 finally stopped after further cries to the crew above. The occupants of Boat No. 13 could already touch the bottom of Lifeboat No. 15, so this shows how lucky they were avoiding another tragedy. When Lifeboat No. 13 was finally free, the passengers realized that no one in particular was in charge of the boat.

Ray remembered that because of that, a fireman took over the command. Since he did not want to leave the side of the boat, he remembered that he had refused to row several times before finally giving in. But because the boat was so fully loaded, he had difficulties using the oars.

Ray survived the sinking and made it aboard the CARPATHIA to New York. He was a witness for the U.S. Investigation of the sinking on Day 9 but was not required to testify for the British Investigation. He returned home to his wife, who had been in North Wales to recover from her illness.

It is not clear how long Ray stayed at sea after the disaster. Later he settled in Newton Abbot, Devon, and began poultry farming.

Frederick became a widower when his wife Annie died in Newton Abbot in mid-1952. Only a few months later, a few months, before the end of the year, he married the widow of his brother Charles, Rose Mary Ray (née Lawrence, born December 4th, 1890).

Frederick and Rose lived in Maidstone, Kent for some time before finally settling in 43 West Park Crescent in Billericay, Essex, where Ray was to spend the rest of his life. In the 1950s he corresponded with Walter Lord while he worked on his book "A Night to Remember".

Frederick died on Saturday, January 15th, 1977 in Basildon Hospital from a hip fracture. He was cremated in the crematorium of South Essex, London, and his ashes were scattered on lawn 37 of the Northern Rose Garden. At 97 years, 6 months and 26 days of age, he was the oldest crew member at his death.

94 years: Olaus Abelseth (10th June 1886 – 4th December 1980)

Olaus Jörgensen Abelseth was born on Thursday, 10th June 1886, on the farm Ovste Kleivane in Alesund (Norway) as the son of Jörgen Andreas Laurits Anderssen and Hanna Petrine Kristine (née Johannsdatter). It is still unknown how he got the surname Abelseth. This is still unclear. Around 1900 he lived with his parents and his five siblings (Inga, Hanna, Gina Jensine, Gurine and Hans) and the foster daughter of the family, Olivie O. Tendfjordnes, in Kleven, Örskog. The servant Anne Olsdatter lived in the household.

Together with his brother Hans, he migrated to America in 1902 or 1903 and lived in Hatton, North Dakota, where he worked on various farms in the Red River Valley. In 1908, he founded a cattle farm in Perkins County, South Dakota. After a very difficult time on his farm, Olaus decided to visit his relatives in Norway. In the late autumn of 1911, he traveled by steamer from New York to Glasgow in Scotland. From there he continued his journey to his old Scandinavian home.

In April 1912, Olaus began his return journey to Minneapolis, USA. Together with him, five other Norwegians traveled: Adolf Humblen, Anna Salkjelsvik, his cousin Peter Søholt, Sigurd Hansen Moen who was married to Olaus' sister Inge, and Karen Marie Abelseth who, despite having the same surname, was not a relative of Olaus Abelseth but the daughter of a neighbor of Olaus when he lived in Norway. Since

Karen was only 16 years old, her father asked, if Olaus could take care of her on the trip to America.

The group sailed from Ålesund via Bergen to Newcastle and finally boarded the TITANIC in Southampton on Wednesday, 10th April 1912. On board, Olaus and Humblen shared a common cabin towards the bow on F Deck (G 63), from where he moved aft along the famous "Scotland Road" to collect Karen on E Deck on the night of the sinking. He found the young woman near the staircase of Third Class, and then the whole group went to the Well Deck in the aft section of the ship.

They then waited on the Poop Deck for instructions from the crew on what to do. At about 1.30 a.m. board time, the Third-Class women were finally allowed on the Boat Deck, followed by the men at 2.00 a.m., twenty minutes before the sinking. While many passengers decided to stay on the Poop Deck, Olaus and his relatives made their way to the Boat Deck. Olaus put Karen Abelseth together with Moen and Soholt into a boat and saved the life of the 16-year-old girl.

Now only collapsibles were on board, and they heard the desperate call of the crew for help of a sailor to free one of the collapsibles. As Olaus had six years of experience as a fisherman, he made arrangements to offer his help, but his brother-in-law and cousin urged him to stay with them.

"I was standing there, and I asked my brother-in-law if he could swim and he said no. I asked my cousin if he could swim and he said no. So, we could see the water coming up, the bow of the ship was going down, and there was a kind of explosion.

We could hear the popping and cracking, and the deck raised up and got so steep that the people could not stand on their feet on the deck, so they fell down and slid on the deck into the water right on the ship.

We were hanging from the davits. We were quite far back on the top deck. My brother-in-law said to me, 'We should jump now, or the suction will pull us down'. I said, 'No, we're not going to jump now. We don't have much of a chance anyway, so we can stay here as long as we can.'

Then, when the water was only five feet away, we jumped. It was not a great jump. Before that, we could see people jumping. The water came up on deck, and they just jumped into the water. My brother-in-law took my hand when we jumped, and my cousin jumped at the same time. When we got into the water, maybe it was the suction, anyway, we dived under, and I swallowed some water. I got caught in a rope and let go of my brother-in-law's hand to free me from the rope. But when I came back up and tried to swim, there was a man - many were floating around - who grabbed me by the neck and pushed me down and tried to climb on top of me. I said to him: 'let go', which he of course didn't pay attention to, but I got rid of him. Then there was another man who was stuck for a while, but he let go. Then I swam. I can't say, but it must have been 15 or 20 minutes. I couldn't have made it more. Then I saw something black in front of me. I didn't know what it was, but I swam that way, and it was one of the collapsible boats.

When I got on this raft or collapsible boat, they didn't try to push me down, but they didn't help me climb up either. All they said when I made it was, 'Don't make the boat capsize.' Before I climbed in, I clung to the boat. Some of them were trying to get up on their feet. They were sitting or lying on the raft. Some of them fell back into the water. Some were frozen *to death, and there were two dead people who were thrown overboard."*

As the passengers rowed through the night, they prayed. And although Olaus was almost waist-deep in the water, he tried to resuscitate a passenger who was lying on the bottom of the lifeboat. When he lifted him up, he discovered that it was a man from New Jersey whom he had met on the train to Southampton.

When the CARPATHIA was sighted, he urged the man to look up, but when the morning dawned, he died. Another man put his arms around Olaus' body to relieve his cramps caused by the cold, but he died, too, and Olaus had to get rid of him.

When he finally reached the deck of the CARPATHIA at 7.00 a.m., he received a warm blanket. Afterwards he went to the dining room to drink schnapps and hot coffee. He slept aboard the CARPATHIA the whole time in the same clothes he had worn the night in the flooded boat. His brother-in-law and cousin had not survived the sinking of the TITANIC.

When he arrived in New York, he stayed at St. Vincent Hospital for a few days. He also testified at the US Senate Inquiry before he finally left for Minneapolis. In 1912 and 1913 he traveled to Canada, Indianapolis, and Montana before returning to his farm in South Dakota. In July 1915 he married Anna Grinde in South Dakota. Anna was his first wife, while he was her second husband. Anna was born in Norway on Wednesday, June 6th, 1877. Her father had died at sea in Norwegian waters near the Sognefjord on Saturday, 19th June 1886.

235

Nine days earlier, Olaus had been born. At that time Anna was eight years old.

Olaus Abelseth worked on his farm for 30 years, and he and Anna had four children during this time. Their second son died at the age of three-and-a-half. The other children were George, Helen, and Mae.

In 1946 he retired to Shipowners, North Dakota. Two years later they moved to Tacoma, Washington, and finally in 1960, to Whetting, North Dakota before settling in Hettinger, Adams Co., North Dakota.

His wife Anna celebrated her 100th birthday in 1977 and died in August 1978. Olaus Abelseth died on Thursday, December 4th, 1980 at the age of 94, making him the oldest male surviving passenger of the TITANIC tragedy.

92 years: Emilio Ilario Guiseppe Portaluppi (15th October 1881 – 18th June 1974)

Emilio Ilario Guiseppe Portaluppi was born on Saturday, 15th October 1881 in Arcisate in the province of Varese in Italy. Shortly after the turn of the century he emigrated to Milford, New Hampshire and settled as a stonemason.

After visiting his old home country Italy, he boarded the TITANIC in Cherbourg as a Second-Class passenger (ticket number 34644).

When the TITANIC collided with the iceberg, he had already retreated into his cabin. At first, he almost had the feeling that the ship had already reached New York and was about to dock. He put on a bathrobe and went on deck. There was no panic there at this point, but he realized that something serious must have happened and returned to his cabin to fully dress. When he returned to the Boat Deck, he saw a lifeboat that was only half full and tried to jump in. However, according to a newspaper interview, he missed it and fell into the water. Other newspapers published different versions of his rescue. The truth is unknown...

The Times published the following sensational report on April 20th, 1912:

"Many people seem to have slept through the shock of the collision, and the tale told by Emilio Portaluppi, a second cabin passenger, shows that he was first awakened by the explosion of one of the ship's boilers. He hurried up to deck one and strapped on a lifebelt. Following the example of others, he then leapt into the sea, and held on to an icefloe, with the help of which he managed to keep afloat until he was seen by those in the lifeboats and rescued.

Portaluppi swam in the water for two hours, and when dawn came, he was pulled aboard by lifeboat number fourteen under the command of Officer Lowe. He was one of only four people rescued by the returning boat. Around them lay hundreds of dead and dying."

If you read a report like this, it is not surprising that there are so many untrue stories about the TITANIC...

After the CARPATHIA had docked in New York on the evening of April 18th, 1912, Emilio Portaluppi was glad that he could avoid the usual formalities for immigration. On Saturday, April 20th, he was brought back to Milford by his friends. This event was even reported in the local press.

Unfortunately, not much is known about his later life. In 1938 he lived in Brooklyn, New York and worked for a company called A. Farranda & Son in Woodside, New York.

Emilio Portaluppi died on Tuesday, 18th June 1974 at the age of 92 and was later buried in his native town of Arcisate in the province of Varese, Italy.

> In his pension application, Emilio Portaluppi stated that he was born on Friday, 15th October 1886 in Varese, Italy, the son of Charles Portaluppi and Josephine Parlatti. That would make him five years younger...

92 years: Michel Navratil (12th June 1908 – 30th January 2001)

Michel Navratil, born on Friday, 12th June 1908 in Nice, France, was without a doubt an important part of the most incredible story about the sinking of the TITANIC.

The remarkable story started on Easter Sunday, April 7th, 1912 in Nice. Together with his younger brother Edmond, he lived with his mother Marcelle, who had separated from her husband, Michel Navratil. His father used the Easter visit to kidnap his two little sons. He brought them to England where he then boarded TITANIC with them under the false name "Hoffman" as a Second-Class passenger. In case he was discovered, he had a loaded revolver in his pocket.

During the journey "Hoffman" kept himself and his two sons away from the other passengers of the luxury liner and hardly let them out of his sight. When they played on deck, he sat nearby and at night he watched over their sleep. Only when he felt the need for a game of cards did he leave his sons to the care of the unsuspecting Swiss woman Bertha Lehmann, who was on her way to Iowa and sat at the table with them during dinner.

Michel later remembered how great the TITANIC was and that his brother and he had played enthusiastically on the Boat Deck of the ship. He also remembered sitting in the Second-Class Dining Room one morning with his father and brother, eating eggs.

At the time of the collision with the iceberg Michel Navratil, alias Hoffman Louis, was in the Second-Class Smoking Room with a friend. When he noticed the vibration of the ship, he immediately ran to his two sons. He dressed Michel very warmly and took him in his arms. A stranger did the same to his brother Edmond. It was later clear to Michel that the two men knew they would die.

The two boys were taken up to the Boat Deck, where they were put into Collapsible D, the last lifeboat that was lowered from the deck of the sinking TITANIC. Before putting his two sons in the boat, he gave his older son Michel a last message, telling him that he loved their mother and still does. He said that he wanted her to follow them so that they could all live happily together in peace and freedom in the New World.

Michel Navratil did not forget these last words of his father for the rest of his life...

Later Michel could vaguely remember his stay in the lifeboat. There he sat with his brother next to the daughter of an American banker who had managed to save his dog without protests from the other passengers in the boat. The two boys sat with their backs to the TITANIC and fell asleep after - according to tradition - playing with the toy pig of First-Class passenger Edith Louise Rosenbaum for quite some time. By turning the tail of this pig, a piece of music called "Maxixe" was played, which was obviously fun for the two boys.

However, it is not clear whether this story is a legend, because Edith Louise Rosenbaum was sitting in another lifeboat that night...

The next morning Michel Navratil saw the CARPATHIA on the horizon. He was then pulled on board, like all children, with a sackcloth bag, which seemed absolutely strange to him.

On board the rescue ship, it was soon realized that the two boys, who did not speak or understand a word of English, were completely alone. First Class passenger Margaret Hays agreed to take care of the children after their arrival in New York until possible family members of the boys contacted her.

Photos of the two boys were printed in the newspapers and went around the world. The fate of the two "Titanic orphans" left no one untouched. Through an advertisement in a French newspaper, the stunned Marcelle Navratil finally learned of the destiny of her two children.

On Thursday, 16th May 1912, she was finally able to embrace her children again and returned with them to France on board the OCEANIC.

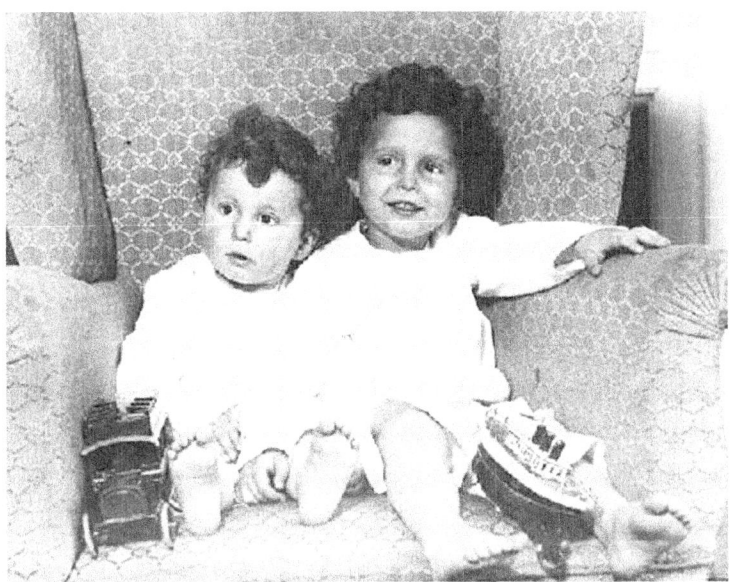

Edmond (left) and Michel (right) Navratil, the two "TITANIC orphans" © public domain

Throughout his life, Michel studied and taught philosophy, obtaining his doctorate in 1952 and teaching as Professor of Philosophy at the University of Montpellier until his retirement in 1969. One year later his wife, who had also studied philosophy, died. In 1974 his mother, who never got over the tragic events of 1912 and had spent many years in psychological treatment, followed her.

His children all followed in the footsteps of their learned father. His son became a urologist, one of his daughters was a psychoanalyst, the other a translator from German and music critic.

His brother Edmond became a successful man. He married and lived in Lourdes (France) as a civil engineer and architect until the outbreak of the Second World War. He volunteered for active duty and was sent to the hard-fought North of France. During the German occupation, Edmond became a prisoner of war and was interned. He managed to escape but did not regain his strength and died in 1953 at the age of 43.

In 1987, on the 75th anniversary of the sinking, Michel returned to the USA for the first time since 1912. Nine years later, Michel, together with other survivors still alive, took part in an expedition of the salvage company RMS Titanic, Inc., to the scene of the disaster. This trip also included a stay in Nova Scotia and a visit to his father's grave.

The body of Michel Navratil Sr. was recovered by the MACKAY-BENNET. In his pockets the crew found the revolver and his ticket. Navatril was erroneously buried at the Jewish cemetery in Halifax, as the officials of the *White Star Line* thought he was a Jew because of his given name.

After his true identity was revealed, the offer was made to move his remains to the Catholic cemetery, but his wife Marcelle did not want to disturb the dead man's peace.

When his son, now 88 years old, came to pay his last respects, he was the first member of the family to ever visit the grave.

Michel Navratil died in Montpellier (France) on Tuesday, 30th January 2001 at the age of 92. He will forever be remembered, like his younger brother Edmond, as one of the two "Titanic orphans." He was the last male survivor of the TITANIC.

92 years: Neshan Krekorian (12th May 1886 – 21st May 1978)

Neshan Krekorian was born on 12th May 1886 in the village of Keghi in the Turkish occupied Armenia.

At the age of 25, he decided to emigrate to Canada, because he was a Christian and was defenseless against the reprisals of the Turkish Muslims. Together with his friends Orsen Siravanian, Ortin Zakarian, Mariededer Zakarian and David Vartanian, he boarded the TITANIC in Cherbourg under ticket number 2654 as a Third-Class passenger with the destination Hamilton, Ontario.

According to another source, (AH) Krekorian originally had no ticket for the TITANIC, and he had to bribe a travel agent in Marseille to get on board the ship.

Neshan Krekorian later complained that he was "*stuffed like a chicken*" in his cabin E 57 on the F Deck. On the evening of the collision, he had been playing cards and had crawled into his bunk dressed, after taking off his shoes, around 11 p.m. He felt a strong draft and noticed that his porthole was open. When he got up to close it, he noticed ice floes in the water: "*Although it was the first time in my life that I saw icebergs, I didn't think much about them because they were barely noticeable.*"

After the collision, Neshan managed to get to the A Deck when Lifeboat No. 10 on port side was just lowered. He ran down the deck, made a jump and landed in the boat. Sailor Frank Evans later testified that Krekorian "*deliberately jumped in and saved himself!*"

This jump into the lifeboat did indeed save his life, but that night, like so many survivors, he suffered pneumonia and was hospitalized immediately after his arrival in New York. When he later made it to Brantford, Ontario, he had to spend several weeks in a hospital again. But finally, he recovered from the stresses and strains of that terrible night. From his four friends with whom he had boarded the luxury liner in Cherbourg, only David Vartanian survived the disaster. Vartanian died on Wednesday, August 3rd, 1966 at the age of 76, in Detroit, Michigan.

In 1918 Neshan Krekorian moved to St. Catherines, Ontario, and married Persa Vartanian on Saturday, July 12th, 1924, with whom he had four children.

All his working life in the USA Neshan worked on the assembly line for automobiles of General Motors. He never went on a ship again after the TITANIC disaster. Whenever he came near a larger area of water, he became restless. His daughter once said about it: *"His face betrayed his thoughts. He stared at the water, and it was obvious he was reliving that night."*

On Sunday, 21st May 1978 Neshan Krekorian died in St Catherine at the age of 92.

The death certificate of Neshan Krekorian states the date of birth as December 1st, 1886 and not May 12th, 1886.

In the list of foreign passengers, he is listed as "Nishan Krikorian", 27 years old and married. The name of his wife is given as "Dilbar Arokian Krikorian."

It is quite possible this was a mistake, as it was always assumed that he was single when he arrived in the USA. A possible explanation for this is that he gave his mother's name on arrival, but this was wrongly recorded by the immigration officials. It is also possible, however, that he was actually married and left his wife behind and then later married to Persa Vartanian, who apparently had no family connection to his friend David Vartanian, who was also rescued.

91 years: Edward Pennington Calderhead (4th June 1869 – 5th April 1961)

Edward Pennington Calderhead was born on Friday, June 4th, 1869 in Philadelphia, Pennsylvania. He was the only child of Edward Calderhead (born in 1844) and Josephine Conrad (born in 1845), both born in Pennsylvania, who married on October 7th, 1867.

His father died on Thursday, December 29th, 1870, when Edward was still a little child. His mother remarried and had two more children with her new husband D. John W. Chew (born 1850 in Gloucester, New Jersey): Elsie D. (1880-1897) and Lilie May (born in 1881).

His mother died in 1904 and his stepfather died in 1919.

In 1897 Edward Calderhead was married to Margaret Pabst (born Saturday, April 9th, 1870). They had a daughter named Margaret who was born on Wednesday, June 22nd, 1898.

The 1910 census shows that Edward, his wife and child, and the servant Estella Coghill lived in Philadelphia. Two years later the family lived in Manhattan. Edward was the buyer of the toy department of Gimbels and Bros.

On Wednesday, 10th April 1912, Edward Calderhead boarded the TITANIC in Southampton as a First-Class passenger (ticket number 17476). On board he shared the cabin E 24 with Spencer Victor Silverthorne.

Together with his cabinmate, who also reached an advanced age and died on Sunday 17th May 1964 at the age of 87, he was rescued in Lifeboat No. 5.

After the disaster, Edward, his wife and daughter continued to live in Manhattan before they moved to San Antonio, Texas, sometime in the 1920s.

According to the 1940 census, they lived in Los Angeles. His wife died on Saturday, August 14th, 1948 at the age of 78.

Edward worked as a stonemason until his retirement and died on Wednesday, April 5th, 1961 at the age of 91 and was buried in Forest Lawn Memorial Park in Glendale, California.
His daughter Margaret was never married and remained in Los Angeles until her own death in 1982.

91 years: Albert Francis Caldwell (8th September 1885 – 10th May 1977)

Albert Francis Caldwell was born on Tuesday, September 8th, 1885 in Sanborn, Iowa, as the son of William E. Caldwell and Fannie Gates.

Albert attended Park College in Missouri, where he met Sylvia Mae Harbaugh. They graduated in 1909 and married on Wednesday, September 1st, 1909 in Colorado Springs, Colorado.

The couple went to Bangkok, Siam (now Thailand), under the auspices of the Presbyterian Board of Foreign

Missions, where they were teachers at the Bangkok Christian College for Boys. There they retained their American citizenship. On Saturday, June 10th, 1911, their son Alden Gates Caldwell was born in Bangkok. Unfortunately, his birth was not registered with the American Consulate. In later years Alden could not find a birth certificate and had no official proof of his American citizenship.

In April 1912, the couple returned to Biggsville, Illinois. Many years later, Albert Caldwell wrote his own account of his family's experiences aboard the TITANIC. In this report Albert told how they traveled through Europe and saw an advertising sign in their hotel in Naples (Italy) for the maiden voyage of the TITANIC. But because it was not possible to do so in Naples, they had to travel to London to make a reservation.

There, they were waiting for someone to cancel their passage on the TITANIC so that they could move up. When passage was available, the Caldwells bought a ticket and then boarded the luxury liner in Southampton under ticket number 248738 as Second-Class passengers.

"It was a carefree and happy throng that sailed with the Titanic on her first and last voyage. The rhythmic beat of her propellers would, as a matter of fact, not cease until the narrow Atlantic had been crossed. The weather was ideal, and the sea was calm. Everyone was having a good time. The tables were piled high with all the luxuries and delicacies that one would desire. All were interested in the record speed that we were making. No mention was made of the icebergs."

Albert also remembered the hymn that was sung during the Sunday service led by the Reverend Ernest Carter in the Second-Class Dining Hall. According to Albert, it was about "the dangers of the sea!"

"How little did that happy group, who with reverent thoughts, were worshipping God, realize that within a few hours the majority of them would meet him."

Around 10 p.m. board time, the Caldwells went to bed, but were awakened by the sound of the collision and the abrupt stopping of the vibrating engines. On deck, a sailor told them about the iceberg, but said that there was no danger for the ship. The Caldwells then went back to bed but were awakened by a steward who knocked on their door and shouted, *"Everyone on deck with life jackets!"*

Albert put on his clothes and was obviously not worried when he left his best suit on the wall and several US gold pieces in his suitcase. Albert and Sylvia went on deck, with little Alden wrapped in a blanket. A large crowd had already gathered on the Boat Deck. There was no panic, and when the order came to fill the lifeboats, the women and children were unwilling to get into the boats at first:

"They felt that it was safer to stay on the big ship. She could not sink. Consequently, the first lifeboats left the ship half filled with women and children who were practically forced into them. I did not want to trust the lives of my wife and baby to a tiny lifeboat and be lowered into the ocean. And so we, like many others, held back."

Only when a stoker, who came up from the Boiler Rooms to the Boat Deck, told him the truth about the water flowing into the Cargo Rooms and the TITANIC was sinking, did the Caldwells enter a lifeboat.

First Sylvia got into Boat No. 13; then little Alden was thrown down into the stern of the boat by Steward Frederick Ray. When the lifeboat was finally lowered, Albert also got in and settled in the bow area of the boat.

From their lifeboat they watched the sinking of the huge ship:

"At first, she seemed unharmed, but as we looked toward the bow of the ship, we could see that the lower line of portholes extended down into the water. The lights on the Titanic burned until a few minutes before she sank. She tipped, headfirst, lower and lower into the water, until all that we could see was the stern of the boat outlined against the starry sky. She hung as if on a pivot and then, with a gentle swish, disappeared from sight. For a moment all was silence and then, across that waste of waters, wafted a sound that will ever ring in my ears, the cries of those perishing in the icy water. They did not drown for they could not withstand the cold water and died, one by one, from exposure."

After being rescued by the CARPATHIA, the Caldwells returned to Illinois where their second son Raymond Milton Caldwell was born on Monday, December 21st, 1914.

The Caldwells' marriage ended several years later, and they were divorced in 1930. Albert later remarried, as did Sylvia, and settled in Richmond, Virginia. On March

10th, 1977 Albert Caldwell died at the age of 91 and was buried in Pinewood Memorial Park in Greenville.

His first wife Sylvia died of pneumonia on Thursday, January 14th, 1965 at the age of 81 years. Their son Alden died on Friday, December 18th, 1992 at the age of 81.

Not quite into the club of the "Nineties" made it:

89 years: Sidney Edward Daniels (19th November 1893 – 25th May 1983)

Sidney Edward Daniels, known as Sid Daniels, was the last surviving member of the crew of the TITANIC. He was born on November 19th, 1893 in Portsmouth, England.

In 1911 he was a member of the crew on the maiden voyage of the OLYMPIC. He was also on board when she collided with the HMS Hawke on Wednesday, September 20th, 1911 and was seriously damaged. Later Sidney moved to the new TITANIC as a steward. When the luxury liner began her maiden voyage, he was 18 years old.

By his own account, everything was quiet as he slept in his bunk until one of the guards came down and said that everyone had to put on their life jackets and climb onto the Boat Beck. Daniels then went on deck and waited there with other crew members for further orders.

Shortly thereafter, they received orders to take all women and children on deck and into the boats. When he had completed his task, only one lifeboat was left.

It was a collapsible boat, which was fixed on the roof of the Wireless Room and had to be cut free before it could be used. When this was done, he went near the Bridge and looked from port side over to starboard where he could see that the water was already reaching the Bridge. He decided to jump when the water reached his knees. After jumping onto the railing, he dived into the freezing cold water. Fearing that the suction of the sinking ship would pull him down, he swam away from the TITANIC as fast as he could. Then he suddenly saw something flashing and swam towards the overturned Collapsible B. Sidney, climbed onto the hull and was able to sit on the keel of the lifeboat.

On the boat they prayed and waited for help. Daniels told an older man that he was tired and would go to sleep, but the man kept him awake and saved his life. Sidney later realized that if he had fallen asleep, he probably never would have woken up again because most people were victims of hypothermia. They sat the entire night on the overturned boat. In the morning, a ship was sighted, and finally the RMS CARPATHIA saved them. On board of the rescue ship Sydney drank coffee for the first time in his life. He said he hated the taste but didn't care as long as it kept him warm. Upon arrival in New York, he was taken to a hospital where he stayed for a long time.

During the First World War, Sidney Daniels joined the Royal Army Service Corps, but he was not involved in any direct fighting, which he says annoyed him. He returned home in 1915 and later gave an interview to a local newspaper in which he said he, *"could do nothing but laugh when I think about everything, I've been through!"* About his further life it is still known that he served in the Merchant Navy during the Second World War.

Sidney Daniels died on May 25th, 1983, at the age of 89, in his Portsmouth home. He thus survived all surviving crew members of the TITANIC.

89 years: Lawrence Beesley (31st December 1877 – 14th February 1967)

One of the most well-known survivors of the TITANIC was Lawrence Beesley, who was born on Monday 31st December 1877 on Steeple Grange Estate near the small community of Wirksworth, Derbshire. He was the third of eight children of the bank employee, and later manager of the Capital & Counties Bank, Henry Beesley and his wife Annie Maria James.

In 1902 he began teaching science at Anthony Gell Grammar School in his hometown of Wirksworth. Two years later he moved to Dulwich College.

In 1911 his wife Gertrude Cecile, who he had married on Monday 17th June 1901, died of consumption, leaving him as a single father of a son. He took a leave of absence from Dulwich College shortly afterwards, and in April 1912, he went to Toronto to visit his brother Frank. He boarded the TITANIC (ticket number 248698) in Southampton on which he had booked a passage for Second Class and was accommodated in cabin D 56.

The days on board the TITANIC were very relaxing and comfortable for Beesley, and among others, he made friends with Reverend Carter, who also traveled in Second Class together with his wife. During the voyage he noticed that the ship had a slight heeling (list) of five degrees to port. However, he did not suspect at this time that this aspect would be important again in his later notes.

Shortly before midnight, on Sunday, he was awakened in his cabin by something that, at first, he could not classify because it no longer seemed to him *"like an additional effort of the machines and another, ordinary, clear movement of the mattress on which he was sitting. There was no cracking noise, no impression of shock, no dissonance as it could be when two heavy bodies meet."*

It was only when he noticed that the machines had stopped running that he became seriously worried, got dressed, and went up to the Boat Deck to see what had happened. When he got dressed, the order was given that all passengers should go on deck with life jackets on. So, he and some other passengers went up with the life jackets on over their clothes.

After all the women and children nearby were in the lifeboat, he also was allowed to get into Lifeboat No. 13, and he was one of only thirteen men from Second Class who were rescued. Sitting in the lifeboat, he watched the sinking of the luxury liner which he described in this way:

"The ship slowly straightened up, apparently turning around her center of gravity a little further back than the middle, until she reached an almost vertical position. Thus, the ship remained - motionless. As the TITANIC swung up, its lights suddenly went out. Those lights that had shone all night without flickering flashed up only once more."

At that moment, there was a noise that many survivors mistakenly described as an explosion, as Beesley believed. To him, it always looked like it was nothing more than the crashing of machinery from its moorings, crashing through the watertight compartments, and smashing everything in its path.

Lawrence Beesley is one of the passengers who thought that the TITANIC did not break apart when she sank. In his memory, the ship stood *"upright as a comma!"* when the noise had stopped. Only the stern part of the luxury liner was still visible and about 150 feet of the hull stood as an indistinctly visible spot in the darkness against the starry sky. The ship remained in this position for a few minutes - Beesley estimated about five minutes - and then the TITANIC glided, sinking a little deeper at the stern at first, slowly down and diving diagonally downwards. Then the sea closed over the TITANIC. She had sunk!

The terrible cries of the passengers fighting for their lives in the freezing cold water remained unforgettable, even for Lawrence Beesley, because according to him, everyone in the lifeboat was extremely surprised to hear these cries at all when the icy waves closed over the TITANIC forever. The lifeboat was fully loaded, so turning back would have put the occupants in great danger. So, the crew member responsible for this boat ordered them to row away from the screams. The screams, which were loud and innumerable at first, gradually died down one by one. According to Beesley, the screams could be heard for about 40 minutes...

At 4.45 a.m. Boat No. 13, with Beesley on board, was picked up by the CARPATHIA and thus saved.

After his arrival in the USA, he started to write down his impressions and memories. In June 1912, the English publisher Houghton Mifflin published his work, "The Loss of SS TITANIC." In Germany, however, this book appeared much later under the title: "Tragedy of the Titanic," or, "Titanic - How I survived the Sinking."

Many years later, Beesley also assisted other authors and historians with his reports on the sinking, supporting the American non-fiction author Walter Lord in his book, "A Night to Remember" ('The Last Night of the Titanic')," which was published in 1935. After his return to England, he never crossed the ocean again, not even the English Channel. He was forever cured of ship travel! Even on bathing trips with his family on the British coast he rarely went into the water.

Privately he found a new happiness. In 1919, he married Muriel "Mollie" Greenwood, who brought a three-year-old daughter named Dinah from her first marriage. With Muriel, Lawrence had three more children: Daughters Laurien and Waveney, and son Hugh. In his spare time, he began to play golf and participated successfully in the British Open several times.

In 1958, when the director Roy Ward Baker filmed Walter Lord's book under the same title, he was, like Joseph Groves Boxhall, a consultant on the set of the movie. The film was a huge success and is considered in professional circles to be the best TITANIC film ever made.
Finally, he died in London on Tuesday, February 14th, 1967, at the age of 89 years.

> On June 12th, 2001, dpa reported from Italy that the 89-year-old Antonio Martinelli, the last TITANIC survivor from Italy, had died:
>
> "The Italian, who was still in diapers when the luxury liner sank, died in a hospital near Isernia, a good 150 kilometres southeast of Rome. According to the information, Martinelli was born in Boston, USA, at the beginning of 1912. His mother brought him to Italy shortly afterwards. A few weeks later, mother and child returned to the USA on a ship considered unsinkable. They survived the sinking because the lifeboats were initially reserved for women and children, the television reported on Tuesday.
> On her maiden voyage, the TITANIC ran into an iceberg on April 14, 1912, and about 1500 people drowned."
>
> Only now the problem begins: There is no Antonio Martinelli on the passenger list of the TITANIC! Also, his mother does not appear there! Martinelli is said to have believed all his life that he was a baby on the TITANIC. How he came up with that remains unclear. The fact is that there was almost certainly no Antonio Martinelli on the TITANIC!

The Scapegoats of the Disaster

Stanley Lord and the CALIFORNIAN

The night of April 14th, 1912 was a date, that would change the lives not only for the surviving passengers and crew members forever. For a man who was completely uninvolved in the disaster and its origin, this night also became a lifelong trauma and he himself became one of the biggest scapegoats of the TITANIC tragedy: Captain Stanley Lord of the steamship CALIFORNIAN!

But how could it have happened, that a man who was completely uninvolved in the collision and sinking of the TITANIC became one of the biggest scapegoats of the TITANIC tragedy?

Stanley Lord, born in Bolton on Thursday, September 13th, 1877, was the captain of the steamship CALIFORNIAN which sailed under the flag of the *Leyland Line*. The CALIFORNIAN had left the Victoria Docks in London on Friday, April 5th, 1912 at six o'clock in the morning with general cargo on board, heading for Boston. On 14th April 1912, the Californian had also run into an ice field and had drawn the attention of other ships to the ice, including the TITANIC, which, however, initially only served as a relay station.

At about 10.20 p.m. the CALIFORNIAN was unable to continue her journey and Stanley Lord did the only right thing for his ship: he stopped the engines!

To warn other ships, Lord had the CALIFORNIAN's position calculated and then passed on to other ships. The position which was passed on was: 42°5°`N, 50°7°`W.

As Captain Lord was about to leave the Bridge, he noticed a light in the east, which he thought was an approaching ship. Shortly after, Lord saw it again and asked if there were other ships near the CALIFORNIAN. His Wireless Operator, Cyril Evans, replied, "*Just the Titanic.*"

But Lord believed that the light had to be from a ship smaller than the Titanic. "*Contact them anyway,*" he ordered Evans, "*and let her know that we are surrounded by ice.*"

But, as you know, that never happened again...

At 11.30 p.m. board time, the green starboard light of the other ship was visible at a distance of five nautical miles, according to Lord. He trued to contact the ship with the morse lamp, but the attempt was unsuccessful.

On board the CALIFORNIAN, Second Officer Herbert Stone took over the watch at midnight. However, he did not consider the ship to be a large steamer like the TITANIC, but rather a so-called tramp ship.

The stoker Ernest Gill, on the other hand, who went on deck of the CALIFORNIAN at the time of the iceberg collision of the TITANIC, insisted that he saw a very large steamer about eight nautical miles away, sailing at full speed!

She became sadly famous: The SS Californian © public domain

Almost 40 minutes later, Gill saw a white rocket rise from about this position. Seven or eight minutes later another followed.

He later put on record: "*I thought it was a shooting star. It wasn't my job to notify the bridge or the lookouts. I went to bed immediately afterwards!*"

What now followed has kept all historians and TITANIC-interested people busy for more than 100 years and has caused the most controversial discussions: The Second Officer Stone also saw white rockets in the sky, five in total, which he assumed came exactly from the direction of the mysterious ship (the TITANIC?).

At 1.15 a.m. ship time, Stone reported his observations to his captain. Lord ordered him to continue to signal with the morse lamp. But again, there was no response.

While Lord was resting in his cabin, Officer Cadet James Gibson joined Stone on the upper Bridge. He pointed his binoculars at the mysterious ship and saw a sixth rocket - a white flash followed by white stars.

Two more rockets followed shortly after, the last one at about 1.40 a.m. Gibson and Stone discussed the reason for the rockets they had seen:

"A ship doesn't launch rockets at sea for no reason," noted Stone.

How right he was. . .

Gibson agreed with Stone and wondered if this was a sign of "some problems". The two men noticed that the ship appeared to be tilting to starboard. The lights on the Quarterdeck now also seemed to be higher than before.

"She looks strange," said Stone. *"It looks as if a large part of it is sticking out of the water."*

At about 2.00 a.m., all they could see was the stern light of the other ship. To Stone, it seemed to turn southwest. However, her green light was not visible, which would have been the case if she had gone in that direction.

Gibson later reported that the ship's lights disappeared at 2.05 a.m., but Stone said they did not disappear until about 2.20 a.m. board time - which is pretty much the time the TITANIC sank!

Inevitably the question arises: Did Stone and Gibson watch the sinking of the TITANIC?

Stone ordered Gibson to wake Captain Lord and inform him that the other ship had fired eight white rockets. Lord later testified that he was asleep and did not remember receiving this information. All he supposedly knew was that Gibson opened the door and immediately closed it again.

It seems like the two officers of the CALIFORNIAN had actually watched the sinking of the TITANIC from their ship. But the problem is: The CQD position of the TITANIC which was calculated by Fourth Officer Joseph Groves Boxhall on that night was wrong!

After the official discovery of the TITANIC wreck in 1985, it is clear that the TITANIC sank about ten nautical miles to the east and southeast of the position indicated in her distress call!

And then of course the question arises whether Stone, Gibson and Gill of the CALIFORNIAN really told the truth before the two Inquirers into the TITANIC tragedy...

For Captain Lord, the invitation to the Committee of Inquiry in New York was practically the end of his career, only he didn't know that when he came before the Inquiry. In the days before his testimony, it became known in the press, that some passengers and also officers of the TITANIC saw the lights of another ship nearby, which did not come to help the sinking ship.

Soon the CALIFORNIAN was identified as that ship, and when it became public that crew members of the CALIFORNIAN presumably saw the distress rockets of the TITANIC, it was immediately clear to everyone: The crew under the leadership of Captain Stanley Lord had not come to help the sinking TITANIC and was therefore responsible for the death of over 1500 people!

The perfect scapegoat for the public was found: Captain Stanley Lord!

He Actually was already prejudiced when he entered the hall in Washington D.C. on Friday, April 26th, 1912 ...

At least Lord must be blamed for not waking his Wireless Operator Cyril Evans when more and more rockets were seen. However, it is not very likely that the CALIFORNIAN would have been at the TITANIC in time to pick up her passengers.

Captain Stanley Lord © public domain

But all attempts at explanation on the part of Stanley Lords were interpreted as excuses at the time, and he had practically no chance against the public opinion (similar to Joseph Bruce Ismay).

For the *White Star Line*, Stanley Lord was like a gift from heaven, because the focus was no longer on the more than obvious negligence of the ship's command that night, but only on the presumed failure of the CALIFORNIAN and her captain to provide assistance.

And so, it happened that a person completely uninvolved in the sinking of the TITANIC, such as Stanley Lord, suddenly became a big bogeyman.

The British Inquiry also had an interest in blaming Stanley Lord for much of the blame for the high number of victims, because if the *White Star Line* had been proved to have been grossly negligent, *White Star* would have been faced with an unimaginable wave of claims for damages from relatives and the survivors, which would almost certainly have led to the bankruptcy of the *White Star Line* and the loss of thousands of jobs. So, Stanley Lord was just in time as a pawn sacrifice to save thousands of lives. The British Committee apparently proceeded on the premise that they would rather destroy one existence (Stanley Lord) than thousands of existences through the bankruptcy of the *White Star Line*.

Thus, the British Inquiry came to the conclusion that the CALIFORNIAN was so close to the sinking TITANIC that it could have reached her before her demise, but it failed to provide this assistance. However, the fact that the CALIFORNIAN was in the middle of a huge ice field and had therefore stopped the engines was not taken into account. It would have taken a considerably long time until she could have made her way to the TITANIC - it is very questionable whether she would have been on the spot in time before the sinking. But nobody really wanted to hear that, because now the ideal scapegoat had been found. Even the position, which was given to all ships at 11.00 p.m. TITANIC board time and which at that time already showed a distance of 19 nautical miles between the two ships, was called a lie by some to exonerate Lord. Only then would Lord have to have had clairvoyant abilities, or did he know of the later sinking of the TITANIC half an hour before she collided with the iceberg? I don't think so...

Lord can be blamed, however, for not seeing any reason to wake up his sleeping wireless operator in order to investigate the observed missiles. Because as his Second Officer Stone said: "*A ship does not fire rockets at sea without a reason*". This fact alone should have perplexed Lord and could have caused him to wake up the wireless operator. By failing to do so, he made probably the biggest mistake of his life...

It took more than 40 years until some movement in the "Stanley Lord case" came again, because after the huge success of the film "A Night to Remember" in 1958 (in this film it is explicitly shown how the CALIFORNIAN did not come to the assistance of the TITANIC) Lord made another attempt to revise the 1912 investigation results.

But all attempts by Lord and his defenders, who continued to fight for the Captain's reputation even after

Lord's death in 1962, to reopen the investigation were rejected on the grounds that there were no new findings.

Only after the official discovery of the wreck of the TITANIC in 1985 did the case begin to move again, because it was now clear that the distress call position of the TITANIC was wrong and that she was much further from the CALIFORNIAN than previously assumed.

So, there was indeed a new investigation which was completed on Thursday, 12th March 1992, 30 years after Lord's death (Wednesday 24th January 1962).

It concluded that if the CALIFORNIAN's position was correct, the two ships could not see each other that night.

The new investigation also states that the CALIFORNIAN's second officer on watch, who had observed a strangely behaving ship and rockets far away, should have called the captain to the Bridge.

Until today the question is not clarified which other ship was seen from the TITANIC, but refused the help...

At least Captain Stanley Lord was rehabilitated to some extent by this investigation.

The Ruined Reputation of Bruce Ismay

One of the most controversial persons in the sinking of the TITANIC is still the Managing Director of the *White Star Line*, Joseph Bruce Ismay.

But why is he considered one of the main guilty persons of the sinking and the terrible number of victims?

In principle, it starts with the planning of the luxury liner, because according to contemporary information, it was Bruce Ismay who insisted that the TITANIC (as well as the OLYMPIC) only fulfilled the legal requirements for the number of lifeboats on board. For the TITANIC, this would have been only 16 lifeboats. Fortunately for the passengers, four additional collapsible boats were taken on board, so that the new luxury liner even exceeded the regulations. The original plans had been based on 64 lifeboats (that would have been enough for all passengers and crew members, author's note). But Ismay, in particular is said to have pushed for fewer boats to be taken along and for more luxury cabins to be built instead. This is more than understandable from a business point of view, but it was absolutely devastating especially with regard to what happened on April 15th, 1912.

On board the TITANIC, Ismay occupied suite B 52 and the two adjacent cabins B 54 and B 56. (The absolute experts on James Cameron's blockbuster "TITANIC" from 1997 are guaranteed to notice that in the film these very cabins were occupied by Rose DeWitt Bukater [alias Kate Winslet] and her entourage. Note of the author.)

This apartment, which was probably the most luxurious on the entire ship, was originally intended to be occupied by J. P. Morgan, the financier of the *White Star Line*. In literally the last second, however, he canceled his participation in the maiden voyage for health reasons. Ismay immediately took advantage of the opportunity and moved into the now vacant suite.

He traveled without his wife and children, who had bid him farewell in Southampton. He was accompanied by his secretary William Henry Harrison, who occupied cabin B 94, and his butler Richard Fry, who occupied cabin B 102 further forward.

In contrast to their superior, both of Bruce Ismay's servants went down with the TITANIC! In the 1990s, the TITANIC documentary "Titanic - The Last Secret" claimed that Bruce Ismay only got his place in the lifeboat because he was forced to give up his place by Ernest Freeman. However, this does not seem to be true...

In deep sorrow and sympathy, Bruce Ismay donated a gravestone to Steward Ernest Freeman at Fairview Cemetery in Halifax after the disaster.

But his behavior on board the ship was disastrous for his reputation. On the sinking day, the TITANIC received the following telegram from the steamer BALTIC at 1.42 p.m. board time:

"Captain Smith, Titanic - Greek steamer Athenia reports passing icebergs and large quantities of field ice today in latitude 41° 51' N, longitude 49° 52' W. Wish you and Titanic all success. Commander".

At this time the ship was at latitude 42° 35° `N, longitude 45° 50° W and had already come very close to the reported ice. The wireless operators immediately transmitted this extremely important message to the Bridge, but then a strange story began. Instead of making the report available to his officers, Captain Smith took it to lunch. On the Promenade Deck he met Bruce Ismay and showed him the message. But why did he do that? Did he perhaps want to make it clear to Ismay that the TITANIC should slow down because she was close to ice?

First Class passenger Miss Elisabeth Lines is one of the reasons for the speculation about a possible involvement of Bruce Ismay in the speed of the TITANIC.

She claims to have heard a conversation between Captain Edward John Smith and Joseph Bruce Ismay in the First-Class Reception Room, sitting at a table next to her, in the course of which Ismay is said to have urged the captain to increase the ship's speed so that the TITANIC would complete her maiden voyage faster than her sister ship OLYMPIC. Ismay is said to have said, that the TITANIC would beat the OLYMPIC and would arrive in New York on Tuesday evening.

Bruce Ismay later vehemently denied that such a conversation with Smith had ever happened. But Miss Elisabeth Lines has not changed her statement...

However, according to the current state of research it is very unlikely that the TITANIC would have been able to arrive in New York on Tuesday evening. Therefore, some researchers see it as a rumor that Ismay urged the captain to go faster. However, this does not explain why the TITANIC went much too fast despite many iceberg warnings...

Joseph Bruce Ismay © public domain

Let us now return to the ice warning of the BALTIC. After Captain Smith had shown him the important message, Ismay immediately put it in his pocket and then showed it only to a few selected passengers, such as Emily Ryerson, whom he met on the Boat Deck on Sunday afternoon, waving the telegram in a cocky manner. To their worried (and also justified) question whether they would slow down, he only replied that it was not necessary, and that additional boilers should be fired up during the day so that *"we can get out of the danger zone faster!"*

It is only because of Emily Ryerson that this story ever became public...

Ismay kept the iceberg warning in his pocket for the next five and a half hours (!!!) until Captain Smith finally demanded it back so he could post it in the Chart Room. But why did Ismay push to go faster? A not inconsiderable reason seems to be, that the maiden voyage threatened to become an economic failure, because due to the coal strike, which only ended shortly before departure, many passengers had refused to travel with the TITANIC. As a result, only about two thirds of the ship (fortunately, as it turned out later) had embarked on her maiden voyage, and that was only because a considerable number of the passengers on board had been transferred from other ships to the TITANIC. So, an earlier arrival of the TITANIC in New York (at least faster than the OLYMPIC on her maiden voyage) would have made a good headline.

> One legend, which is particularly very popular in Germany, is, that on her maiden voyage the TITANIC wanted to achieve the so-called "Blue Band" for the fastest speed on the Atlantic crossing. This is complete nonsense, however, because the recordholder at that time was the legendary MAURETANIA of the *Cunard Line*, which reached 26 knots. The TITANIC, even if all the boilers had really been put into operation, would only have been able to reach a speed of 24 knots - far away from the 26

knots of the MAURETANIA. But where did the misbelief come from, especially in Germany, that the TITANIC wanted to break the record? This is probably mainly due to the film "Titanic", produced by the Nazis in 1943, in which it is claimed that the "Jewish-led" *White Star Line* wanted to break the record out of pure greed (of course "typically Jewish"). This shows impressively how such feeble-minded propaganda can still haunt the minds of people many decades later...

When the TITANIC had hit the iceberg, Ismay is said to have insisted on continuing the journey. (see chapter "The collision with the Iceberg") Only when it obviously made no more sense did the ship finally stop.

During the evacuation of the ship, Ismay helped actively, even if he sometimes overshot the target. For example, he shouted at the Fifth Officer Harold Lowe when, in Ismay's eyes, he was taking too long to lower the lifeboats.

For the young and impulsive Welsh Lowe, this went decidedly too far, as he ordered Ismay not to interfere in a rather crude tone of voice:

"You want me to launch the boat quickly? Then they will all drown!"

After this rude admission, Ismay walked away without a word.

In Collapsible C, one of the last lifeboats lowered by First Officer William McMaster Murdoch, Bruce Ismay finally disembarked. That should ruin his life forever. Because the fact that the manager of the shipping line disembarked the ship although there were still more than 1500 people on board the sinking ship (and lost their lives in the process) was interpreted as cowardice.

When the TITANIC finally sunk into the sea, Ismay turned his back on her. Later he did not make any attempt to persuade the passengers of his boat to return.

After Collapsible C was docked at the CARPATHIA at 6.30 a.m, he was one of the first to climb aboard. He is said to have spoken only one sentence:

"I am Ismay, I am Ismay."

The ship's doctor of the CARPATHIA, Dr. McGhee, suggested that he go down to the Dining Room and have a hot soup or something to drink.

"No, I don't want anything."
"Why don't you go and get something?"
"I would be more comfortable here if you would leave me alone... No, wait, if you could just get me to any room where I could rest. It would be nice if you could do that."
"Please go in the salon and get something hot to drink."
"I'd rather not."

The doctor finally gave up and led Ismay to his own cabin, where he could retire until CARPATHIA's arrival in New York, which he did.

This self-imposed isolation, however, was to indirectly feed later rumors about Ismays behavior before and after the tragedy, until public opinion punished him so much, that he finally sought refuge in anonymity. Perhaps he didn't know it himself yet, but Bruce Ismay was a ruined man.

After his arrival in New York, the American authorities were already waiting for Ismay, who summoned him directly as an important witness for the forthcoming Committee of Inquiry into the TITANIC disaster. The Senator responsible, William Alden Smith, feared that Ismay wanted to escape the American authorities, as he had already wanted to send a number of telegrams on board the CARPATHIA which allowed precisely this conclusion to be drawn (the telegrams were not transmitted by the completely overloaded wireless operator, however):

Wednesday, April 17, 1912, 17:35 NYZ
"Most desirable Titanic crew aboard Carpathia should be returned home earliest moment possible. Suggest you hold Cedric, sailing her daylight Friday unless you see any reason contrary. Propose returning in her myself. Please send outfit of clothes, including shoes, for me to Cedric. Have nothing on my own. Please reply. YAMSI"

Thursday, April 18, 1912, 8:00 NYZ
"Very important you should hold Cedric daylight Friday for Titanic crew. Reply. YAMSI"

Thursday, April 18, 1912, no time given
"Unless you have good and substantial reason for not holding Cedric, please arrange to do so. Most undesirable have crew New York so long."

These telegrams could only give the impression that Bruce Ismay wanted to get away as quickly as possible. So, the decision of the US Senate to hold him is more than understandable.

Bruce Ismay was directly heard as the first witness before the Inquiry Committee. He was already considered by the vast majority of the public as the absolutely ideal scapegoat. He had finally survived the tragedy, while so many others had to die. The extremely nationalistic New York newspaper American had already successfully stirred up public opinion against Ismay when it published a picture of him surrounded by pictures of the victims' widows.

This photo was decorated with the headline, which left no doubt about the contempt for Ismay:
J. BRUTE ISMAY

It was obvious to everyone, that Ismay was very exhausted, but this was not taken into account in any way. He stressed again and again that he had *"absolutely nothing to hide"* and that he was *"just a normal passenger on board the TITANIC"*.

He vehemently defended himself against the rumors and suspicions openly expressed before the committee, according to which the TITANIC had wanted to set a record for the crossing.

The committee also asked him how he had finally managed to get into a lifeboat when so many women and children had not made it. To which he replied:

"The boat was there. There were some men in the boat and the officer asked if there were any women left, but there were no more passengers on deck. "They were going to lower the boat, so I got in."

He also had to defend himself against the rumors that he had naturally demanded the best cabin on board the CARPATHIA:

"On board I stood with my back against the bulkhead. Someone came up to me and asked if I wanted to come into the salon and have some soup or something to drink. I said, 'No, I don't want anything... If I could just get a room where I could rest, please'... Then he took me with him and gave me a room. I didn't know whose cabin it was." (It was the ship's doctor's cabin, author's note)

Joseph Bruce Ismay before the American Inquiry at the Walldorf Astoria Hotel © Library of Congress

277

Bruce Ismay had also been summoned as a witness at the British Inquiry where he again said that he had no control over the speed of the TITANIC, which was also confirmed by Captain Henry Arthur Rostron of the CARPATHIA. Rostron stated that no captain at sea, least of all Smith, could be given any instructions.

Asked about the ice warning he had taken, Ismay tried to deny any blame and justify Captain Smith's decision not to reduce speed. Bruce Ismay contradicted himself, but his statement was accepted as he was not a sailor after all, but rather to cover up the unpleasant truth.

The presiding Judge Lord Mersey said about the fact that Ismay had saved himself:

"If he hadn't jumped into the boat, he would have added only one name to the list of victims, his own."

This was a very questionable formulation, but it is not entirely incorrect. But in principle Lord Mersey let him off very lightly.

But the public never forgave him for not going down with the TITANIC, like John Jacob Astor, Benjamin Guggenheim, Thomas Andrews or Captain Edward John Smith. His reputation was completely ruined.

When a horse sponsored by him won a horse race sometime later, he was disqualified for flimsy reasons...

Already in 1913, one year after the TITANIC disaster, he retired as president of the *International Mercantile Marine Company*. However, there are also sources that report that on Wednesday, 10th January 1912 he announced his retirement at the end of the year.

However, he continued to advise his successors behind the scenes for several years. His health caused him more and more problems in his later years and on October 17th, 1937 he died at the age of 74 in Mayfair near London after a long illness due to a blood clot in his brain. He was buried at Putney Vale Cemetery in London

The "Incompetent" Captain Smith

Since the freezing North Atlantic closed over the TITANIC at 2.20 a.m. on 15th April 1912, the blame of Captain Edward John Smith for the terrible disaster has been disputed. In recent years, however, the impression is growing, that it seems to be becoming popular to blame him for absolutely everything that went wrong back then. But what mistakes did E. J. Smith really make? Here is an attempt to bring some light into his "mistakes":

1. His management with the ice warnings

A huge controversy is understandably the way Smith (and his officers) dealt with the ice warnings they have received from other ships. But the problem begins here. Did Smith really have been informed of all ice warnings that reached the Wireless Room with Jack Phillips and Harold Bride during the crossing?

As already mentioned in the chapter "The Ice Warnings", it is assumed that not all messages from the Wireless Room reached the Bridge. We have only to remember the controversial message from the MESEBA which allegedly never reached the Bridge and thus Captain Smith. In this case, however, it seems more likely that this very decisive warning was dropped by the *White Star Line* leadership after the sinking, because if the Bridge was aware of this message, it was grossly negligent to ignore it! And that could have cost *White Star Line* a million dollars in damages to the bereaved...

Even if Smith had no knowledge of this warning, the TITANIC was still sailing too fast in view of the lurking danger, especially since the ship's command was informed of the other messages warning of ice on the ship's course. But E. J. Smith acted like any other captain who was sailing the world's oceans at the time: He drove faster, so that the ship could get out of the danger zone faster! If the weather was good, as on the TITANIC, then the custom of not slowing down was followed. The speed was maintained until an obstacle in the way of the ship was sighted. And this is exactly what the TITANIC did! According to today's knowledge this may be completely absurd, but in 1912 it was done...

On Sunday, 14th April 1912, sight was good, and the sea was calm ("like a village pond"), so Smith was not forced to reduce speed.

In the final report of the American Committee of Inquiry of Tuesday, May 28th, 1912, Senator William Alden Smith condemned his namesake *"for his indifference to danger, his self-confidence and his failure to respond to the frequent warnings of his friends!"*

It should be noted here that the handling of the ice warnings by the ship's command around Captain Smith (but also his officers, who cannot be released from liability here) was very lax and careless.

2. Was Smith on the Bridge during the collision?

It is very controversial whether Smith was on the Bridge, or in his cabin during the collision of the TITANIC with the iceberg. Well, there are very conflicting details as to where he was at the crucial time. It is generally assumed that he appeared on the Bridge immediately after the collision with the iceberg. But there's no certainty of that either...

However, if Smith was not on the Bridge during the fatal collision with the iceberg, this is not a valid reason to blame him for the disaster or even to accuse him of a lack of leadership qualities, as some experts have repeatedly done in recent years.

All higher-ranking officers were in possession of their own captain's license and had ambitions to command a liner like the TITANIC. According to the rules of the *White Star Line* shipping company, the captain should be on the Bridge in critical situations. But how critical was the ice situation considered to be? That remains the big question...

Furthermore, Smith had clearly instructed his officers to inform him immediately if problems arose. So, in principle there is no reason to accuse him of not being on the Bridge during the collision. After all, he trusted his highly qualified officers.

3. Captain Smith could no longer handle the new types of ships and was only the captain of the TITANIC for marketing reasons

This is probably the most popular accusation made against E. J. Smith here: He could no longer cope with the new and larger ships and was basically no longer able to command them, as he was still a "captain from the old times" who learned his job on sailing ships. He was only given command of the large ships for representational purposes. He was practically the advertising locomotive to attract the rich passengers, "who only sailed because E. J. Smith was the captain!" The word "millionaire captain", which is very popular with Smith, probably originated here.

It should be noted that the *White Star Line* would hardly have commissioned an "incompetent" captain like Smith to command all new ships such as the OLYMPIC and the TITANIC on their maiden voyages.

Examples of Smith's "incompetence" are usually the collision of the OLYMPIC with the HMS HAWKE and the narrowly avoided collision with the NEW YORK when the TITANIC left Southampton. This is not really fair because the collision with the HMS HAWKE was not necessarily Smith's only mistake as already described in the chapter "The Construction of the TITANIC in Belfast".

Much more significant is Smith's much quoted statement after the maiden voyage of the ADRIATIC in 1907: "*I say that I cannot imagine any circumstances that could cause a ship to fail. I cannot imagine any threatening misfortune that could befall this ship. Modern shipbuilding has overcome that point.*"

This statement, made five years before the sinking of the TITANIC, shows how much Smith, too, had confidence in the technology of the new ships - perhaps too much.

4. His behavior during the evacuation of the TITANIC

The biggest point of contention, however, is his behavior during the evacuation of TITANIC. Smith is massively accused that he gave the order much too late to put the passengers in the lifeboats and evacuate the ship.

Indeed, it took a very long time, 35 minutes, before the first distress signal of the TITANIC was given, but Smith had to make sure that these distress signals were really necessary. When Thomas Andrews finally made it clear to him that the TITANIC would not survive the night, he gave the order for the ship to call for help. Should Smith have had CQD or SOS sent even before the damage report by Andrews and the situation assessment?

Today we know that the TITANIC was irreparably damaged by the collision and that she had only two hours and 40 minutes left until her sinking, but immediately after the collision nobody on board knew or could seriously imagine that. So, this accusation is somewhat weak.

During the evacuation of the TITANIC Smith is said to have been quite absent-minded and not to have been of much help. But isn't that humanly understandable? What must have been going on in Smith's mind when he realized that the Titanic would sink? The largest and safest ship in the world which, he commands is going down on its maiden voyage and he is more than aware that there was only a lifeboat place available for half of the people on board.

In the course of the night, a ship is sighted nearby, and hope arises that although the ship is lost, at least the passengers can be brought to safety. But this ship in the proximity simply does not react to the fired distress rockets and the sent emergency call. That must have been the pure horror and that Smith must have "broken internally" as the TITANIC historian Claes-Göran Wetterholm once said, is understandable.

If you now add up all the points against each other, Smith cannot be described as " incompetent". Unfortunately, the TITANIC disaster brought together some very unfortunate points that cannot be blamed on Smith:

- Presumably not all the ice warnings were known to Smith
- Flooding pattern of the ship
- Foreign ship nearby does not respond to the distress signals

Only the undeniable fact that the TITANIC went too fast through the night, although it was known that a considerable amount of ice fields would probably be on her course, is to blame on Smith, even if he acted exactly like all captains of that time.

The sinking of the TITANIC on April 15th, 1912 was the result of simply too many things that led to the disaster and the loss of 1496 lives, but certainly not "incompetence" of her Captain Edward John (E.J.) Smith.

Interesting Conspiracy Theories and Bad Omens

Since the sinking of the TITANIC over 100 years ago, there have been many theories about the reasons for this terrible disaster. Some were very close to the truth, some rather absurd and some almost bizarre. In this chapter, some of these theories and "bad omens" are mentioned. But there is no claim to be complete...

1. It's all a giant insurance scam?

In his book "The Titanic Conspiracy, "the author Robin Gardiner had put forward the theory that the OLYMPIC had suffered such serious damage after its collision with the HMS HAWKE, that she was only fit for scrap and was therefore sunk as the TITANIC disguised for insurance reasons (there are indeed insurance documents in which the OLYMPIC was certified unfit for sea. Note of the author).

In Belfast, the two ships are said to have been switched during the repairs. Since almost everything on board of both ships was pretty much identical, including the tableware, which cannot be assigned to any particular ship of the *White Star Line*, since it was used on all ships of the line, the opportunity to switch the identity of the ships would have been very convenient there.

However, the following things are at least a little curious:

On historical photos of the TITANIC the tugboats on the starboard side always bump just in front of the spot where the OLYMPIC was damaged.

Furthermore, the TITANIC is usually moored astern in the harbor - maybe so that people walking past the pier will see a clean port side and no possibly patched starboard side?

What is really mysterious is the fact that the TITANIC was not pulled out of the harbor stern first, as is usual with other ships of the *White Star Line* (also on the maiden voyage of the OLYMPIC), but bow first.

Should this perhaps mean that visible damage to the stern of the ship would not become public, which would identify her as the OLYMPIC?

However, Thomas Andrews seems to have suggested already in 1911, after the maiden voyage of the OLYMPIC, to moor the liners of the so-called "Olympic-class" on the port side, among other things to avoid the time-consuming maneuvering when leaving port!

However, the salvage teams played into Gardiner's hands for years, because for many years only pictures of the starboard propeller of the wreck had been published, but none of the port propeller. Probably because the number 401 can be seen so clearly on the starboard propeller. However, this is not definite proof that the TITANIC and not the OLYMPIC lies on the seabed at a depth of 3,800 meters. Because if the OLYMPIC was really lying down there, which number would have her starboard screw which she had received from the TITANIC: Right, the number 401 of the TITANIC!

However, one must take into account Gardiner's theory: How should an exchange of the ships have taken place? The two ships were very similar but there were also many differences between the sisters. In view of the many changes which should have been done, and the less time for that, it's nearly impossible that the switch theory is actually true.
And moreover: How could a very large number of shipyard employees have been prevented from talking about the exchange of the two ships during all these years?

That is simply impossible, and that's where the whole switch theory becomes more and more problematic.

Only in the years following the publication of Gardiner's book were photographs of the luxury liner's starboard propeller published. Unfortunately, these pictures are always a bit blurred, so that it is not possible to see exactly which construction number this propeller has. It looks like 401, but it would be desirable to finally show clearer pictures, so that Gardiner's thesis is refuted once and for all.

2. The fire in the coal bunker has speed up the sinking.

The fact, that there was a smoldering fire on board the luxury liner in one of the coal bunkers, which had been raging for several days and was probably only extinguished on the day of the collision, has been known since the committees of inquiry after the disaster. But the Irish journalist and author Senan Molony ("A Ship Accused ") assumes that this fire was much bigger and more serious than previously assumed.

Molony backs up his theory with photos taken of the TITANIC as she was lying in the port of Belfast in Northern Ireland. On the starboard side of the ship's hull, two photos show a dark spot about ten meters long at the point where the iceberg hit the ship. These photos were first shown to the public in 2014 at the Ulster Folk and Transport Museum in Ireland. In a documentary on the British Channel 4 in January 2017, Molony shows what he believes actually happened: The fire broke out during a test run in one of the coal bunkers, and all attempts to extinguish it failed. Had it not burned there with temperatures of more than 1,000 degrees for weeks, the TITANIC would have survived the collision with the iceberg. For Molony it is also the explanation why the TITANIC was so fast on the way.

It was common practice to fight fires in the coal bunker by burning the coal faster to get to the source of the fire. This way the steam engine has more power and the ships are faster, In the case of the TITANIC, too fast to avoid the iceberg.

Molony told the "Independent": "*The official TITANIC investigation explains the sinking as an act of God. But it was not simply a collision with an iceberg and subsequent sinking. It was a chain of unfortunate circumstances: fire, ice and criminal negligence.*"

In order to deceive the passengers, the TITANIC was therefore also deliberately parked upside down on the quay wall, so that nobody could see the damaged side of the ship's hull.

This seems quite familiar to the inclined reader now, doesn't it? Right, that was one of the points Robin Gardiner used in his book almost 20 years ago as a hanger for his conspiracy theory.

On each of the two photos there is indeed a dark spot, but was it really damage to the ship? Or is it simply due to the image quality of the more than one-hundred-year-old photos?

In expert circles, Molony's theory is viewed very critically and is considered rather improbable. Also, the assumption that the fire in the coal bunker was responsible for the tragedy is not really new, because already in 2004, the American engineer Robert Essenhigh from Ohio State University had made the claim, that a fire in the coal bunker was responsible for the sinking of the TITANIC. Like Molony 13 years later, Essenhigh argued that the increased burning of the coal produced so much steam, that the luxury liner subsequently became faster and faster and finally could not be stopped by Captain Smith in time before reaching the well-known ice field.

It therefore remains to be seen whether the history of the TITANIC really has to be rewritten.

3. Did the author Morgan Robertson foresee the tragedy?

One of the most incredible stories about the sinking of the TITANIC is about the author Morgan Robertson (30th September 1861 – 24th March 1915) who published his novel Futility ("Titan - A love story on the high seas") in 1898. In this book Robertson describes a ship called TITAN which collides with an iceberg and sinks on a night in April while sailing in the Atlantic Ocean. Whoever reads this will be amazed, because the size of the ship TITAN, the number of people on board, the number of lifeboats and the number of dead is incredibly similar to the TITANIC, which was not supposed to sink until 14 years later. It is even described exactly with which side the ship hits the iceberg - on the starboard side, like the TITANIC! Truly mysterious...

These parallels earned Robertson the reputation of a clairvoyant, although the stories of the two ships also differ greatly in many respects. In esoteric circles the opinion is still held today that Robertson had a vision.

Even those who should not believe in such forebodings, this incredible story seems quite fantastic to them.

4. Already the hull number of the TITANIC was damned

A widespread myth is, that even when the ship was being built in Belfast, there were fears among shipyard workers that the TITANIC was " damned." The reason for this was that her hull number was 3909 04, which read mirror-inverted and means "No Pope," so, without Christian blessing and therefore damned.

This is very far-fetched, but it remained a myth for a very long time.

But there are at least two problems with this story: The number 3909 04 was not assigned to the TITANIC as hull number, and also as a somehow different number, the official identification number of the Board of Trade for the TITANIC was 131 428 and the construction number at Harland & Wolff was 401.

Furthermore, most of the shipyard workers in Belfast were Protestants, so why should they be upset about "No Pope"?

With a lot of fantasy, you can really read a "No Pope" from 3909 04...

Passenger and Crew List of the TITANIC

The task of compiling a complete passenger and crew list of the TITANIC proved to be very difficult over many decades. The following list was compiled by Hermann Söldner in long and meticulous research and is today considered the complete passenger and crew list of the TITANIC.

Passenger List

Abbing, Anthony, 42, 3rd Class †
Abbott, Rosa *Hunt, 36, 3rd Class
Abbott, Rossmore Edward, 16, 3rd Class †
Abbott, Eugene Joseph, 14, 3rd Class †
Abelseth, Karen Marie, 16, 3rd Class
Abelseth, Olaus Jørgensen, 25, 3rd Class
Abelson, Samuel, 30, 2nd Class †
Abelson, Hannah *Wizosky, 28, 2nd Class
Abilmona/Balman, Nassif Cassam, 26, 3rd Class
Abrahamsson, Abraham August Johannes, 20, 3rd Class
Abrahim/Joseph, Mary Sophie *Easu, 18, 3rd Class
Ådahl, Mauritz Nils Martin, 30, 3rd Class †
Ahlin, Johanna Persdotter *Larsson, 40, 3rd Class †
Ahmed, Ali, 24, 3rd Class †
Aks, Leah *Rosen, 18, 3rd Class
Aks, Frank Philip, 10M, 3rd Class
Aldworth, Charles Augustus, 30, 2nd Class †
Alexander, William, 23, 3rd Class †
Alhomäki, Ilmari Rudolf, 19, 3rd Class †
Ali, William, 25. 3rd Class †

294

Allen, Elizabeth Walton, 29, 1st Class
Allen, William Henry, 35, 3rd Class †
Allison, Hudson Joshua Creighton, 30, 1st Class †
Allison, Bessie Waldo *Daniels, 25, 1st Class †
Allison, Helen Loraine, 2, 1st Class †
Allison, Hudson Trevor, 11M, 1st Class
Allum, Owen George, 18, 3rd Class †
Andersen, Albert Kaurin, 33, 3rd Class †
Andersen, Carla Christine Nielsine, 19, 3rd Class
Anderson, Harry, 47, 1st Class
Andersson (alias Wennerström), August Edvard, 27, 3rd Class
Andersson, Erna Alexandra, 17, 3rd Class
Andersson, Johan Samuel, 26, 3rd Class †
Andersson, Ida Augusta Margareta, 38, 3rd Class†
Andersson, Anders Johan, 39, 3rd Class †
Andersson, Alfrida Konstantia *Brogren, 39, 3rd Class †
Andersson, Sigrid Elizabeth, 11, 3rd Class †
Andersson, Ingeborg Constanzia, 9, 3rd Class †
Andersson, Ebba Iris Alfrida, 6, 3rd Class †
Andersson, Sigvard Harald Elias, 4, 3rd Class †
Andersson, Ellis Anna Maria, 2, 3rd Class †
Andreasson, Paul Edvin, 20, 3rd Class †
Andrew, Edgardo Samuel, 17, 2nd Class †
Andrew, Frank Thomas, 25, 2nd Class †
Andrews, Kornelia Theodosia, 62, 1st Class
Andrews, Thomas jr., 39, 1st Class †
Angheloff, Minko, 26, 3rd Class †
Angle, William A., 32, 2nd Class †
Angle, Florence Agnes *Hughes, 36, 2nd Class
Appleton, Charlotte *Lamson, 53, 1st Class
Arnold-Franchi, Josef, 25, 3rd Class †
Arnold-Franchi, Josefine *Franchi, 18, 3rd Class †
Aronsson, Ernst Axel Algot, 24, 3rd Class †

Artagaveytia Gomez, Ramón, 71, 1st Class †
Ashby, John, 57, 2nd Class †
Asim, Adola, 35, 3rd Class †
Asplund, Johan Charles, 23, 3rd Class
Asplund, Carl Oscar Vilhelm Gustafson, 40, 3rd Class †
Asplund, Selma Augusta Emilia *Johansson, 38, 3rd Class
Asplund, Carl Edgar, 5, 3rd Class †
Asplund, Filip Oscar, 13, 3rd Class †
Asplund, Clarence Gustaf Hugo, 9, 3rd Class †
Asplund, Lillian Gertrud, 5, 3rd Class
Asplund, Edvin Rojj Felix, 3, 3rd Class
Assaf, Mariana Khalil, 45, 3rd Class
Assam, Ali, 23, 3rd Class †
Astor, John Jacob, 47, 1st Class †
Astor, Madeleine Talmadge *Force, 18, 1st Class
Attalah, Malaka, 17, 3rd Class †
Attalah Khalil, Sleiman, 27, 3rd Class †
Aubart, Léontine Pauline, 24, 1st Class
Augustsson, Albert, 23, 3rd Class †
Ayoub Daher, Banoura, 15, 3rd Class
Backström, Karl Alfred, 32, 3rd Class †
Backström, Marie Mathilda *Gustafson, 33, 3rd Class
Baclini, Latifie *Qurban, 24, 3rd Class
Baclini, Marie Catherine, 5. 3rd Class
Baclini, Eugenie, 3, 3rd Class
Baclini, Helene Barbara, 9M, 3rd Class.
Badman, Emily Louisa, 18, 3rd Class...
Badt/Badr, Mohamed, 40, 3rd Class †
Bailey, Percy Andrew, 18, 2nd Class †
Bainbrigge, Charles Robert, 23, 2nd Class †
Balkic, Cerin, 26, 3rd Class †
Ball, Ada Anna *Hall, 36, 2nd Class.
Banfield, Frederick James, 28, 2nd Class †
Banski, Mara *Osman, 31, 3rd Class.

Barbarah, Catherine *David, 45, 3rd Class †
Barbarah, Saiide, 18, 3rd Class †
Barber, Ellen, 26, 1st Class.
Barkworth, Algernon Henry Wilson, 47, 1st Class
Barry, Julia, 26, 3rd Class †
Barton, David John, 22, 3rd Class †
Bateman, Robert James, 51, 2nd Class †
Baumann, John D.? 1st Class †
Baxter, Hélène *De Lanaudière Chaput, 50, 1st Class
Baxter, Quigg Edmond, 24, 1st Class †
Bazi/Razi, Rashid, 30, 3rd Class †
Bazzani, Albina *? 36, 1st Class.
Beane, Edward, 32, 2nd Class
Beane, Ethel *Clarke, 19, 2nd Class
Beattie, Thomson, 36, 1st Class †
Beauchamp, Henry James, 28, 2nd Class †
Beavan, William Thomas, 18, 3rd Class †
Becker, Ellen Elizabeth *Baumgardner, 35, 2nd Class
Becker, Marion Louise, 4th, 2nd Class
Becker, Richard F., 1st, 2nd Class
Becker, Ruth Elizabeth, 12, 2nd Class
Beckwith, Richard Leonard, 37, 1st Class
Beckwith, Sallie *Monypeny, 46, 1st Class
Beesley, Lawrence, 34, 2nd Class
Behr, Karl Howell, 26, 1st Class
Bengtsson, Johan Viktor, 26, 3rd Class †
Bentham, Lilian W., 19, 2nd Class
Berglund, Karl Ivar Sven, 22, 3rd Class †
Berriman, William John, 23, 2nd Class †
Bessette, Nellie Mayo, 39, first Class
Betros Kaouy, Tannous, 20, 3rd Class †
Bidois, Rosalie, 46, 1st Class
Bing, Lee, 32, 3rd Class.
Bird, Ellen, 31, 1st Class

Birkeland, Hans Martin Monsen, 21, 3rd Class †
Birnbaum, Jakob, 24, 1st Class †
Bishop, Dickinson H., 25, 1st Class
Bishop, Helen Margaret *Walton, 19, 1st Class
Björklund, Ernst Herbert, 18, 3rd Class †
Björnström-Steffansson, Mauritz Håkan, 28, 1st Class
Blackwell, Stephen Weart, 45, 1st Class †
Blank Henry, 39, 1st Class
Bonnell, Caroline, 30, 1st Class
Bonnell, Elizabeth, 61, 1st Class
Borebank, John James, 42, 1st Class †
Bostandyeff, Guentcho, 26, 3rd Class †
Botsford, William Hull, 25, 2nd Class †
Boulos, Sultana *Rizq, 40, 3rd Class †
Boulos, Nourelain, 7, 3rd Class †
Boulos, Akar, 9, 3rd Class †
Bourke, John, 42, 3rd Class †
Bourke, Catherine *McHugh, 32, 3rd Class †
Bourke, Mary, 40, 3rd Class †
Bowen, David John, 26, 3rd Class †
Bowen, Grace Scott, 45, 1st Class
Bowenur, Solomon, 42, 2nd Class †
Bowerman, Elsie Edith, 22, 1st Class
Bracken, James H., 29, 2nd Class †
Bradley, Bridget Delia, 22, 3rd Class.
Brady, John Bertram, 41, 1st Class †
Braf, Elin Ester Maria, 20, 3rd Class †
Brailey, Ronald, 24, 2nd Class †
Brandeis, Emil, 48, 1st Class †
Braund, Lewis Richard, 29, 3rd Class †
Braund, Owen Harris, 22, 3rd Class †
Brereton (aka Brayton), George Andrew, 37, 1st Class
Brewe, Arthur Jackson, 45, 1st Class †
Bricoux, Roger, 20, 2nd Class †

Brobeck, Carl Rudolf, 22, 3rd Class †
Brocklebank, William Alfred, 35, 3rd Class †
Brown, Amelia, 20, 2nd Class
Brown, Caroline Lane *Lamson, 59, 1st Class
Brown, Margaret *Tobin, 44, 1st Class
Brown, Thomas William Solomon, 60, 2nd Class †
Brown, Elizabeth Catherine *Ford, 40, 2nd Class
Brown, Edith Eileen, 15, 2nd Class
Bryhl, Curt Arnold Gottfrid, 25, 2nd Class †
Bryhl, Dagmar Jenny Ingeborg, 20, 2nd Class
Buckley, Daniel, 21, 3rd grade
Buckley, Katherine, 22, 3rd Class †
Bucknell, Emma Eliza *Ward, 59, 1st Class
Burke, Jeremiah, 19, 3rd Class †
Burns, Elizabeth Margaret, 41, 1st Class
Burns, Mary Delia, 17, 3rd Class †
Buss, Kate, 36, 2nd Class
Butler, Reginald Fenton, 25, 2nd Class †
Butt, Archibald Willingham, 46, 1st Class †
Byles, Thomas Roussel Davids, 42, 2nd Class †
Byström, Carolina *Jonsson, 42, 2nd Class
Cacic, Jego Grgo, 18, 3rd Class †
Cacic, Luka, 38, 3rd Class †
Cacic, Mara, 36, 3rd Class †
Cacic, Manda, 20, 3rd Class †
Cairns, Alexander, 1st Class †
Calderhead, Edward Pennington, 42, 1st Class
Caldwell, Albert Francis, 26, 2nd Class
Caldwell, Sylvia Mae *Harbaugh, 28, 2nd Class
Caldwell, Alden Gates, 10M, 2nd Class
Calic, Petar, 17, 3rd Class †
Calic (alias Uzelac), Jovo, 17, 3rd Class †
Cameron, Clear Annie, 35, 2nd Class
Campbell, William Henry, 21, 2nd Class †

Canavan, Mary, 22, 3rd Class †
Canavan, Patrick, 21, 3rd Class †
Candee, Helen Churchill *Hungerford, 52, 1st Class
Cann, Ernest Charles, 21, 3rd Class †
Caram, Joseph, 28, 3rd Class †
Caram, Maria *Elias, 18, 3rd Class †
Carbines, William, 19, 2nd Class †
Cardeza, Charlotte Wardle *Drake, 58, 1st Class
Cardeza, Thomas Drake Martinez, 36, 1st Class
Carlsson, August Sigfrid, 28, 3rd Class †
Carlsson, Carl Robert, 24, 3rd Class †
Carlsson, Frans Olof, 33, 1st Class †
Carr, Jane, 45, 3rd Class †
Carrau y Rovira, Francisco M., 31, 1st Class †
Carrau Estévez, José Pedro, 17, 1st Class †
Carter, Ernest Coutenay, 54, 2nd Class †
Carter, Lillian *Hughes, 45, 2nd Class †
Carter, William Ernest, 36, 1st Class
Carter, Lucile *Polk, 36, 1st Class
Carter, Lucile Polk, 13, 1st Class
Carter William Thornton II, 11, 1st Class
Carver, Alfred John, 28, 3rd Class †
Case, Howard Brown, 49, 1st Class †
Cassebeer, Eleanor Geneviève *Fosdick, 36, 1st Class
Cavendish, Tyrell William, 36, 1st Class †
Cavendish, Julia Florence *Seal, 25, 1st Class
Celotti, Francesco, 24, 3rd Class †
Chaffee, Herbert Fuller, 46, 1st Class †
Chaffee, Carrie Constance *Toogood, 47, 1st Class
Chambers, Norman Campbell, 27, 1st Class
Chambers, Bertha *Griggs, 32, 1st Class
Chang, Chip, 32, 3rd Class
Chapman, Charles Henry, 52, 2nd Class †
Chapman, John Henry, 36, 2nd Class †

Chapman, Sarah Elizabeth *Lawry, 28, 2nd Class †
Charters, David, 20, 3rd Class †
Chaudanson, Victorine, 36, 1st Class
Chehab/Shihab, Farres, 29, 3rd Class †
Cherry, Gladys, 30, 1st Class
Chevré, Paul Romain Marie Léonce, 45, 1st Class
Chibnall, Edith Martha Bowerman *Barber, 48, 1st Class
Chisholm, Roderick Robert Crispin, 40, 1st Class †
Christmann, Emil, 29, 3rd Class †
Christy, Alice Frances *Jones, 42, 2nd Class
Christy/Cohen, Rachel Julie, 25, 2nd Class
Chronopoulos, Apostolos, 26, 3rd Class †
Chronopolous, Demetrios, 18, 3rd Class †
Clark, Walter Miller, 27, 1st Class †
Clark, Virginia Estelle *McDowell, 26, 1st Class
Clarke, Charles Valentine, 29, 2nd Class †
Clarke, Ada Maria *Winfield, 28, 2nd Class
Clarke, John Frederick Preston, 30, 2nd Class †
Cleaver, Alice Catherine, 22, 1st Class
Clifford, George Quincy, 40, 1st Class †
Coelho, Domingos Fernandes, 20, 3rd Class †
Cohen, Gershon, 18, 3rd Class
Colbert, Patrick, 24, 3rd Class †
Coleff, Totio, 24, 3rd Class †
Coleridge, Reginald Charles, 29, 2nd Class †
Collander, Erik Gustaf, 27, 2nd Class †
Collett, Sidney Clarence Stuart, 25, 2nd Class
Colley, Edward Pomeroy, 37, 1st Class †
Collyer, Harvey, 31, 2nd Class †
Collyer, Charlotte Annie *Tate, 31, 2nd Class
Collyer, Marjorie Lottie, 8, 2nd Class
Coltcheff, Peyu, 36, 3rd Class †
Compton, Mary Eliza *Ingersoll, 64, 1st Class
Compton, Sara Rebecca, 39, 1st Class

Compton, Alexander Taylor Jr., 37, 1st Class †
Conlin/Conlon, Thomas Henry, 31, 3rd Class †
Connaughton, Michael, 31, 3rd Class †
Connolly, Kate, 23, 3rd Class
Connolly, Kate, 35, 3rd Class †
Connors/O'Connor, Patrick, 66, 3rd Class †
Cook, Jacob, 43, 3rd Class †
Cook, Selena *Rogers, 22, 2nd Class
Cor, Bartol, 35, 3rd Class †
Cor, Ivan, 27, 3rd Class †
Cor, Liudevit, 19, 3rd Class †
Corbett, Irene *Colvin, 30, 2nd Class †
Corey, Mary Phyllis Elizabeth *Miller, 30, 2nd Class †
Corn/Cornblatt, Henry, 30, 3rd Class †
Cornell, Malvina Helen *Lamson, 55, 1st Class
Corr, Ellen, 16, 3rd Class
Cotterill, Harry, 20, 2nd Class †
Coutts, Mary (Minnie) *Treanor, 36, 3rd Class
Coutts, William Loch, 9th, 3rd Class
Coutts, Neville Leslie, 3rd, Class
Coxon, Daniel, 59, 3rd Class †
Crafton, John Bertram, 59, 1st Class †
Crease, Ernest James, 19, 3rd Class †
Cribb, John Hatfield, 44, 3rd Class †
Cribb, Laura Mae, 16, 3rd Class
Crosby, Edward Gifford, 70, 1st Class †
Crosby, Catherine Elizabeth *Halstead, 64, 1st Class
Crosby, Harriette R., 39, 1st Class
Culumovic (alias Ecimovic), Joso, 17, 3rd Class †
Cumings, John Bradley, 39, 1st Class †
Cumings, Florence Briggs *Thayer, 35, 1st Class
Cunningham, Alfred Flemming, 21, 2nd Class †
Dahl, Charles Edward, 45, 3rd Class
Hence, Tannous, 28, 3rd Class †

Dahlberg, Gerda Ulrika, 22, 3rd Class †
Dakic, Branko, 19, 3rd Class †
Daly, Eugene Patrick, 29, 3rd Class
Daly, Margaret, 30, 3rd Class
Daly, Peter Denis, 51, 1st Class
Danbom, Ernst Gilbert, 34, 3rd Class †
Danbom, Anna Sigrid Maria *Brogren, 28, 3rd Class †
Danbom, Gilbert Sigvard Emanuel, 4M, 3rd Class †
Daniel, Robert Williams, 27, 1st Class
Daniels, Sarah, 33, 1st Class
Danoff, Yoto, 27, 3rd Class †
Dantcheff, Christo, 25, 3rd Class †
Davidson, Thornton, 31, 1st Class †
Davidson, Orian *Hays, 27, 1st Class
Davies, Charles Henry, 21, 2nd Class †
Davies, Evan, 21, 3rd Class †
Davies, Elizabeth Agnes Mary *White, 48, 2nd Class
Davies, John Morgan, 8, 2nd Class
Davies, Alfred J., 24, 3rd Class †
Davies, John Samuel, 21, 3rd Class †
Davies, Joseph, 17, 3rd Class †
Davis, Mary, 28, 2nd Class
Davison, Thomas Henry, 32, 3rd Class †
Davison, Mary Elizabeth *Finck, 34, 3rd Class.
Deacon, Percy William, 20, 2nd Class †
Dean, Bertram Frank, 25, 3rd Class †
Dean, Eva Georgetta *Light, 32, 3rd Class.
Dean, Bertram Vere, 1st, 3rd Class.
Dean, Elizabeth Gladys, 2nd, 3rd Class.
de Brito, José Joaquim, 32, 2nd Class †
Delalic, Redjo, 25, 3rd Class †
Del Carlo, Sebastiano, 29, 2nd Class †
Del Carlo, Argene *Genovese, 24, 2nd Class
De Messemaeker, Guillaume Joseph, 36, 3rd Class

De Messemaeker, Anna *De Becker, 36, 3rd Class
De Mulder, Theodoor, 30, 3rd Class
Denbouy, Albert, 25, 2nd Class †
Denkoff, Mito, 30, 3rd Class †
Dennis, Samuel, 22, 3rd Class †
Dennis, William, 26, 3rd Class †
De Pelsmaeker, Alfons/Alphonse, 16, 3rd Class †
Devaney, Margaret Delia, 19, 3rd Class
Dibden, William, 18, 2nd Class †
Dick, Albert Adrian, 31, 1st Class
Dick, Vera Agnes *Gillespie, 17, 1st Class
Dika, Mirko, 17, 3rd Class †
Dimic, Jovan, 42, 3rd Class †
Dintcheff, Valtcho, 43, 3rd Class †
Dodge, Henry Washington, 52, 1st Class
Dodge, Ruth *Vidaver, 34, 1st Class
Dodge, Washington Jr., 4th, 1st Class
Doherty (aka Moran), William John (aka James), 22, 3rd Class †
Doling, Ada Julia Elizabeth *Bone, 36, 2nd Class
Doling, Elsie, 18, 2nd Class
Donohue, Bridget, 21, 3rd Class †
Dooley, Patrick, 38, 3rd Class †
Dorkings, Edward Arthur, 18, 3rd Class
Douglas, Walter Donald, 50, 1st Class †
Douglas, Mahala *Dutton, 48, 1st Class
Douglas, Mary-Hélène Jane *Baxter, 27, 1st Class
Douton, William James, 54, 2nd Class †
Dowdell, Elizabeth, 31, 3rd Class
Doyle, Elizabeth, 24, 3rd Class †
Drazenovic, Jozef/Joso, 33, 3rd Class †
Drew, James Vivian, 42, 2nd Class †
Drew, Lulu Thorne *Christian, 34, 2nd Class
Drew, Marshall Brines, 8, 2nd Class.

Driscoll, Bridget, 27, 3rd Class
Dropkin, Jennie, 24, 3rd Class
Duff-Gordon (alias Morgan), Cosmo Edmund, 49, 1st Class
Duff-Gordon (alias Morgan), Lucy Christiana *Sutherland, 48, 1st Class
Dulles, William Crothers, 39, 1st Class †
Duquemin, Joseph Pierre, 19, 3rd Class
Duran y More, Florentina, 30, 2nd Class
Duran y More, Asuncion, 27, 2nd Class
Dwan, Frank, 65, 3rd Class †
Dyker, Adolf Fredrik, 23, 3rd Class †
Dyker, Anna Elizabeth Judith, 22, 3rd Class
Earnshaw, Olive *Potter, 23, 1st Class
Edvardsson, Gustaf Hjalmar, 18, 3rd Class †
Eitemiller, George Floyd, 23, 2nd Class †
Eklund, Hans Linus, 16, 3rd Class †
Ekström, Johan, 45, 3rd Class †
Elias, Dibo, 29, 3rd Class †
Elias Nassrallah, Tannous, 22, 3rd Class †
Elias, Joseph jr., 15, 3rd Class †
Elsbury, William James, 47, 3rd Class †
Emanuel, Virginia Ethel, 5th, 3rd Class
Enander, Ingvar, 21, 2nd Class †
Endres, Caroline Louise, 39, 1st Class
Estanislau, Manuel Gonçalves, 37, 3rd Class †
Eustis, Elizabeth Mussey, 54, 1st Class
Evans, Edith Corse, 36, 1st Class †
Everett, Thomas James, 39, 3rd Class †
Fahlstrøm, Arne Joma, 18, 2nd Class †
Fardon (alias Franklin), Charles, 38, 3rd Class †
Farrell, James, 25, 3rd Class †
Farthing, John, 57, 1st Class †
Faunthorpe, Harry Bartram, 40, 2nd Class †

"Faunthorpe", Elizabeth Anne *Wilkinson, 35, 2nd Class
Fillbrook, Joseph Charles, 18, 2nd Class †
Finoli, Luigi, 34, 3rd Class
Fischer, Eberhard Thelander, 18, 3rd Class †
Flegenheim(er), Antoinette *Wendt, 48, 1st Class
Fleming, Honora, 22, 3rd Class †
Fleming, Margaret, 42, 1st Class
Flynn, James, 28.3rd Class †
Flynn, John, 42, 3rd Class †
Flynn, John Irwin, 36, 1st Class
Foley, Joseph, 19, 3rd Class †
Foley, William, 20, 3rd Class †
Foo, Cheong, 32, 3rd Class
Ford, Arthur, 22, 3rd Class †
Ford, Margaret Ann *Watson, 48, 3rd Class †
Ford, Dollina Margaret, 20, 3rd Class †
Ford, Ernest Watson, 18, 3rd Class †
Ford, William Neal Thomas, 16, 3rd Class †
Ford, Robina Maggie, 7, 3rd Class †
Foreman, Benjamin Laventall, 30, 1st Class †
Fortune, Mark, 64, 1st Class †
Fortune, Mary *McDougald, 60, 1st Class
Fortune, Ethel Flora, 28, 1st Class
Fortune, Alice Elizabeth, 24, 1st Class
Fortune, Mabel Helen, 23, 1st Class
Fortune, Charles Alexander, 19, 1st Class †
Fox, Patrick, 28, 3rd Class †
Fox, Stanley Hubert, 38, 2nd Class †
Francatelli, Laura Mabel, 31, 1st Class
Franklin, Thomas Parnham, 37, 1st Class †
Frauenthal, Isaac Gerald, 43, 1st Class
Frauenthal, Henry William, 49, 1st Class
Frauenthal, Clara *Heinsheimer, 42, 1st Class
Frölicher, Hedwig Margaritha, 22, 1st Class

Frölicher-Stehli, Maximilian Josef, 60, 1st Class
Frölicher-Stehli, Margaretha Emerentia *Stehli, 48, 1st Class
Frost, Antony Wood, 37, 2nd Class †
Fry, John Richard, 38, 1st Class †
Radio, Annie Clemmer, 38, 2nd Class †
Futrelle, Jacques Heath, 37, 1st Class †
Futrelle, Lily May *Peel, 35, 1st Class
Fynney, Joseph J., 35, 2nd Class †
Gale, Harry, 38, 2nd Class †
Gale, Shadrach, 33, 2nd Class †
Gallagher, Martin, 29, 3rd Class †
Garfirth, John, 21, 3rd Class †
Garside, Ethel, 34, 2nd Class
Gaskell, Alfred, 16, 2nd Class †
Gavey, Laurence, 26, 2nd Class †
Gee, Arthur Henry, 47, 1st Class †
George/Joseph, Shawneene Whabee *Abi-Saab, 38, 3rd Class
Gerios Tamah, Assaf, 21, 3rd Class †
Gheorgheff, Stanio, ?, 3rd Class †
Gibson, Pauline C. #Boeson, 45, 1st Class
Gibson, Dorothy Winifred, 22, 1st Class
Gieger, Amalie Henriette, 39, 1st Class
Giglio, Victor Gaeton A., 24, 1st Class †
Gilbert, William, 47, 2nd Class †
Giles, Edgar, 21, 2nd Class †
Giles, Frederick Edward, 20, 2nd Class †
Giles, Ralph, 24, 2nd Class †
Gilinsky, Eliezer, 22, 3rd Class †
Gill, John William, 24, 2nd Class †
Gillespie, William Henry, 34, 2nd Class †
Gilnagh, Mary Katherine, 17, 3rd Class
Givard, Hans Christensen, 30, 2nd Class †

Glynn, Mary Agatha, 19, 3rd Class.
Goldenberg, Samuel L., 47, 1st Class
Goldenberg, Nella *Wiggens, 43, 1st Class
Goldschmidt, George B., 71, 1st Class †
Goldsmith, Frank John, 33, 3rd Class †
Goldsmith, Emily Alice *Brown, 31, 3rd Class
Goldsmith, Frank John William, 9, 3rd Class
Goldsmith, Nathan, 41, 3rd Class †
Goodwin, Frederick Joseph, 40, 3rd Class †
Goodwin, Augusta *Tyler, 43, 3rd Class †
Goodwin, Lillian Augusta, 16, 3rd Class †
Goodwin, Charles Edward, 14, 3rd Class †
Goodwin, William Frederick, 13, 3rd Class †
Goodwin, Jessie Allis Mary, 12, 3rd Class †
Goodwin, Harold Victor, 10, 3rd Class †
Goodwin, Sidney Leslie, 19M, 3rd Class †
Gracie, Archibald IV, 53, 1st Class
Graham, George Edward, 38, 1st Class †
Graham, Edith Ware *Junkins, 59, 1st Class
Graham, Margaret Edith, 19, 1st Class
Green, George Henry, 40, 3rd Class †
Greenberg, Samuel, 52, 2nd Class †
Greenfield, Blanche *Strouse, 45, 1st Class
Greenfield, William Bertram, 23, 1st Class
Grønnestad, Daniel Danielsen, 32, 3rd Class †
Guest, Robert, 23, 3rd Class †
Guggenheim, Benjamin, 46, 1st Class †
Gustafsson, Karl Gideon, 19, 3rd Class †
Gustafsson, Alfred Ossian, 19, 3rd Class †
Gustafsson, Anders Vilhelm, 37, 3rd Class †
Gustafsson, Johan Birger, 28, 3rd Class †
Haas, Aloisia, 24, 3rd Class †
Hagland, Ingvald Olai Olsen, 28, 3rd Class †
Hagland, Konrad Mathias Reiersen, 19, 3rd Class †

Hakkarainen, Pekka Pietari, 28, 3rd Class †
Hakkarainen, Elin Matilda *Dolck, 24, 3rd Class
Hale, Reginald, 30, 2nd Class †
Hämäläinen, Anna *? 23, 2nd Class
Hämäläinen, Wiljo, 8M, 2nd Class
Hamad, Hassab, 27, 1st Class
Hampe, Léon Jérome/Leo Jerôme, 19, 3rd Class †
Hanna Dib, Boulos, 18, 3rd Class †
Hanna, Mansour, 35, 3rd Class †
Hannah, Barak Sleiman Assi, 27, 3rd Class
Hansen, Claus Peter, 41, 3rd Class †
Hansen, Jennie Louise *Howard, 45, 3rd Class
Hansen, Henry Damgaard, 21, 3rd Class †
Hansen, Henrik Juul, 26, 3rd Class †
Harbeck, William H., 48, 2nd Class †
Harder, George Achilles, 25, 1st Class
Harder, Dorothy *Annan, 21, 1st Class
Hargardon, Kate, 17, 3rd Class †
Harknett, Alice Phoebe, 21, 3rd Class †
Harper, Henry Sleeper, 48, 1st Class
Harper, Myra *Haxtun, 49, 1st Class
Harper, John, 39, 2nd Class †
Harper, Anna Jessie, 6, 2nd Class
Harrington, Charles Henry, 37, 1st Class †
Harris, George, 62, 2nd Class
Harris, Henry Burkhardt, 45, 1st Class †
Harris, Irene *Gelding, 35, 1st Class
Harris, Walter, 30, 2nd Class †
Harrison, William Henry, 45, 1st Class †
Hart, Benjamin, 47, 2nd Class †
Hart, Esther Ada *Bloomfield, 48, 2nd Class
Hart, Eva Miriam, 7, 2nd Class
Hart, Henry, 28, 3rd Class †
Hartley, Wallace Henry, 33, 2nd Class †

Hassan Abilmona, Houssein Mohamed, 11, 3rd Class †
Hawksford, Walter James, 45, 1st Class
Hays, Charles Melville, 55, 1st Class †
Hays, Clara Jennings *Gregg, 52, 1st Class
Hays, Margaret Bechstein, 24, 1st Class
Head, Christopher, 42, 1st Class †
Healy, Honora, 29, 3rd Class
Hedman, Oskar Arvid, 27, 3rd Class
Hee, Ling, 24, 3rd Class
Hegarty, Hanora, 18, 3rd Class †
Heikkinen, Laina, 26, 3rd Class
Heininen, Wendla Maria, 23, 3rd Class †
Hellström, Hilda Maria, 22, 3rd Class
Hendekovic, Ignjac, 28, 3rd Class †
Henriksson, Jenny Lovisa, 28, 3rd Class †
Henry, Bridget Delia, 21, 3rd Class †
Herman, Samuel, 49, 2nd Class †
Herman, Jane *Laver, 48, 2nd Class
Herman, Alice, 24, 2nd Class.
Herman, Kate, 24, 2nd Class
Hewlett, Mary Dunbar *Kingcome, 56, 2nd Class
Hickman, Leonard Mark, 24, 2nd Class †
Hickman, Lewis, 32, 2nd Class †
Hickman, Stanley George, 20, 2nd Class †
Hilliard, Herbert Henry, 44, 1st Class †
Hiltunen, Martta, 18, 2nd Class †
Hipkins, William Edward, 55, 1st Class †
Hippach, Ida Sophia *Fischer, 44, 1st Class
Hippach, Jean Gertrude, 17, 1st Class
Hirvonen, Helga Elisabeth *Lindqvist, 22, 3rd Class
Hirvonen, Hildur Elisabeth, 2nd, 3rd Class
Hocking, Richard George, 23, 2nd Class †
Hocking, Elizabeth *Needs, 54, 2nd Class
Squat, Ellen, 20, 2nd Class

Hocking, Samuel James Metcalfe, 36, 2nd Class †
Hodges, Henry Price, 50, 2nd Class †
Hogeboom, Anna Louisa *Andrews, 51, 1st Class
Hold, Stephen, 44, 2nd Class †
Hold, Annie Margaret *Hill, 29, 2nd Class
Holm, John Frederik Alexander, 43, 3rd Class †
Holten, Johan Martin, 28, 3rd Class †
Holverson, Alexander Oskar, 42, 1st Class †
Holverson, Mary Aline *Towner, 35, 1st Class
Homer (aka Haven), Harry, 40, 1st Class
Honkanen, Eliina, 27, 3rd Class
Hood, Ambrose Jr., 22, 2nd Class †
Hosono, Masabumi, 41, 2nd Class
Howard, Benjamin, 63, 2nd Class †
Howard, Ellen Turelove *Arman, 60, 2nd Class †
Howard, May Elizabeth, 27, 3rd Class
Hoyt, Frederick Maxfield, 38, 1st Class
Hoyt, Jane Anne *Forby, 31, 1st Class
Hoyt, William Fisher, 42, 1st Class †
Humblen, Adolf Mathias Nikolai Olsen, 42, 3rd Class †
Hume, John Law, 28, 2nd Class †
Hunt, George Henry, 33, 2nd Class †
Hyman, Abraham, 34, 3rd Class
Ibrahim Shawah, Yousseff, 33, 3rd Class †
Icard, Amelie, 40, 1st Class
Ilett, Bertha, 17, 2nd Class
Ilieff, Ilyu, 32, 3rd Class †
Ilmakangas, Ida Livija, 27, 3rd Class †
Ilmakangas, Pieta Sofia, 25, 3rd Class †
Isham, Anne Elizabeth, 50, 1st Class †
Ismay, Joseph Bruce, 49, 1st Class
Ivanoff, Konio, 20, 3rd Class †
Jabbur, Thamine, 19, 3rd Class †
Jabbur, Hilena, 16, 3rd Class †

Jacobsohn, Sidney Samuel, 40, 2nd Class †
Jacobsohn, Amy Frances *Cohen, 24, 2nd Class
Jalsevac, Ivan, 29, 3rd Class
Jansson, Carl Olof, 21, 3rd Class
Jardim, José Netto, 21, 3rd Class †
Jarvis, John Denzil, 47, 2nd Class †
Jefferys, Clifford Thomas, 24, 2nd Class †
Jefferys, Ernest Wilfred, 22, 2nd Class †
Jenkin, Stephen Curnow, 32, 2nd Class †
Jensen, Hans Peder, 20, 3rd Class †
Jensen, Svend Lauritz, 17, 3rd Class †
Jensen, Nils Peder (Rasmus), 48, 3rd Class †
Jermyn, Annie Jane, 26, 3rd Class.
Jerwan, Marie Marthe *Thuillard, 23, 2nd Class
Johannesen, Bernt Joahnnes, 29, 3rd Class
Johansson, Jakob Alfred, 34, 3rd Class †
Johansson, Nils, 29, 3rd Class †
Johansson, Erik, 22, 3rd Class †
Johansson, Gustaf Joel, 33, 3rd Class †
Johansson, Karl Johan, 31, 3rd Class †
Johansson Palmquist, Oskar Leander, 26, 3rd Class
Johnson, Alfred, 49, 3rd Class †
Johnson, William Cahoon Jr., 19, 3rd Class †
Johnson/Johansson, Malkolm Joackim, 33, 3rd Class †
Johnson, Elisabeth Vilhelmina *Backberg, 26, 3rd Class
Johnson, Harold Theodor, 4th, 3rd Class
Johnson, Eleonor Ileen, 1st, 3rd Class
Johnston, Andrew Emslie, 35, 3rd Class †
Johnston, Elizabeth *Watson, 34, 3rd Class †
Johnston, William Andrew, 8, 3rd Class †
Johnston, Catherine Nellie, 7, 3rd Class †
Jones, Charles Cresson, 46, 1st Class †
Jonkoff, Lalyu, 23, 3rd Class †
Jonsson, Carl, 25, 3rd Class

Jönsson, Nils Hilding, 27, 3rd Class †
Joseph Shahin, Elias, 39, 3rd Class †
Julian, Henry Forbes, 50, 1st Class †
Jussila, Katriina, 20, 3rd Class †
Jussila, Mari Aina, 21, 3rd Class †
Jussila, Eiriik/Erckki, 32, 3rd Class
Kallio, Nikolai Erland, 17, 3rd Class †
Kalvik, Johannes Halvorsen, 21, 3rd Class †
Cantor, Sinai (Sehua), 34, 2nd Class †
Kantor, Miriam *Sternichev, 24, 2nd Class
Karaic, Milan, 30, 3rd Class †
Karlsson, Einar Gervasius, 21, 3rd Class
Karlsson, Julius Konrad Eugen, 33, 3rd Class †
Karlsson, Nils August, 22, 3rd Class †
Karnes, Claire *Bennett, 28, 2nd Class †
Karun, Franz, 39, 3rd Class
Karun, Manca, 4th, 3rd Class
Kassem Houssein, Fared, 18, 3rd Class †
Katavelas, Vassilios, 19, 3rd Class †
Keane, Andrew, 23, 3rd Class †
Keane, Daniel, 35, 2nd Class †
Keane, Nora A., 46, 2nd Class
Keefe, Arthur, 39, 3rd Class †
Keeping, Edwin Herbert, 33, 1st Class †
Kelly, Fanny Lydia *? 45, 2nd Class
Kelly, James, 19, 3rd Class †
Kelly, James, 44, 3rd Class †
Kelly, Anna Katherine, 20, 3rd Class.
Kelly, Mary, 22, 3rd Class.
Kennedy, John Joseph, 24, 3rd Class
Kent, Edward Austin, 58, 1st Class †
Kenyon, Frederick R., 41, 1st Class †
Kenyon, Marion *Stauffer, 31, 1st Class
Khalil Khoury, Betros, 25, 3rd Class †

Khalil, Zahie *Badr, 20, 3rd Class †
Kiernan, John, 25, 3rd Class †
Kiernan, Phillip, 22, 3rd Class †
Kilgannon, Thomas Joseph, 22, 3rd Class †
Kimball, Edwin Nelson Jr., 42, 1st Class
Kimball, Gertrude *Parsons, 45, 1st Class
Kink, Anton, 29, 3rd Class
Kink, Luise *Heilmann, 26, 3rd Class
Kink, Luise Gretchen, 4th, 3rd Class
Kink, Maria, 22, 3rd Class †
Kink, Vinzenz, 26, 3rd Class †
Kirkland, Charles Leonard, 52, 2nd Class †
Klaber, Herman, <40, 1st Class †
Klasén, Klas Albin, 18, 3rd Class †
Klasén, Gertrud Emilia, 1st, 3rd Class †
Klasén, Hulda Kristina Eugenia *Löfquist, 36, 3rd Class †
Knight, Robert J., 39, 2nd Class †
Kraeff, Thodor? 3rd Class †
Kramaric, Matilda *Peteranec, 28, 3rd Class †
Krekorian, Neshan, 25, 3rd Class
Kreuchen, Emilie Louise Auguste, 29, 1st Class
Krins, Georges Alexandre, 23, 2nd Class †
Coachman (alias Lithman), Simon, 26, 3rd Class †
Kvillner, Johan Henrik Johanesson, 31, 2nd Class †
Lahoud Ishaq, Sarkis, 30, 3rd Class †
Lahtinen, William, 35, 2nd Class †
Lahtinen, Anna Amelia *Sylfvén, 34, 2nd Class †
Laitinen, Kristina Sofia, 37, 3rd Class †
Laleff, Christo, 23, 3rd Class †
Lam, Ah, 38, 3rd Class
Lam, Len, 23, 3rd Class †
Lamb, John James, 30, 2nd Class †
Lambert-Williams, Fletcher Fellows, ca.50, 1st Class †
Landergren, Aurora Adelia, 22, 3rd Class

Landers (alias Horgan), (aka John), 22, 3rd grade †
Lane, Patrick, 16, 3rd Class †
Lang, Fang, 32, 3rd Class
Laroche, Joseph Philippe Lemercier, 25, 2nd Class †
Laroche, Juliette Marie Louise *Lafargue, 22, 2nd Class
Laroche, Louise, 1st, 2nd Class
Laroche, Simonne Marie Anne Andrée, 3rd, 2nd Class
Larsson, August Viktor, 29, 3rd Class †
Larsson, Bengt Edvin, 29, 3rd Class †
Larsson-Rondberg, Edvard A., 22, 3rd Class †
Leader, Alice *Farnham, 49, 1st Class
Lefebvre, Marie *Daumont, 40, 3rd Class †
Lefebvre, Henri, 5, 3rd Class †
Lefebvre, Ida, 3rd, Class †
Lefebvre, Jeanne, 8, 3rd Class †
Lefebvre, Mathilde, 12, 3rd Class †
Lehmann, Bertha, 17, 2nd Class
Leinonen, Antii Gustaf, 32, 3rd Class †
Leitch, Jessie Wills, 31, 2nd Class
Lemberopoulos, Peter Leni, 30, 3rd Class †
Lemore, Amelia *Hunt, 34, 2nd Class
Lennon, Denis, 20, 3rd Class †
Leonard, Lonel, 36, 3rd Class †
Leroy, Berthe, 27, 1st Class
Lester, James, 26, 3rd Class †
Lesueur, Gustave J., 36, 1st Class
Lévy, René Jacques, 36, 2nd Class †
Lewy, Erwin G., 31, 1st Class †
Leyson, Robert William Norman, 25, 2nd Class †
Lievens, René Aimé, 24, 3rd Class †
Lind, Erik Gustaf (alias Edward Lingrey), 42, 1st Class †
Lindahl, Agda Thorilda Viktoria, 25, 3rd Class †
Lindblom, Augusta Charlotta, 45, 3rd Class †
Lindell, Edvard Bengtsson, 36, 3rd Class †

Lindell, Elin Gerda *Persson, 30, 3rd Class †
Lindqvist, Eino William, 20, 3rd Class
Lindström, Sigrid *Posse, 55, 1st Class
Linehan, Michael, 21, 3rd Class †
Lines, Elizabeth Lindsey *James, 50, 1st Class
Lines, Mary Conover, 16, 1st Class
Ling, Lee, 28, 3rd Class †
Lingane, John, 61, 2nd Class †
Linhart, Wenzel, 27, 3rd Class †
Livshin (aka Harmer), David (aka Abraham), 25, 3rd Class †
Lobb, William Arthur, 30, 3rd Class †
Lobb, Cordelia *Stanlick, 26, 3rd Class †
Lockyer, Edward Thomas, 21, 3rd Class †
Long, Milton Clyde, 29, 1st Class †
Longley, Gretchen Fiske, 21, 1st Class
Loring, Joseph Holland, 30, 1st Class †
Louch, Charles Alexander, 50, 2nd Class †
Louch, Alice Adelaide *Slow, 42, 2nd Class
Lovell, John Henry, 20, 3rd Class †
Lulic, Nikola, 29, 3rd Class
Lundahl, Johan Svensson, 51, 3rd Class †
Lundin, Olga Elida, 23, 2nd Class
Lundström, Thure Edvin, 32, 3rd Class
Lurette, Eugénie Elise, 59, 1st Class
Lyntakoff, Stanko, 44, 3rd Class †
Mack, Mary *Lacy, 57, 2nd Class †
MacKay, George William, 20, 3rd Class †
Madigan, Margaret, 21, 3rd Class
Madsen, Fridtjof Arne, 24, 3rd Class
Madill, Georgette Alexandra, 16, 1st Class
Mäenpää, Matti Alexanteri, 22, 3rd Class †
Maguire, John Edward, 30, 1st Class †
Mäkinen, Kalle Edvard, 29, 3rd Class †

Mahon, Bridget Delia, 20, 3rd Class †
Maioni, Roberta Elizabeth Mary, 19, 1st Class
Maisner, Simon, 34, 3rd Class †
Malachard, Jean-Noël, 25, 2nd Class †
Mallet, Albert, 31, 2nd Class †
Mallet, Antonine Marie *Magnin, 24, 2nd Class
Mallet, André Clément, 1st, 2nd Class
Mama, Hanna, 20, 3rd Class
Manganese, Mary, 32, 3rd Class †
Mangiavacchi, Serafino Emilio, >30, 2nd Class †
Mannion, Margaret, 28, 3rd Class
Mardirossian, Sarkis, 25, 3rd Class †
Maréchal, Pierre, 28, 1st Class
Marinko, Dimitri, 23, 3rd Class †
Markoff, Marin, 35, 3rd Class †
Markun, Johann, 33, 3rd Class †
Marvin, Daniel Warner, 18, 1st Class †
Marvin, Mary Graham Carmichael *Farquharson, 18, 1st Class
Matinoff, Nicola, 30, 3rd Class †
Matthews, William John, 30, 2nd Class †
May (aka Adams), Richard (aka John), 26, 3rd Class †
Maybery, Frank Hubert, 36, 2nd Class †
Mayné (alias de Villiers), Bertha Antonine, 24, 1st Class
McCaffry, Thomas Francis, 46, 1st Class †
McCarthy, Catherine, 24, 3rd Class
McCarthy, Timothy John, 54, 1st Class †
McCormack, Thomas Joseph, 19, 3rd Class
McCoy, Agnes, 29, 3rd Class
McCoy, Alicia, 26, 3rd Class
McCoy, Bernard, 24, 3rd Class
McCrae, Arthur Gordon, 32, 2nd Class †
McCrie, James Matthew, 30, 2nd Class †
McDermott, Bridget Delia Kate, 31, 3rd Class.

McEvoy, Michael, 19, 3rd Class †
McGough, James Robert, 35, 1st Class
McGovern, Mary, 22, 3rd Class
McGowan, Katherine, 42, 3rd Class †
McGowan, Annie, 17, 3rd Class
McKane, Peter David, 46, 2nd Class †
McMahon, Martin, 20, 3rd Class †
McNamee, Neal, 27, 3rd Class †
McNamee, Eileen *O'Leary, 19, 3rd Class †
McNeill, Bridget, 27, 3rd Class †
Meanwell, Mary Ann *Ogden, 63, 3rd Class †
Meehan, John, 22, 3rd Class †
Meek, Annie Louise *Rowley, 31, 3rd Class †
Mellinger, Elizabeth Anne *Maidment, 41, 2nd Class
Mellinger, Madeleine Violet, 13, 2nd Class
Mellors, William John, 19, 2nd Class
Meo Martino, Alfonzo, 48, 3rd Class †
Mernagh, Robert, 28, 3rd Class †
Meyer, August, 31, 2nd Class †
Meyer, Edgar Joseph, 28, 1st Class †
Meyer, Leila *Saks, 25, 1st Class
Midtsjø, Karl Albert, 21, 3rd Class
Mihoff, Stoytcho, 28, 3rd Class †
Miles, Frank, 23, 3rd Class †
Millet, Francis Davis, 65, 1st Class †
Milling, Jacob Christian, 48, 2nd Class †
Minahan, William Edward, 44, 1st Class †
Minahan, Lillian Mae *Thorpe, 37, 1st Class
Minahan, Daisy E., 33, 1st Class
Mineff, Ivan, 24, 3rd Class †
Minkoff, Lazar, 21, 3rd Class †
Mitchell, Henry Michael, 71, 2nd Class †
Mitkoff, Mito, 23, 3rd Class †
Mock, Philip Edmund, 30, 1st Class

Mockler, Ellen Mary, 23, 3rd Class
Moen, Sigurd Hansen, 27, 3rd Class †
Molson, Harry Markland, 55, 1st Class †
Montvila, Juozas, 27, 2nd Class †
Moore, Bella *Shapiro, 29, 3rd Class
Moore, Meyer, 7, 3rd Class
Moore, Clarence Bloomfield, 47, 1st Class †
Moore, Leonard Charles, 19, 3rd Class †
Moran, Bertha Bridget, 28, 3rd Class.
Moran, Daniel James, 27, 3rd Class †
Moraweck, Ernest, 54, 2nd Class †
Morley (alias Marshall), Henry Samuel, 38, 2nd Class †
Morley, William, 34, 3rd Class †
Morrow, Thomas Rowan, 30, 3rd Class †
Moss, Albert Johan, 29, 3rd Class
Moubarek/George, Mefeosikor Amina *Alexander, 24, 3rd Class
Moubarek/George, Gerios Youssef, 7th, 3rd Class
Moubarek/George, Halim Gonios, 4th, 3rd Class
Mouselmany, Fatima, 22, 3rd Class
Moussa, Mantoura *Boulos, 35, 3rd Class
Moutal, Rahamin Haim, 28, 3rd Class †
Mudd, Thomas Charles, 16, 2nd Class †
Mullen, Katherine, 21, 3rd Class.
Mullin (alias Lennon), Mary, 18, 3rd Class †
Mulvihill, Bridget Elizabeth, 25, 3rd Class
Murdlin, Joseph, 22, 3rd Class †
Murphy, Nora, 34, 3rd Class
Murphy, Margaret Jane, 25, 3rd Class
Murphy, Katherine, 18, 3rd Class
Myhrman, Per Fabian Oliver Malkolm, 18, 3rd Class †
Myles, Thomas Francis, 63, 2nd Class †
Naidenoff, Penko, 22, 3rd Class †
Najib Kiamie, Adal/Adele Jane, 15, 3rd Class.

Nakhli Khoury, Toufik, 17, 3rd Class †
Nakid, Said, 20, 3rd Class
Nakid, Wadia *Mowad, 19, 3rd Class
Nakid, Maria, 18M, 3rd Class
Nancarrow, William Henry, 34, 3rd Class †
Nankoff, Minko, 32, 3rd Class †
Nasrallah/Nasser, Niqula/Nicholas, 28, 2nd Class †
Nasrallah/Nasser, Adal/Adele *Achem/Hakim, 14, 2nd Class
Nasr Alma, Mustafa, 20, 3rd Class †
Nassr Rizq, Saade Hanna/Jean, 20, 3rd Class †
Natsch, Charles H., 36, 1st Class †
Naughton, Hannah, 21, 3rd Class †
Navratil (aka Hoffman), Michael (aka Louis M.), 32, 2nd Class †
Navratil, Edmond Roger, 2nd, Class
Navratil, Michel Marcel, 3rd, 2nd Class
Nenkoff, Christo, 22, 3rd Class †
Nesson, Israel, 26, 2nd Class †
Newell, Arthur Webster, 58, 1st Class †
Newell, Marjorie Anne, 23, 1st Class
Newell, Madeleine, 31, 1st Class
Newsom, Helen Monypeny, 19, 1st Class
Nicholls, Joseph Charles, 19, 2nd Class †
Nicholson, Arthur Ernest, 64, 1st Class †
Nicola-Yarad, Jamilia, 14, 3rd Class
Nicola-Yarad, Elias, 11, 3rd Class
Nieminen, Manta Josefina, 29, 3rd Class †
Niklasson, Samuel, 28, 3rd Class †
Nilsson, August Ferdinand, 21, 3rd Class †
Nilsson, Berta Olivia, 18, 3rd Class
Nilsson, Helmina Josefina, 26, 3rd Class
Nirva, Iisakki Antino Äijö, 41, 3rd Class †
Niskänen, Juha, 39, 3rd Class

Nofal, Mansour, 20, 3rd Class †
Norman, Robert Douglas, 28, 2nd Class †
Nosworthy, Richard Cater, 21, 3rd Class †
Nourney, Alfred, 20, 1st Class (alias Baron von Drachstedt)
Nye, Elizabeth *Ramell, 29, 2nd Class
Nysten, Anna Sofia, 22, 3rd Class
Nysveen, Johannes Hansen, 60, 3rd Class †
O'Brien, Denis, 21, 3rd Class †
O'Brien, Thomas, 27, 3rd Class †
O'Brien, Johanna *Godfrey, 26, 3rd Class.
O'Connell, Patrick Denis, 17, 3rd Class †
O'Connor, Maurice, 16, 3rd Class †
O'Connor, Patrick, 23, 3rd Class †
Ödahl, Nils Martin, 23, 3rd Class †
O'Dwyer, Ellen, 25, 3rd Class
Öhman, Velin, 22, 3rd Class
O'Keefe, Patrick, 21, 3rd Class
O'Leary, Hanora, 16, 3rd Class
Oliva y Ocaña, Fermina, 39, 1st Class
Olsen, Carl Siegwart Andreas, 42, 3rd Class †
Olsen, Arthur Carl, 9, 3rd Class
Olsen, Henry Margido, 28, 3rd Class †
Olson, Ole Martin, 27, 3rd Class †
Olsson, Oscar Wilhelm, 32, 3rd Class
Olsson, Nils Johan Göransson, 28, 3rd Class †
Olsson, Elina, 31, 3rd Class †
Olsvigen, Thor Andersen, 20, 3rd Class †
Omont, Alfred Fernand, 29, 1st Class
Oreskovic, Luka, 20, 3rd Class †
Oreskovic, Jeka, 21, 3rd Class †
Oreskovic, Marija, 19, 3rd Class †
Osén, Olof Elon, 16, 3rd Class †
Østby, Engelhart Cornelius, 64, 1st Class †

Østby, Helen Ragnhild, 22, 1st Class
O'Sullivan, Bridget Mary, 21, 3rd Class †
Otter, Richard, 38, 2nd Class †
Ovies y Rodriguez, Servando José Florentino, 36, 1st Class †
Oxenham, Percy Thomas, 22, 2nd Class
Padro y Manent, Julian, 26, 2nd Class
Pain, Alfred, 23, 2nd Class †
Pallas y Castillo, Emilio, 29, 2nd Class
Pålsson, Alma Cornelia *Berglund, 29, 3rd Class †
Pålsson, Gösta Leonard, 2nd, 3rd Class †
Pålsson, Paul Folke, 6, 3rd Class †
Pålsson, Stina Viola, 3rd, 3rd Class †
Pålsson, Torborg Danira, 8, 3rd Class †
Panula, Maria Emilia *Ojala, 41, 3rd Class †
Panula, Jaako Arnold, 14, 3rd Class †
Panula, Ernesti Arvid, 16, 3rd Class †
Panula, Juha Niilo, 7, 3rd Class †
Panula, Urho Abraham, 2nd, 3rd Class †
Panula, Eino Viljami, 1st, 3rd Class †
Parker, Clifford Richard, 28, 2nd Class †
Parkes, Francis, 18, 2nd Class †
Parr, William Henry Marsh, 29, 1st Class †
Parrish, Lucinda Davis *Temple, 59, 2nd Class
Partner, Austin, 40, 1st Class †
Pasic, Jakob, 21, 3rd Class †
Patchett, George, 19, 3rd Class †
Pavlovic, Stefo, 32, 3rd Class †
Payne, Vivian Arthur Ponsonby, 22, 1st Class †
Peacock, Edith *Nile, 26, 3rd Class †
Peacock, Alfred Edward, 7M, 3rd Class †
Peacock, Treasteall, 3rd, 3rd Class †
Pearce, Ernest, 32, 3rd Class †
Pears, Thomas Clinton, 29, 1st Class †

Pears, Edith *Wearne, 22, 1st Class
Pedersen, Olaf, 28, 3rd Class †
Peduzzi, Joseph/Giuseppe, 24, 3rd Class †
Pekoniemi, Edvard, 21, 3rd Class †
Peltomäki, Nikolai Johannes, 25, 3rd Class †
Peñasco y Castellana, Victor de Satode, 24, 1st Class †
Peñasco y Castellana, Maria Josefa Perez de Soto y Vallejo, 22, 1st Class
Pengelly, Frederick William, 19, 2nd Class †
Perkin, John Henry, 22, 3rd Class †
Pernot, René, 39, 2nd Class †
Perrault, Mary Anne, 33, 1st Class
Persson, Ernst Ulrik, 25, 3rd Class
Peruschitz, Joseph Benedikt, 41, 2nd Class †
Peter/Joseph, Catherine *Rizk, 24, 3rd Class
Peter/Joseph, Michael, 4th 3rd Class
Peter/Joseph, Anna/Mary, 2nd, 3rd Class
Peters Katie, 26, 3rd Class †
Petersen, Marius, 24, 3rd Class †
Petroff, Nedyalco, 19, 3rd Class †
Petroff, Pentcho, 29, 3rd Class †
Pettersson, Johan Emil, 25, 3rd Class †
Pettersson, Ellen Natalia, 18, 3rd Class †
Peuchen, Arthur Godfrey, 52, 1st Class
Phillips, Escott Robert, 42, 2nd Class †
Phillips, Alice Frances Louisa, 21, 2nd Class
Phillips (alias Marshall), Kate Florence, 19, 2nd Class
Pickard, Berk Trembisky, 32, 3rd Class
Pinsky, pink *?, 32, 2nd Class
Plotcharsky, Vasil, 27, 3rd Class †
Pocrnic, Mate, 17, 3rd Class †
Pocrnic, Tomo, 24, 3rd Class †
Ponesell, Martin, 24, 2nd Class †
Portaluppi, Emilio Ilario Giuseppe, 30, 2nd Class

Porter, Walter Chamberlain, 46, 1st Class †
Potter, Lily Alexenia *Wilson, 56, 1st Class
Pulbaum, Franz, 27, 2nd Class †
Pulner, Usher, 16, 3rd Class †
Quick, Jane *Richards, 33, 2nd Class
Quick, Winifred Vera, 8, 2nd Class
Quick, Phyllis May, 2nd, Class
Radeff, Alexander, 27, 3rd Class †
Rafful Boulos, Baccos, 20, 3rd Class †
Rasmussen, Lena Jakobsen *Solvang, 63, 3rd Class †
Reed, James George, 19, 3rd Class †
Reeves, David, 36, 2nd Class †
Rekic, Tido, 38, 3rd Class †
Renouf, Peter Henry, 33, 2nd Class †
Renouf, Lillian Elizabeth *Jefferys, 30, 2nd Class
Reuchlin, Johan George, 37, 1st Class †
Reynaldo/Reinardo, Encarnación, 28, 2nd Class
Reynolds, Harold J., 21. 3rd Class †
Rheims, George Alexander Lucien, 33, 1st Class
Richard, Emile Philippe, 23, 2nd Class †
Richards, Emily *Hocking, 24, 2nd Class
Richards, William Rowe, 3rd, 2nd Class
Richards, George Sibley, 9M, 2nd Class
Rice, Margaret *Norton, 39, 3rd Class †
Rice, Albert, 10, 3rd Class †
Rice, Georges Hugh, 8, 3rd Class †
Rice, Eric, 7, 3rd Class †
Rice, Arthur, 4th, 3rd Class †
Rice, Eugene Francis, 2nd, 3rd Class †
Ridsdale, Lucy, >50, 2nd Class
Righini, Sante, 28, 1st Class †
Riihiivuuri, Susanna Juhantytär, 22, 3rd Class †
Rintamäki, Matti, 35, 3rd Class †
Riordan, Hannah, 18, 3rd Class

Risien, Samuel Beard, 69, 3rd Class †
Risien, Emma *Lellyet, 58, 3rd Class †
Robbins, Viktor, 42, 1st Class †
Robert, Elizabeth Walton *McMillan, 43, 1st Class
Robins, Alexander A., 50, 3rd Class †
Robins, Grace Charity *Laury, 47, 3rd Class †
Roebling, Washington Augustus 2nd, 31, 1st Class †
Rogers, Reginald Harry, 18, 2nd Class †
Rogers, William John, 29, 3rd Class †
Romaine (alias Rolmane), Charles Hallace, 45, 1st Class
Rommetvedt, Knud Paust, 49, 3rd Class †
Rood, Hugh Roscoe, 38, 1st Class †
Rosblom, Helena Wilhelmina *, 41, 3rd Class †
Rosblom, Salli Helena, 2nd, 3rd Class †
Rosblom, Viktor Rikard, 18, 3rd Class †
Rosenbaum (alias Russell), Edith Louise, 34, 1st Class
Rosenshine (alias Thorne), George, 46, 1st Class †
Ross, John Hugo, 36, 1st Class †
Roth, Sara A., 26, 3rd Class
Rothes, Noëlle Lucy *Dyer-Edwards, 33, 1st Class
Rothschild, Martin, 46, 1st Class †
Rothschild, Elizabeth Jane Anne *Barrett, 54, 1st Class
Rouse, Richard Henry, 53, 3rd Class †
Rowe, Alfred Graham, 59, 1st Class †
Rugg, Emily, 21, 2nd Class
Rush, Alfred George John, 16, 3rd Class †
Ryan, Patrick, 29, 3rd Class †
Ryan, Edward, 24, 3rd Class
Ryerson, Arthur Larned, 61, 1st Class †
Ryerson, Emily Maria *Borie, 48, 1st Class
Ryerson, Emily Borie, 18, 1st Class
Ryerson, Suzette Parker, 21, 1st Class
Ryerson, John Borie, 13, 1st Class
Saad, Amin, 30, 3rd Class †

Saad, Khalil, 27, 3rd Class †
Saalfeld, Adolphe, 47, 1st Class
Sadlier, Matthew, 20, 3rd Class †
Sadowitz, Harry, 17, 3rd Class †
Sawyer, Emma, 24, 1st Class
Sæther, Simon Sivertsen, 43, 3rd Class †
Sage, John George, 44, 3rd Class †
Sage, Annie Elizabeth *Cazaly, 44, 3rd Class †
Legend, Stella Anne, 20, 3rd Class †
Sage, George John, 19, 3rd Class †
Legend, Douglas Bullen, 18, 3rd Class †
Sage, Frederick, 16, 3rd Class †
Legend, Dorothy Florence, 14, 3rd Class †
Sage, Anthony William, 12, 3rd Class †
Legend, Elizabeth Ada, 10, 3rd Class †
Sage, Constance Gladys, 7, 3rd Class †
Legend, Thomas Henry, 4th, 3rd Class †
Salander, Karl Johan, 24, 3rd Class †
Salkjelsvik, Anna Kristine, 21, 3rd Class.
Solomon, Abraham Lincoln, 43, 1st Class
Salonen, Johan Werner, 29, 3rd Class †
Samaan, Hanna Elias, 40, 3rd Class †
Samaan, Elias, 17, 3rd Class †
Samaan, Youssef Omar, 15, 3rd Class †
Sandström, Agnes Charlotta *Bengtsson, 24, 3rd Class
Sandström, Beatrice Irene, 1st, 3rd Class
Sandström, Marguerite Ruth, 4th, 3rd Class
Sap, Jules/Julius, 21, 3rd Class
Saundercock, William Henry, 19, 3rd Class †
Sawyer, Frederick Charles, 33, 3rd Class †
Scanlan, james, 22, 3rd Class †
Schabert, Emma *Mock, 35, 1st Class
Scheerlinck, Jean Baptiste/Joannes Baptist, 29, 3rd Class
Sdykoff, Todor, 42, 3rd Class †

Sedgwick, Charles Frederick Waddington, 25, 2nd Class †
Seman/Samaan, Betros, 10, 3rd Class †
Serraplan, Augusta, 30, 1st Class
Seward, Frederic Kimber, 34, 1st Class
Sharp, Percival James Richard, 27, 2nd Class †
Shaughnessy, Patrick, 24. 3rd Class †
Shedid, Hence Nahil, 19, 3rd Class †
Shellard, Frederick William Blainey, 55, 3rd Class †
Shelley, Imanita Parrish *Hall, 24, 2nd Class
Shine, Ellen Natalia, 17, 3rd Class
Shorney, Charles Joseph, 22, 3rd Class †
Shute, Elizabeth Weed, 40, 1st Class
Sihvola/Sivola, Antti Wilhelm, 21, 3rd Class †
Silvén, Lyyli Karoliina, 17, 2nd Class
Silverthorne, Spencer Victor, 35, 1st Class
Silvey, William Baird, 50, 1st Class †
Silvey, Alice *Munger, 39, 1st Class
Simmons, John, 39, 3rd Class †
Simonius-Blumer, Alfons, 56, 1st Class
Sincock, Maude, 20, 2nd Class
Sinkkonen, Anna, 30, 2nd Class
Siraganian, arsenic, 22, 3rd Class †
Sirota, Maurice, 20, 3rd Class †
Sivic, Husein, 40, 3rd Class †
Sjöblom, Anna Sofia, 18, 3rd Class
Sjöstedt, Ernst Adolf, 59, 2nd Class †
Skoog, Wilhelm Johansson, 40, 3rd Class †
Skoog, Anna Bernhardina *Karlsson, 43, 3rd Class †
Skoog, Karl Thorsten, 11, 3rd Class †
Skoog, Harald, 5, 3rd Class †
Skoog, Mabel, 9, 3rd Class †
Skoog, Margit Elizabeth, 2nd, 3rd Class †
Slabenoff, Petco/Peko, 42, 3rd Class †

Slayter, Hilda Mary, 30, 2nd Class
Slemen, Richard James, 35, 2nd Class †
Slocovsky, Selman Francis, 20, 3rd Class †
Sloper, William Thomson, 28, 1st Class
Smart, John Montgomery, 56, 1st Class †
Smiljanic, Mile, 37, 3rd Class †
Smith/Schmidt, Augustus/August, 26, 2nd Class †
Smith, James Clinch, 56, 1st Class †
Smith, Richard William, 57, 1st Class †
Smith, Lucian Philip, 24, 1st Class †
Smith, Mary Eloise *Hughes, 18, 1st Class
Smith, Marion Elsie, 49, 2nd Class
Smith, Thomas, 26, 3rd Class †
Smyth, Julia, 17, 3rd Class.
Snyder, John Pillsbury, 24, 1st Class
Snyder, Nelle *Stevenson, 23, 1st Class
Sobey, Hayden Samuel James, 25, 2nd Class †
Søholt, Peter Andreas Laurits Andersen, 19, 3rd Class †
Somerton, Francis William, 31, 3rd Class †
Spector, Woolf, 23, 3rd Class †
Spedden, Frederick Oakley, 45, 1st Class
Spedden, Margaretta Corning *Stone, 39, 1st Class
Spedden, Robert Douglas, 6, 1st Class
Spencer, William Augustus, 57, 1st Class †
Spencer, Maria Eugenie *, 45, 1st Class
Spinner, Henry John, 32, 3rd Class †
Staehelin-Maeglin, Max, 32, 1st Class
Staneff, Ivan, 23, 3rd Class †
Stankovic, Ivan, 33, 3rd Class †
Stanley, Amy Zillah Elsie, 24, 3rd Class.
Stanley, Ernest Rowland, 21, 3rd Class †
Stanton, Samuel Ward, 42, 2nd Class †
Stead, William Thomas, 62, 1st Class †
Stengel, Charles Emil Henry, 54, 1st Class

Stengel, Annie May *Morris, 44, 1st Class
Stephenson, Martha *Eustis, 52, 1st Class
Stewart, Albert Ankeny, 54, 1st Class †
Stokes, Phillip Joseph, 25, 2nd Class †
Stone, Martha Evelyn *Stevens, 62, 1st Class
Storey, Thomas, 51, 3rd Class †
Stoytcheff, Ilya, 19, 3rd Class †
Strandberg, Ida Sofia, 22, 3rd Class †
Strandén, Juho Niilosson, 30, 3rd Class
Straus, Isidor, 67, 1st Class †
Straus, Rosalie Ida *Blun, 63, 1st Class †
Strilic, Ivan, 26, 3rd Class †
Ström, Elna Matilda Persdotter *Persson, 29, 3rd Class †
Ström, Selma Matilda, 2nd, 3rd Class †
Sunderland, Victor Francis, 20, 3rd Class
Sundman, Johan Julian, 44, 3rd Class
Sutehall, Henry jr., 25, 3rd Class †
Sutton, Frederick, 61, 1st Class †
Svensson, Olof, 24, 3rd Class †
Svensson, Johan, 74, 3rd Class †
Svensson, Johan Cervin, 14, 3rd Class
Swane, George, 26, 2nd Class †
Sweet, George Frederick, 14, 2nd Class †
Swift, Margaret Welles *Barron, 46, 1st Class
Taussig, Emil, 52, 1st Class †
Taussig, Tillie *Almond tree, 39, 1st Class
Taussig, Ruth, 18, 1st Class
Taylor, Elmer Zelby, 48, 1st Class
Taylor, Juliet Cummings *Wright, 49, 1st Class
Taylor, Percy Cornelius, 32, 2nd Class †
Tenglin, Gunnar Isidor, 25, 3rd Class
Thayer, John Borland, 49, 1st Class †
Thayer, Marian Longstreth *Morris, 39, 1st Class
Thayer, John Borland Jr., 17, 1st Class

Theobald, Thomas Leonard, 34, 3rd Class †
Thomas/Tannous, John, 34, 3rd Class †
Thomas/Tannous, Tannous, 16, 3rd Class †
Thomas, Charles R'ad, 31, 3rd Class †
Thomas/Scunda, Thamine *Khoury, 16, 3rd Class
Thomas, Assad Alexander, 5M, 3rd Class
Thompson, Alexander Morrison, 36, 3rd Class †
Thorne, Gertrude Maybelle, 38, 1st Class
Thorneycroft, Percival, 36, 3rd Class †
Thorneycroft, Florence Kate *Stears, 32, 3rd Class
Tikkanan, Juho, 32, 3rd Class †
Tobin, Roger, 20, 3rd Class †
Todoroff, Lalyu, 23, 3rd Class †
Törber, Ernst Wilhelm, 41, 3rd Class †
Törnquist, William Henry, 25, 3rd Class
Tomlin, Ernest Portage, 22, 3rd Class †
Toomey, Ellen, 48, 2nd Class
Torfa, Assad, 20, 3rd Class †
Touma/Darwish, Hanne Youssef *Razi, 27, 3rd Class
Touma/Darwish, Mariana Youssef, 9th, 3rd Class
Touma/Darwish, Georges Youssef, 8th, 3rd Class
Troupeansky, Moses Aaron, 23, 2nd Class †
Trout, Jessie L. *Bruce, 26, 2nd Class
Troutt, Edwina Celia, 27, 2nd Class
Tucker, Gilbert Milligan Jr., 31, 1st Class
Turcin, Stjepan, 36, 3rd Class †
Turya, Anna Sofia, 18, 3rd Class
Turkula, Hedvig *Holma, 63, 3rd Class
Turpin, William John Robert, 29, 2nd Class †
Turpin, Dorothy Ann *Wonnacott, 27, 2nd Class †
Uruchurtu, Manuel E., 40, 1st Class †
van Billiard, Austin Blyler, 35, 3rd Class †
van Billiard, James William, 10, 3rd Class †
van Billiard, Walter John, 9, 3rd Class †

Van Den Steen, Leo Peter, 28, 3rd Class †
Vandercruyssen, Victor, 46, 3rd Class †
Van der Hoef, Wyckoff, 61, 1st Class †
Vanderplancke, Jules/Julius, 31, 3rd Class †
Vanderplancke, Emelie Maria *Vandemoortele, 31, 3rd Class †
Vanderplancke, Augusta Maria, 18, 3rd Class †
Vanderplancke, Leo Edmondus, 15, 3rd Class †
Van de Velde, Johannes Jozef, 35, 3rd Class †
Vande walle, Nestor Cyriel, 28, 3rd Class †
Van Impe, Jean Baptiste/Jan Baptist, 36, 3rd Class †
Van Impe, Rosalie Paula *Govaert, 30, 3rd Class †
Van Impe, Catharina, 10, 3rd Class †
Van Melckebeke, Philemon, 23, 3rd Class †
Vartanian, David, 22, 3rd Class
Veal, James, 40, 2nd Class †
Vendel, Olof Edvin, 20, 3rd Class †
Veström, Hulda Amanda Adolfina, 14, 3rd Class †
Vovk, Janko, 21, 3rd Class †
Waelens, Achille/Achiel, 22, 3rd Class †
Walker, William Anderson, 48, 1st Class †
Wallcroft, Ellen, 36, 2nd Class
Ward, Annie Moore, 38, 1st Class
Ware, Frederick William, 34, 3rd Class †
Ware, John James, 45, 2nd Class †
Ware, Florence Louise *Long, 31, 2nd Class
Ware, William Jeffrey, 23, 2nd Class †
Warren, Charles William, 30, 3rd Class †
Warren, Frank Manley, 63, 1st Class †
Warren, Anna Sophia Bates *Atkinson, 60, 1st Class
Watson, Ennis Hastings, 18, 2nd Class †
Watt, Elizabeth Inglis *Milne, 40, 2nd Class
Watt, Robertha Josephine, 12, 2nd Class
Wazli, Yousif Ahmed, 25, 3rd Class †

Webber, James, 66, 3rd Class †
Webber, Susan, 37, 2nd Class
Weir, John, 60, 1st Class †
Weisz, Leopold, 28, 2nd Class †
Weisz, Mathildis Francisca *Pede, 37, 2nd Class
Wells, Adelaide Dart *Trevaskis, 29, 2nd Class
Wells, Joan, 4th, 2nd Class
Wells, Ralph Lester, 2nd, Class
West, Edwy Arthur, 36, 2nd Class †
West, Ada Mary *Worth, 33, 2nd Class
West, Constance Miriam, 4th, 2nd Class
West, Barbara Joyce, 11M, 2nd Class
Wheadon, Edward Herbert, 66, 2nd Class †
Wheeler, Edwin Frederic, 24, 2nd Class †
Whilems, Charles, 32, 2nd Class
White, Percival Wayland, 54, 1st Class †
White, Richard Frasar, 21, 1st Class †
White, Ella *Holmes, 55, 1st Class
Wick, George Dennick, 57, 1st Class †
Wick, Mary *Hitchcock, 45, 1st Class
Wick, Mary Natalie, 31, 1st Class
Widegren, Carl Peter, 51, 3rd Class †
Widener, George Dunton, 50, 1st Class †
Widener, Eleanor *Elkins, 50, 1st Class
Widener, Harry Elkins, 27, 1st Class †
Wiklund, Karl Johan, 21, 3rd Class †
Wiklund, Jakob Alfred, 18, 3rd Class †
Wilkes, Ellen *Needs, 47, 3rd Class.
Willard, Constance, 21, 1st Class
Willer, Aaron, 37, 3rd Class †
Willey, Edward, 18, 3rd Class †
Williams, Charles Duane, 51, 1st Class †
Williams, Richard Norris II, 21, 1st Class
Williams, Charles Eugene, 23, 2nd Class

Williams, Howard Hugh, 28, 3rd Class †
Williams, Leslie, 28, 3rd Class †
Wilson, Helen Alice, 31, 1st Class
Windeløv, Einar, 21, 3rd Class †
Wirz, Albert, 27, 3rd Class †
Wiseman, Philippe, 54, 3rd Class †
Wittevrongel, Camille/Camiel Aloysius, 36, 3rd Class †
Woodward, John Wesley, 32, 2nd Class †
Woolner, Hugh, 45, 1st Class
Wright, George, 62, 1st Class †
Wright, Marion, 26, 2nd Class
Yazbeck Moussa, Antoni (Fraza), 27, 3rd Class †
Yazbeck, Salini *Alexander, 15, 3rd Class
Young, Marie Grice, 36, 1st Class
Youssef Abi Saab, Gerios, 45, 3rd Class †
Youssif Sam'aan, Gerios, 28, 3rd Class †
Yrois, Henriette, 24, 2nd Class †
Zakarian, Haroutioun D., 27, 3rd Class †
Zakarian, Mampré D., 22, 3rd Class †
Zenni, Fahim/Philip Rohanna Assad, 22, 3rd Class
Zimmermann, Leo, 29, 3rd Class †

Crew

Abbott, Ernest Owen, 21, Lounge Pantry Steward †
Abrams, William, 33, Fireman †
Adams, R., 26, Fireman †
Ahier, Percy Snowden, 20, Saloon Steward †
Akerman, Albert, 28, Steward †
Akerman, Joseph Francis, 35, Assistant Pantryman Steward †
Allan, Robert Spencer, 36, Bed Room Steward †

Allaria, Battista Antonio, 22, Assistant Waiter †
Allen, Ernest Frederick, 24, Trimmer
Allen, Frederick, 17, Lift Steward †
Allen, Gorge, 26, Scullion †
Allen, Henry, 32, Fireman †
Allsop, Frank Richard, 41, Saloon Steward †
Allsopp, Alfred Samuel, 34, 2nd. Electrician †
Anderson, James, 40, A. B. Seaman
Anderson, Walter J., 48, Bed Room Steward †
Andrews, Charles Edward, 19, Assistant Saloon Steward
Archer, Ernest Edward, 36, A. B. Seaman
Ashcroft, Austin Aloysius, 26, Clerk †
Ashe, Henry Wellesley, 32, Glory Hole Steward †
Aspeslagh, Georges, 26, Assistant Plateman †
Avery, James Frank, 22, Trimmer
Ayling, George Edwin, 22, Assistant Vegetable Cook †
Back, Charles F., 32, Assistant Lounge Steward †
Baggott, Allen Marden, 28, Saloon Steward
Bagley, Edward Ernest, 31, Saloon Steward †
Bailey, George Francis, 36, Saloon Steward †
Bailey, George W., 46, Fireman †
Bailey, Joseph Henry, 43, Master-at-arms
Baines, Richard, 24, Greaser †
Ball, Percy, 19, Plate Steward
Banfi, Ugo, 24, Waiter †
Bannon, John, 32, Greaser †
Barker, Albert Vale, 19, Assistant Baker †
Barker, Ernest T., 37, Saloon Steward †
Barker, Reginald Lomond, 40, 2nd. Purser †
Barlow, Charles, 30, Fireman †
Barlow, George, 36, Bed Room Steward †
Barnes, Charles, 29, Fireman †
Barnes, Frederick, 29, Fireman †
Barnes, Frederick, 37, Assistant Baker †

Barratt, Arthur, 15, Bell Boy Steward †
Barrett, Frederick, 28, Leading Fireman
Barrett, Frederick William, 33, Fireman †
Barringer, Arthur William, 33, Saloon Steward †
Barrow, Harry, 35, Assistant Butcher †
Barrows, William, 32, Saloon Steward †
Barton, Sidney John, 25, Steward †
Basilico, Giovanni, 27, Waiter †
Baxter, Harry Ross, 51, Steward †
Baxter, Thomas Ferguson, 48, Linen Steward †
Bazzi, Narciso, 33, Waiter †
Beattie, Joseph, 35, Greaser †
Beauchamp, George William, 24, Fireman
Bedford, William Bessant, 31, Assistant Roast Cook †
Beedem, George, 34, Bed Room Steward †
Beere, William, 19, Kitchen Porter †
Bell, Joseph, 50, Chief Engineer †
Bendell, F., 24, Fireman †
Benham, Frederick, 29, Saloon Steward †
Bennett, George Alfred, 30, Fireman †
Bennett, Mabel, 30, Stewardess
Benville, E., 42, Fireman †
Bernardi, Battista, 22, Assistant Waiter †
Bessant, Edward, 31, Baggage Steward †
Bessant, William Edward, 39, Fireman †
Best, Alfred Edwin, 38, Saloon Steward †
Beux, David, 26, Assistant Waiter †
Bevis, Joseph Henry, 22, Trimmer †
Biddlecombe, Charles, 33, Fireman †
Biétrix, George Baptiste, 28, Sauce Cook †
Biggs, Edward Charles, 20, Fireman †
Billow, J., 20, Trimmer †
Binstead, Walter, 19, Trimmer
Bird (alias Morgan), C. F., 42, Storekeeper †

Bishop, Walter Alexander, 34, Bed Room Steward †
Black, Alex, 28, Fireman †
Black, D., 41, Fireman †
Blackman, H., 24, Fireman †
Blake, Percival Albert, 22, Trimmer
Blake, Seaton, 26, Mess Steward †
Blake, Thomas, 36, Fireman †
Blaney, J., 29, Fireman †
Blann, Eustace Horatius, 21, Fireman †
Bliss, Emma *Junod, 45, Stewardess
Blumet, Jean Baptiste, 26, Plateman †
Bochatay, Alexis Joseph, 30, Assistant Chef †
Bochet, Pietro Giuseppe, 43, 2nd. Head Waiter †
Bogie, Norman Leslie, 29, Bed Room Steward †
Bolhuis, Hendrik, 21, Larder Cook †
Bond, William John, 40, Bed Room Steward †
Boothby, W., 36, Bed Room Steward †
Boston, William John, 30, Assistant Deck Steward †
Bott, W., 44, Greaser †
Boughton, B., 24, Saloon Steward †
Bowker, Ruth, 27, 1st. Cashier
Boxhall, Joseph Charles, 28, 4th Mate
Boyd, John, 35, Saloon Steward †
Boyes, John Henry, 36, Saloon Steward †
Bradley, Patrick Joseph, 39, Fireman †
Bradley, T., 29, A. B. Seaman †
Bradshaw, J. A., 43, Plate Steward †
Brewer, Harry, 30, Trimmer †
Brewster, George H., 48, Bed Room Steward †
Brice, Walter Thomas, 42, A. B. Seaman
Bride, Harold Sidney, 22, Assistant Telegraphist
Bright, Arthur John, 41, Quartermaster
Bristow, Robert Charles, 31, Steward †
Bristow, Harry, 33, Saloon Steward †

Brookman, John, 27, Steward †
Brooks, J., 25, Trimmer †
Broom, H., 33, Bath Steward †
Broome, Athol Frederick, 30, Verandah Steward †
Brown, Edward, 34, Saloon Steward
Brown, John, 25, Fireman †
Brown, Joseph James, 25, Fireman †
Brown, Walter James, 28, Saloon Steward †
Bryant (alias Stafford), M., 37, Greaser †
Buckley, H. E., 34, Assistant Vegetable Cook †
Buley, Edward John, 27, A. B. Seaman
Bull, W., 30, Scullion †
Bully, Henry Ashburnham, 21, Boots Steward †
Bunnell, Wilfred, 20, Plate Steward †
Burgess, Charles Reginald, 18, Extra 3rd Baker
Burke, Richard E., 30, Lounge Steward †
Burke, William, 31, 2nd Saloon Steward
Burr, Ewart Sydenham, 29, Saloon Steward †
Burrage, Alfred, 20, Plate Steward
Burroughs, Arthur, 35, Fireman †
Burton, Edward John, 32, Fireman †
Butt, Robert Henry, 21, Saloon Steward †
Butt, William John, 30, Fireman †
Butterworth, John, 23, Saloon Steward †
Byrne, J. E., 38, Bed Room Steward †
Calderwood, Hugh, 30, Trimmer †
Campbell, Donald S., 25, Clerk (2nd Class) †
Canner, J., 40, Fireman †
Carney, William, 31, Lift Steward †
Carr, Richard Stephen, 37, Trimmer †
Carter (alias Ball), James (alias W.), 46, Fireman †
Cartwright, James Edward, 32, Saloon Steward †
Casali, Giulio, 32, Waiter †
Casey, T., 28, Trimmer †

Casswill, Charles, 34, Saloon Steward †
Castleman, Edward, 37, Greaser †
Caton, Annie, 33, Turkish Bath Stewardess
Caunt, William Ewart, 27, Grill Cook †
Cave, Herbert, 34, Saloon Steward †
Cavell, George Henry, 22, Trimmer
Cecil, C., 20, Steward †
Chaboisson, Adrien Firmin, 25, Roast Cook †
Chapman, Joseph Charles, 32, Boots Steward
Charman, John, 25, Saloon Steward †
Cherrett, William Victor, 24, Fireman †
Cheverton, William Edward, 27, Saloon Steward †
Chisnall, George Alexander, 35, Boilermaker †
Chitty, Archibald George, 28, Steward †
Chitty, George Henry, 52, Assistant Baker †
Chorley, John, 25, Fireman †
Christmas, H., 33, Assistant Saloon Steward †
Clark, William, 39, Fireman
Clench, Frederick, 34, A. B. Seaman
Clench, George, 31, A. B. Seaman †
Coe, Harry, 21, Trimmer †
Coffey, John, 23, Fireman (deserted ship in Queenstown!)
Coleman, Albert Edward, 28, Saloon Steward †
Coleman, John, 57, Mess Steward †
Colgan, E. Joseph, 33, Scullion
Collins, John, 17, Scullion
Collins, Samuel J., 35, Fireman
Combes, George, 34, Fireman
Conway, P. W., 25, Saloon Steward †
Cook, George, 32, Saloon Steward †
Coombs, Augustus Charles, 42, Assistant Cook †
Cooper, Harry, 26, Fireman †
Cooper, James, 25, Trimmer †

Copperthwaite, B., 22, Fireman †
Corben, Ernest Theodore, 27, Assistant Printer Steward †
Corcoran, Denny, 33, Fireman †
Cornaire, Marcel Raymond André, 19, Assistant Roast Cook †
Cotton, A., ?, Trimmer †
Couch, Frank, 28, A. B. Seaman †
Couch, Joseph Henry, 45, Greaser †
Couper, Robert, 30, Fireman
Coutin, Auguste Louis, 28, Entre Cook †
Cox, William Denton, 29, Steward †
Coy, Francis Ernest George, 26, Junior Assistant 3rd Engineer †
Crabb, H., 23, Trimmer †
Crafter, Frederick, 27, Saloon Steward
Crawford, Alfred, 36, Bed Room Steward
Creese, Henry Philip, 44, Deck Engineer †
Crimmins, James, 21, Fireman
Crisp, Albert Hector, 39, Saloon Steward †
Crispin, William, 32, Glory Hole Steward †
Crosbie, J. Bertram, 42, Turkish Bath Attendant †
Cross, W., 39, Fireman †
Crovella, Luigi/Louis, 17, Assistant Waiter †
Crowe, George Frederick, 30, Saloon Steward
Crumplin, Charles, 35, Bed Room Steward †
Cullin, Charles, 45, Bed Room Steward
Cunningham, Andrew, 35, Bed Room Steward
Cunningham, B., 30, Fireman †
Curtis, Arthur, 25, Fireman †
Daniels, Sidney Edward, 18, Steward
Dashwood, William George, 19, Saloon Steward †
Davies, Gordon Raleigh, 33, Bed Room Steward †
Davies, John James, 27, Extra 2nd Baker †
Davies, Robert J., 26, Saloon Steward †

Davi(e)s Thomas, 33, Leading Fireman †
Davis, Stephen James, 39, A. B. Seaman †
Dawson, Joseph, 23, Trimmer †
Dean, George H., 19, Assistant Saloon Steward †
Debreuq, Maurice Emile Victor, 18, Assistant Waiter †
Deeble, Alfred Arnold, 29, Saloon Steward †
De Marsico, Giovanni, 20, Assistant Waiter †
Derrett, Albert, 26, Saloon Steward †
Deslands, Percival Stainer, 36, Saloon Steward †
Desvernine, Louis Gabriel, 20, Assistant Pastry Cook †
Diaper, J., 24, Fireman
Dickson, W., 36, Trimmer †
Dilley, John, 30, Fireman
Dillon, Thomas Patrick, 24, Trimmer
Dinneage, James Richard, 47, Saloon Steward †
Dodd, Edward Charles, 38, Junior 3rd Engineer †
Dodd, George Charles, 44, 2nd Steward †
Dodds, Henry Watson, 27, Junior Assistant 4th Engineer †
Doel, Frederick, 22, Fireman
Dolby, Joseph, 36, Reception Steward †
Donati, Italo Francesco, 17, Assistant Waiter †
Donoghue, Frank, 35, Bed Room Steward †
Dore, A., 22, Trimmer
Dornier, Louis Auguste, 20, Assistant Fish Cook †
Doughty, W., 22, Saloon Steward †
Doyle, Laurence, 27, Fireman †
Duffy, William Luke, 28, Writer †
Dunford, William, 41, Hospital Steward †
Dyer, Henry Ryland, 24, Senior Assistant 4th Engineer †
Dyer, William, 31, Saloon Steward †
Dymond, Frank, 25, Fireman
Eagle, A. J., 22, Trimmer †
Eastman, Charles, 44, Greaser †

Edbrooke, F., 24, Steward †
Ede, George B., 22, Steward †
Edge, Frederick William, 39, Deck Steward †
Edwards, 39, Assistant Pantryman Steward †
Egg, W. H., 34, Steward †
Elliott, Everett Edward, 24, Trimmer †
Ellis, John Bertram, 30, Assistant Vegetable Cook
Ennis, Walter, 35, Turkish Bath Attendant †
Ervine, Albert George, 18, Assistant Electrician †
Etches, Henry Samuel, 41, Bed Room Steward
Evans, Alfred Frank, 24, Lookout
Evans, Frank Olliver, 27, A. B. Seaman
Evans, George Richard, 27, Saloon Steward †
Evans, William, 30, Trimmer †
Fairall, Henry, 38, Saloon Steward †
Farquharson, William Edward, 39, Senior 2nd Engineer †
Farrenden, Ernest John, 22, Confectioner †
Faulkner, William Stephen, 37, Bed Room Steward
Fay, Thomas Joseph, 30, Greaser †
Fellowes, Alfred J., 29, Assistant Boots Steward †
Feltham, G., 36, Vienna Baker †
Ferrary, Anton, 34, Trimmer †
Ferris, W., 38, Leading Fireman †
Fey, Carlo, 30, Scullion †
Finch, Harry, 18, Steward †
Fioravante, Giuseppe Bertoldo, 23, Assistant Scullion †
Fitzpatrick, Charles William N., 21, Mess Steward
Fitzpatrick, Hugh J., 27, Junior Boilermaker †
Flarty, Edward, 43, Fireman
Fleet, Frederick, 24, Lookout
Fletcher, Peter W., 26, Bugler Steward †
Foley, John, 44, Storekeeper
Foley, William C., 26, Steward
Ford, Ernest, 32, Steward †

Ford, F., 37, Bed Room Steward †
Ford, H., 22, Trimmer †
Ford, Thomas, 30, Leading Fireman †
Forward, James, 27, A. B. Seaman
Foster, A. C., 37, Storekeeper †
Fox, William Thomas, 27, Steward †
Franklin, Alan Vincent, 29, Saloon Steward †
Fraser, James, 29, Junior 3rd Engineer †
Fraser J., 30, Fireman †
Fredericks, W., 20, Trimmer
Freeman, Ernest Edward Samuel, 43, Deck Steward †
Fryer, Albert Ernest, 26, Trimmer
Gatti, Gaspare Antonio Pietro, 37, Manager (Restaurant) †
Geddes, Richard Charles, 31, Bed Room Steward †
Geer, Alfred Ernest, 24, Fireman †
Gibbons, Jacob William, 36, Saloon Steward
Gilardino, Vincenzo Pio, 31, Waiter †
Giles, John Robert, 33, 2nd Baker †
Gill, Joseph Stanley, 34, Bed Room Steward †
Gill, Patrick, 38, Ship's Cook †
Godley, George, 34, Fireman
Godwin, Frederick Walter, 34, Greaser †
Gold, Katherine *Cook, 42, Stewardess
Golder, M. W., 32, Fireman †
Gollop, F., 28, Assistant Passage Cook †
Gordon, J., 29, Trimmer †
Goree, Frank, 42, Greaser †
Goshawk, Arthur James, 31, 3rd Saloon Steward †
Gosling, Bertram James, 22, Trimmer †
Gosling, S., 26, Trimmer †
Gradidge, Ernest Edward, 22, Fireman †
Graham, Thomas G., 28, Fireman
Green, George, 20, Trimmer †

Gregory, David, 40, Greaser †
Gregson, Mary, 44, Stewardess
Grosclaude, Gérald, 24, Assistant Coffee Man †
Gumery, George, 24, Mess Steward †
Gunn, Joseph Alfred, 28, Assistant Saloon Steward †
Guy, Edward John, 28, Assistant Boots Steward
Gwynn, William Logan, 37, US Postal Clerk †
Haggan, John, 35, Fireman
Haines, Albert, 31, Boatswain Mate
Halford, Richard, 22, Steward
Hall, F. A. J., 38, Scullion †
Hall, J., 32, Fireman †
Hallett, George, 22, Fireman †
Hamblyn, Ernest William, 41, Bed Room Steward †
Hamilton, Ernest, 25, Assistant Smoke Room Steward †
Hands, Bernard, 53, Fireman †
Hannam, George, 30, Fireman †
Harder, William, 39, Window Cleaner
Harding, A., 20, Assistant Pantry Steward †
Hardwick, Reginald, 21, Kitchen Porter
Hardy, John W., 37, Chief 2nd Class Steward
Harris, Amos Fred, 21, Trimmer †
Harris, Charles William, 19, Saloon Steward †
Harris, Clifford Henry, 16, Bell Boy Steward †
Harris, E., 18, Assistant Pantryman Steward †
Harris, Edward, 28, Fireman †
Harris, Frederick, 39, Fireman
Harrison, Aragon D., 40, Saloon Steward
Harrison, Norman E., 38, Junior 2nd Engineer †
Hart, John Edward, 31, Steward
Hart, Thomas, 49, Fireman †
Hartnell, Frederick, 21, Saloon Steward
Harvey, Herbert Gifford, 34, Junior Assistant 2nd Engineer †

Haslin, James, 45, Trimmer †
Hatch, Hugh, 23, Scullion †
Hawkesworth, James, 38, Saloon Steward †
Hawkesworth, William Walter, 43, Assistant Deck Steward †
Hayter, Arthur, 44, Bed Room Steward †
Head, A., 24, Fireman †
Hebb, A., 20, Trimmer
Heinen, Joseph, 30, Saloon Steward †
Hemming, Samuel Ernest, 43, Lamp Trimmer
Hendrickson, Charles George, 29, Leading Fireman
Hensford, Herbert George, 27, Assistant Butcher †
Hendy, Edward Martin, 38, Saloon Steward †
Hesketh, John Henry, 33, 2nd Engineer †
Hewett, Thomas, 37, Bed Room Steward †
Hichens, Robert, 29, Quartermaster
Hill, H. P. 36, Steward †
Hill, James, 25, Trimmer †
Hill, James Colston, 38, Bed Room Steward †
Hinckley, George, 35, Bath Steward †
Hine, William Edward, 36, 3rd Baker †
Hinton, Stephen William, 30, Trimmer †
Hiscock, S., 22, Plate Steward †
Hoare, Leonard James, 16, Saloon Steward †
Hodge, Charles, 29, Senior Assistant 3rd Engineer †
Hodges, W., 26, Fireman †
Hodgkinson, Leonard, 45, Senior 4th Engineer †
Hogan (alias King), G., 20, Scullion †
Hogg, Charles William, 37, Bed Room Steward †
Hogg, George Alfred, 29, Lookout
Hogue, E., 22, Plate Steward †
Holland, Thomas, 28, Reception Steward †
Holloway, Sidney, 20, Assistant Clothes Presser Steward †

Holman, Harry, 27, A. B. Seaman †
Hopgood, Roland, 22, Fireman †
Hopkins, F., 16, Plate Steward †
Hopkins, Robert John, 40, A. B. Seaman
Horswill, Albert Edward James, 33, A. B. Seaman
Hosgood, Richard, 22, Fireman †
Hosking, George Fox, 36, Senior 3rd Engineer †
House, William, 38, Saloon Steward †
Howell, Arthur Albert, 31, Saloon Steward †
Hughes, William Thomas, 36, Assistant 2nd Steward †
Humby, Frederick, 16, Plate Steward †
Humphreys, Thomas Humphrey, 31, Assistant Saloon Steward †
Humphreys, Sidney James, 48, Quartermaster
Hunt, Albert, 22, Trimmer
Hunt, Tom, 28, Fireman †
Hurst, Charles John, 40, Fireman †
Hurst, Walter, 27, Fireman
Hutchinson, James, 28, Vegetable Cook †
Hutchinson, John Hall, 26, Joiner †
Hyland, Lee James, 19, Steward
Ide, Harry John, 32, Bed Room Steward †
Ingram, Charles, 20, Trimmer †
Ings, William Ernest, 20, Scullion †
Ingrouille, Henry, 21, Steward †
Instance, T., 33, Fireman †
Jackson, Cecil, 22, Assistant Boots Steward †
Jacobson, John, 29, Fireman †
Jago, Joseph, 27, Greaser †
Jaillet, Henri Marie, 28, Pastry Cook †
James, Thomas, 27, Fireman †
Janaway, William Frank, 35, Bed Room Steward †
Janin, Claude Marie, 29, Soup Cook †
Jarvis, W., 37, Fireman †

Jeffery, William Alfred, 28, Controller †
Jenner, Harry, 41, 2nd Class Saloon Steward †
Jensen, Charles Valdemar, 25, Saloon Steward †
Jessop, Violet Constance, 24, Stewardess
Jewell, Archie, 23, Lookout
Joas, N., 38, Fireman †
Johnson Thorne, Harry, 25, Assistant Ship's Cook †
Johnston, James, 41, Saloon Steward
Jones, Albert, 17, Saloon Steward †
Jones, Arthur Ernest, 38, Plate Steward †
Jones, H., 29, Roast Cook †
Jones, Reginald V., 20, Saloon Steward †
Jones, Thomas William, 32, A. B. Seaman
Jouannault, Georges Jules, 24, Assistant Sauce Cook †
Joughin, Charles John, 32, Chief Baker
Judd, Charles E., 32, Fireman
Jukes, James, 35, Greaser †
Jupe, Herbert, 30, Assistant Electrician †
Kasper, F., 40, Fireman
Kearl, Charles Henry, 43, Greaser †
Kearl, G., 24, Trimmer †
Keegan, James, 38, Leading Fireman †
Keen, Percy Edward, 28, Saloon Steward
Kelland, Thomas, 21, Library Steward †
Kelly, James, 44, Greaser †
Kelly, William, 23, Assistant Electrician †
Kemish, George, 24, Fireman
Kemp, Thomas Hulman, 43, Extra Assistant 4th Engineer †
Kenchenten, Frederick, 37, Greaser †
Kennell, Charles, 30, Hebrew Cook †
Kenzler, Augustus, 43, Storekeeper †
Kerley, William Thomas, 28, Assistant Saloon Steward †
Kerr, Thomas, 26, Fireman †

346

Ketchley, Henry, 30, Saloon Steward †
Kieran, James W., 32, Chief 3rd Class Steward †
Kieran, Michael, 31, Storekeeper †
King, Alfred, 18, Lift Steward †
King, Ernest Waldron, 28, Clerk †
King, Thomas W., 43, Master-at-arms †
Kingscote, William Ford, 42, Saloon Steward †
Kinsella, Louis, 30, Fireman †
Kirkaldy (alias Clark), Thomas, 39, Bed Room Steward †
Kirkham, J., 39, Greaser †
Kitching, Arthur Alfred, 30, Saloon Steward †
Klein, Herbert, 33, 2nd Class Barber †
Knight, George, 44, Saloon Steward
Knight, Leonard George, 21, Steward †
Knowles, Thomas, 45, Fireman Messman
Lacey, Bert W., 21, Assistant Saloon Steward †
Lake, William, 35, Saloon Steward †
Laley, T., 32, Fireman †
Lane, Albert Edward, 34, Saloon Steward †
Latimer, Andrew J., 55, Chief Steward †
Laurence, Arthur, 35, Saloon Steward †
Lavington, Bessie, 38, Stewardess
Leader, Archie, 22, Assistant Confectioner †
Leather, Elizabeth May *Edwards, 41, Stewardess
Lefebvre, Paul Georges, 35, Saloon Steward †
Lee, H., 18, Trimmer †
Lee, Reginald Robinson, 41, Lookout
Leonard, Matthew, 26, Steward †
Levett, George Alfred, 21, Assistant Pantryman Steward †
Lewis, Arthur Ernest Read, 27, Steward
Light, C., 21, Fireman †
Light, C., 23, Plate Steward †
Light, W., 47, Fireman †

347

Lightoller, Charles Herbert, 38, 2nd Mate
Lindsay, William Charles, 30, Fireman
Littlejohn, Alexander James, 40, Saloon Steward
Lloyd, Humphrey I., 32, Saloon Steward †
Lloyd, W., 29, Fireman †
Locke, A., 33, Scullion †
Long, F., 28, Trimmer †
Long, W., 30, Trimmer †
Longmuir, John Dickson, 19, Assistant Pantry Steward †
Lovell, John, 38, Grill Cook †
Lowe, Harold Godfrey, 29, 5th Mate
Lucas, William, 34, Saloon Steward
Lucas, William A., 25, A. B. Seaman
Lydiatt, Charles, 38, Saloon Steward †
Lyons, William Henry, 26, A. B. Seaman †
Mabey, J., 23, Steward †
Mac Kay, Charles Donald, 34, Saloon Steward
Mackie, William Dickinson, 32, Junior 5th Engineer †
Mac Kie, George William, 34, Bed Room Steward †
Major, Edgar Thomas, 35, Bath Steward †
Major, William James, 32, Fireman
Mantle, Roland Frederick, 36, Steward †
March, John Starr, 50, US Postal Clerk †
Marks, J., 26, Assistant Pantryman Steward †
Marrett, G., 22, Fireman †
Marriott, J. W., 20, Assistant Pantryman Steward †
Marsden, Evelyn, 28, Stewardess
Marsh, Frederick Charles, 39, Fireman †
Martin, Annie *?, 33, Stewardess
Martin, F., 29, Scullion
Martin, Mabel Edwina, 20, 2nd Cashier
Maskell, Leopold Adolphus, 25, Trimmer †
Mason, Frank Archibald Robert, 32, Fireman
Mason, J., 39, Leading Fireman †

Matherson, David, 30, A. B. Seaman †
Mathias, Montague Vincent, 27, Mess Steward †
Mattmann, Adolf, 20, Ice Man †
Maugé, Paul Achille Maurice, 25, Kitchen Clerk
Maxwell, John, 31, Carpenter †
May, Arthur, 24, Fireman †
May, Arthur William, 60, Fireman Messman †
Maynard, Isaac, 31, Entre Cook
Mayo, William Peter, 27, Leading Fireman †
Maytum, Alfred, 52, Chief Butcher †
Mayzes, Thomas, 25, Fireman
McAndrew, Thomas, 36, Fireman †
McAndrews, William, 23, Fireman †
McCarthy, Frederick James, 36, Bed Room Steward †
McCarthy, William, 47, A. B. Seaman
McCastlan, W., 38, Fireman †
McCawley, Thomas W., 36, Gymnasium Steward †
McElroy, Hugh Walter, 37, Purser †
McGann, James, 26, Trimmer
McGarvey, Edward Joseph, 34, Fireman †
McGaw, Eroll V., 30, Fireman †
McGough, James R., 25, A. B. Seaman
McGrady, James, 27, Saloon Steward †
McGregor, J., 30, Fireman †
McInerney, Thomas, 37, Greaser †
McIntyre, William, 21, Trimmer
McLaren, Harriet Elizabeth *Allsop, 40, Stewardess
McMicken, Arthur, 23, Saloon Steward
McMicken, Benjamin Tucker, 21, 2nd Pantryman Steward †
McMullin, James, 32, Saloon Steward †
McMurray, William Ernest, 43, Bed Room Steward †
McQuillan, William, 26, Fireman †
McRae, William Alexander, 32, Fireman †

McReynolds, William, 22, Junior 6th Engineer †
Mellor, Arthur, 34, Saloon Steward †
Middleton, Alfred Pirrie, 26, Assistant Electrician †
Middleton, M. V., 24, Saloon Steward †
Milford, George, 28, Fireman †
Millar, Robert, 26, Extra 5th Engineer †
Millar, Thomas, 33, Assistant Deck Engineer †
Mills, Christopher, 51, Assistant Butcher
Mintram, William, 46, Fireman †
Mishellany, A., 52, Printer Steward †
Mitchell, Lawrence, 18, Trimmer †
Monteverdi, Giovanni, 23, Assistant Entre Cook †
Moody, James Paul, 24, 6th Mate †
Moore, Alfred Ernest, 39, Saloon Steward †
Moore, George Alfred, 32, A. B. Seaman
Moore, John J., 29, Fireman
Moore, Ralph William, 21, Trimmer †
Moores, Richard Henry, 44, Greaser †
Morgan, Arthur Herbert, 27, Trimmer †
Morgan, Thomas A., 26, Fireman †
Morell, R., 21, Trimmer †
Morris, A., 30, Greaser †
Morris, Frank Herbert, 28, Bath Room Steward
Morris, W., 24, Trimmer †
Moss, William, 34, 1st Saloon Steward †
Mouros, Jean/Javier, 20, Assistant Waiter †
Moyes, William Young, 23, Senior 6th Engineer †
Müller, L., 36, Interpreter Steward †
Mullen, Thomas A., 20, Steward †
Murdoch, William John, 33, Fireman
Murdoch, William McMaster, 39, 1st Mate †
Nannini, Francesco Luigi Arcangelo, 42, Head Waiter †
Neal, Henry, 25, Assistant Baker
Nettleton, Gorge, 28, Fireman †

Newman, Charles Thomas, 33, Assistant Storekeeper †
Nicholls, Sidney, 39, Saloon Steward †
Nichols, Alfred, 42, Boatswain †
Nichols, A. D., 34, Steward †
Nichols, Walter Henry, 35, Assistant Saloon Steward
Noon, John, 35, Fireman †
Norris, J., 23, Fireman †
Noss, Bertram Arthur, 21, Fireman †
Noss, Henry, 30, Fireman
Nutbean, William, 30, Fireman
O'Connor, John, 25, Trimmer
O'Connor, Thomas Peter, 39, Bed Room Steward †
Olive, Charles, 31, Greaser †
Olive, Ernest Roskelly, 28, Clothes Presser Steward †
Oliver, Harry, 32, Fireman
Olliver, Alfred, 27, Quartermaster
O'Loughlin, Dr., William Francis Norman, 62, Surgeon †
Orpet, Walter Hayward, 31, Saloon Steward †
Orr, J., 40, Assistant Vegetable Cook †
Osborne, William Edward, 32, Saloon Steward †
Osman, Frank, 28, A. B. Seaman
Othen, Charles Alfred, 36, Fireman
Owen, Lewis, 49, Assistant Saloon Steward †
Pacey, Reginald Ivan, 17, Lift Steward †
Pachéra, Jean Baptiste Stanislas, 19, Assistant Larder Cook †
Paice, Richard Charles John, 32, Fireman †
Painter, Charles, 31, Fireman †
Painter, Frank Frederick, 29, Fireman †
Paintin, James Arthur, 29, Captain's Steward †
Palles, Thomas, 42, Greaser †
Parsons, Edward, 35, Chief Storekeeper †
Parsons, Frank Alfred, 26, Senior 5th Engineer †
Parsons, Richard, 18, Saloon Steward †

Pascoe, Charles H., 43, A. B. Seaman
Pearce, Alfred Ernest, 24, Steward †
Pearce, John, 28, Fireman
Pearcey, Albert Victor, 32, III. Class Pantry Steward
Pedrini, Alessandro, 21, Assistant Waiter †
Pelham, George, 39, Trimmer
Pennal, Thomas Francis, 33, Bath Steward †
Penny, William C., 30, Assistant Saloon Steward †
Penrose, John Poole, 49, Bed Room Steward †
Peracchio, Alberto, 20, Assistant Waiter †
Peracchio, Sebastiano, 17, Assistant Waiter †
Perkins, Laurence, Alexander, 22, Telephone Steward †
Perkis, Walter John, 37, Quartermaster
Perotti, Alfonso, 20, Assistant Waiter †
Perrin, William Charles, 39, Boots Steward †
Perriton, Hubert Prouse, 31, Saloon Steward †
Perry, Edgar Lionel, 19, Trimmer
Perry, H., 23, Trimmer †
Peters, William Chapman, 26, A. B. Seaman
Petty, Edwin Henry, 25, Bed Room Steward †
Pewsey, John E., 35, Saloon Steward †
Pfropper, Richard, 30, Saloon Steward
Phillimore, Harold Charles William, 23, Saloon Steward
Phillips, A. G., 27, Greaser †
Phillips, John George, 25, Telegraphist †
Phillips, Walter John, 35, Storekeeper †
Piatti, Louis, 17, Assistant Waiter †
Piazza, Pompeo, 30, Waiter †
Pitfield, William James, 25, Greaser †
Pitman, Herbert John, 34, 3rd Mate
Platt, W., 18, Scullion †
Podesta, John Alexander, 24, Fireman
Poggi, Emilio, 28, Waiter †
Poigndestre, John Thomas, 33, A. B. Seaman

Pond, George, 32, Fireman †
Pook, P., 34, Assistant Pantry Steward †
Port, Frank, 22, Steward
Porteus (alias Parker), Thomas, 32, Assistant Butcher †
Prangnell, George Alexander, 30, Greaser
Prentice, Frank Winnold, 22, Storekeeper
Preston, Thomas Charles Alfred, 20, Trimmer †
Price, Ernest, 17, Barman †
"Prichard", Alice *?, 33, Stewardess
Prideaux, Jack Arthur, 23, Steward †
Priest, Arthur John, 24, Fireman
Prior, Harold John, 21, Steward
Proctor, Charles, 40, Chef †
Proudfoot, Richard, 23, Trimmer †
Pryce, Charles William, 22, Saloon Steward †
Pugh, Alfred, 20, Steward
Pugh, Percy, 31, Leading Fireman †
Pusey, Robert William, 24, Fireman
Randall, Frank Henry, 29, Saloon Steward †
Ranger, Thomas, 29, Greaser
Ransom, James, 33, Saloon Steward †
Ratti, Enrico, 21, Waiter †
Rattonbury, William Henry, 36, Assistant Boots Steward †
Ray, Frederick Dent, 32, Saloon Steward
Read, J., 21, Trimmer †
Read, Robert, 30, Trimmer †
Reed, Charles, 43, Bed Room Steward †
Reeves, F., 31, Fireman †
Revell, William, 31, Saloon Steward †
Ricaldone, Rinaldo Renato, 22, Assistant Waiter †
Rice, Charles, 32, Fireman
Rice, John Reginald, 25, Clerk †
Rice, Percy, 19, Steward †

Richards, Joseph James, 28, Fireman †
Rickman, George Albert, 36, Fireman †
Ricks, Cyril G., 23, Storekeeper †
Ridout, W., 29, Saloon Steward †
Rigozzi, Abele, 22, Assistant Waiter †
Roberts, Frederick, 36, 3rd Butcher †
Roberts, Hugh H., 40, Bed Room Steward †
Roberts, Mary Keziah *Humphreys, 41, Stewardess
Roberts, Robert George, 35, Fireman †
Robertson, George Edward, 19, Assistant Saloon Steward †
Robinson, James William, 30, Saloon Steward †
Robinson, Annie *, 40, Stewardess
Rogers, Edward James William, 32, Storekeeper †
Rogers, Michael, 27, Saloon Steward †
Ross, Horace Leopold, 36, Scullion
Rotta, Angelo Mario, 23, Waiter †
Rous, Arthur J., 26, Plumber †
Rousseau, Pierre, 49, Chef (Restaurant) †
Rowe, Edward M., 31, Saloon Steward †
Rowe, George Thomas, 32, Quartermaster
Rudd, Henry, 23, Assistant Storekeeper †
Rule, Samuel James, 58, Bath Room Steward
Rummer, Gilbert, 27, Saloon Steward †
Russell, Boysie Richard, 19, Saloon Steward †
Rutter (alias Graves), Sidney Frank, 30, Fireman †
Ryan, Tom, 27, Steward †
Ryerson, William Edwy, 32, Saloon Steward
Saccaggi, Giovanni Giuseppe Emilio, 24, Assistant Waiter †
Salussolia, Giovanni, 25, Glass Man †
Samuel, Owen Wilmore, 41, Saloon Steward †
Sangster, Charles, 32, Fireman †
Sartori, Lazar, 24, Assistant Glass Man †

Saunders, D. E., 26, Saloon Steward †
Saunders, F., 23, Fireman †
Saunders, W., 23, Fireman †
Saunders, Walter Edward, 23, Trimmer †
Savage, Charles J., 23, Steward
Sawyer, Robert James, 30, Window Cleaner †
Scarrott, Joseph George, 33, A. B. Seaman
Scavino, Candido, 42, Carver †
Scott, Archibald, 40, Fireman †
Scott, Frederick William, 28, Greaser
Scott, John, 21, Assistant Boots Steward †
Scovell, Robert, 42, Saloon Steward †
Sedunary, Sidney Francis, 25, 2nd III. Class Steward †
Self, Alfred Henry, 39, Greaser †
Self, Edward, 25, Fireman
Senior, Harry, 31, Fireman
Sesia, Giacomo, 24, Waiter †
Seward, Wilfred Deable, 25, Chief Pantry Steward
Shaw, Henry, 39, Kitchen Porter †
Shea, John, 39, Saloon Steward †
Shea, Thomas, 32, Fireman †
Sheath, Frederick, 20, Trimmer
Shepherd, Jonathan, 32, Junior Assistant 2nd Engineer †
Shiers, Alfred Charles, 25, Fireman
Shillabeer, Charles Frederick, 20, Trimmer †
Siebert, Sidney Conrad, 29, Bed Room Steward †
Simmons, Alfred, 31, Scullion
Simmons, Frederick C., 25, Saloon Steward †
Simmons, W., 32, Passage Cook †
Simpson, Dr., John Edward, 37, Assistant Surgeon †
Sivier, William, 23, Steward †
Skeates, William, 26, Trimmer †
Skinner, Edward, 33, Saloon Steward †
Slight, Harry John, 32, Steward †

Slight, William H., 37, Larder Cook †
Sloan, Mary, 28, Stewardess
Sloan, Peter, 31, Chief Electrician †
Slocombe, Maud Louise *Walden, 30, Turkish Bath Stewardess
Small, William, 40, Leading Fireman †
Smillie, John, 29, Saloon Steward †
Smith, Charles, 38, Kitchen Porter †
Smith, Charles Edwin, 38, Bed Room Steward †
Smith, Edward John, 62, Master †
Smith, Ernest George, 26, Trimmer †
Smith, F., 20, Assistant Pantryman Steward †
Smith, J., 24, Assistant Baker †
Smith, James M., 35, Junior 4th Engineer †
Smith, John Richard Jago, 35, British Postal Clerk †
Smith, Katherine Elizabeth, 42, Stewardess
Smith, Robert G., 30, Saloon Steward †
Smith, William, 26, Seaman †
Smither, Harry John, 22, Fireman †
Snape, Lucy Violett *Leonard, 22, Stewardess †
Snellgrove, G., 40, Fireman †
Snooks, W., 26, Trimmer †
Snow, Eustace Philip, 21, Trimmer
Sparkman, H., 30, Fireman
Stagg, John Henry, 34, Saloon Steward †
Stanbrook, Alfred Augustus, 30, Fireman †
Stap, Sarah Agnes, 47, Stewardess
Steel, Robert Edward, ?, Trimmer †
Stebbings, Sydney Frederick, 34, Chief Boots Steward †
Stewart, John, 27, Verandah Steward
Stocker, H., 20, Trimmer †
Stone, Edmond J., 33, Bed Room Steward †
Stone, Edward Thomas, 30, Bed Room Steward †
Street, Thomas Albert, 25, Fireman

Strout, Edward Alfred Orlando, 19, Saloon Steward †
Stroud, Harry John, 35, Saloon Steward †
Strugnell, John H., 34, Saloon Steward †
Stubbings, Harry Robert, 31, 2nd Class Cook †
Stubbs, James Henry, 28, Fireman †
Sullivan, S., 25, Fireman †
Swan, W., 46, Bed Room Steward †
Symonds, J., 38, Saloon Steward †
Symons, George Thomas Macdonald, 24, Lookout
Talbot, George Frederick Charles, 27, Steward †
Tamlyn, Frederick, 23, Mess Steward †
Taylor, C., 35, A. B. Seaman †
Taylor, Cuthbert, 26, Steward †
Taylor, J., 42, Fireman †
Taylor, James, 24, Fireman
Taylor, John, 50, Fireman †
Taylor, Leonard, 23, Turkish Bath Attendant †
Taylor, William Henry, 26, Fireman
Taylor, William John, 30, Saloon Steward †
Taylor (alias Turner), George Frederick, 32, Stenographer †
Terrell, Bertram, 20, Seaman †
Terrell, Frank, 27, Assistant Saloon Steward
Testoni, Ercole, 23, Assistant Glass Man †
Teuton, Thomas Moore, 32, Saloon Steward †
Thaler, Montague Donald, 17, Steward †
Theissinger, Franz Alfred Daniel, 46, Bed Room Steward
Thomas, Albert Charles, 23, Saloon Steward
Thomas, Benjamin James, 32, Saloon Steward
Thomas, Joseph, 25, Fireman †
Thompson, Herbert Henry, 25, 2nd Storekeeper †
Thompson, John William, 35, Fireman
Thorley, William, 39, Assistant Cook †
Threlfall, Thomas, 44, Leading Fireman

Thresher, George Terrill, 25, Fireman
Tietz, Carlo/Karl, 27, Kitchen Porter †
Tizard, Arthur, 31, Fireman †
Toms, Francis A., 31, Saloon Steward
Topp, Thomas Frederick, 28, 2nd Butcher †
Tozer, James, 30, Greaser †
Triggs, Robert, 40, Fireman
Turley, Richard, 35, Fireman †
Turner, L., 28, Saloon Steward †
Turvey, Charles, 16, Page Boy †
Urbini, Roberto, 22, Waiter †
Valvassori, Ettore Luigi, 35, Waiter †
Van der Brugge, Wessel Adrianus, 42, Fireman †
Veal, Arthur, 35, Greaser †
Veal, Thomas Henry Edom, 38, Saloon Steward †
Vear, H., 32, Fireman †
Vear, William, 33, Fireman †
Vicat, Alphonse Jean Eugène, 21, Fish Cook †
Vigott, Philip Francis, 32, A. B. Seaman
Villvarlange, Pierre Léon Gabriel, 19, Assistant Soup Cook †
Vine, H., 18, Assistant Controller †
Vioni, Roberto, 31, Waiter †
Vögelin-Dubach, Johannes, 35, Coffee Man †
Wake, Percy, 37, Assistant Baker †
Wallis, Catherine Jane *Moore, 35, Matron †
Walpole, James, 48, Chief Pantryman Steward †
Walsh, Catherine, 32, Stewardess †
Ward, Arthur, 24, Junior Assistant 4th Engineer †
Ward, Edward, 34, Bed Room Steward †
Ward, J., 31, Leading Fireman †
Ward, Percy Thomas, 38, Bed Room Steward †
Ward, William, 36, Saloon Steward
Wardner, Albert, 39, Fireman †

Wareham, Robert Arthur, 36, Bed Room Steward †
Warwick, Tom, 35, Saloon Steward †
Wateridge, Edward Lewis, 25, Fireman †
Watson, W., 27, Fireman †
Watson, W. A., 14, Bell Boy Steward †
Watts or Witts, F., 36, Trimmer †
Weatherstone, Thomas Herbert, 24, Saloon Steward †
Webb, Brooke Holding, 50, Smoke Room Steward †
Webb, S., 28, Trimmer †
Webber, Francis Albert, 31, Leading Fireman †
Welch, W. H., 23, Assistant Cook †
Weller, William, 30, A. B. Seaman
Wheat, Joseph Thomas, 29, Assistant 2nd Steward
Wheelton, Edneser Edward, 29, Saloon Steward
White, Alfred, 32, Greaser
White, Arthur, 37, 1st Class Assistant Barber †
White, Frank Leonard, 28, Trimmer †
White, J. W., 27, Glory Hole Steward †
White, Leonard Lisle Oliver, 31, Saloon Steward †
White, William George, 23, Trimmer
Whiteley, Thomas, 18, Saloon Steward
Whiteman, August H., 51, 1st Class Barber
Whitford, Alfred Henry, 39, Saloon Steward †
Widgery, James George, 37, Bath Steward
Wilde, Henry Tingle, 39, Chief Mate †
Williams, Arthur J., 38, Storekeeper †
Williams, Samuel S., 26, Fireman (used his brother Edward's Discharge Book) †
Williams, Walter John, 28, Assistant Saloon Steward
Williamson, James Bertram, 35, British Postal Clerk †
Willis, W., 46, Steward †
Willsher, William Audrey, 33, Assistant Butcher †
Wilson, Bert, 28, Senior Assistant 2nd Engineer †
Wilton, William, 45, Trimmer †

Windebank, Alfred Edgar, 38, Sauce Cook
Winser, Rowland (alias Evans, George), 33, Steward †
Witcher, Albert Ernest, 39, Fireman †
Witt, Henry Dennis, 37, Fireman †
Witter, James William Cheetham, 31, Smoke Room Steward
Wittman, Henry, 34, Bed Room Steward †
Wood, H., 30, Trimmer †
Wood, J. T., 40, Assistant Saloon Steward †
Woodford, Frederick, 40, Greaser †
Woody, Oscar Scott, 44, US Postal Clerk †
Wormald, Frederick William, 36, Saloon Steward †
Wrapson, Frederick Bernard, 19, Assistant Pantryman Steward †
Wright, Frederick, 24, Racquet Steward †
Wright, William, 40, Glory Hole Steward
Wyeth, James, 26, Fireman †
Wynn, Walter, 41, Quartermaster
Yearsley, Harry, 41, Saloon Steward
Yoshack, James Adamson, 30, Saloon Steward †
Young, Francis James, 30, Fireman †
Zanetti, Mario, 20, Assistant Waiter †
Zarracchi, L., 26, Wine Butler †

Sources:

Anatomy of the Titanic – Tom McCluskie

Titanic Voices, Memories from the Fateful Voyage – Donald Hyslop, Alastair Forsyth

German Titanic Society

Titanic: Triumph and Tragedy- John P. Eaton & Charles A. Haas

A Night to Remember-Walter Lord

American and British Inquiry

The Titanic Disaster Hearings – Tom Kuntz

TITANIC Voices – Hannah Holman

Spiegel TV-Die letzten Stunden der Titanic (2012)

Titanic– Geoff Tibbals

Titanic: Legacy of the World`s Greatest Ocean Liner – Susan Wels

The Irish Aboard the Titanic - Senan Molony

Mission TITANIC-James Cameron

Encyclopedia Titanica

Unsinkable: the full story of the RMS Titanic - Daniel Allen Butler

Reise auf der Titanic – Günter Bäbler

Titanic- Signals of the Disaster – John Booth & Sean Coughlan

Titanic-Zeugen des Untergangs (Discovery Channel, 1997)

Titanic- Die Ausstellung 2010

The Daily Mail, 1st August 2007

The two pennies-Susie Millar

American Inquiry, 23rd April 1912

Southampton Echo, 11th January 1965

Japan Today, 9 thApril 2014

Westmeath Independente, 25th November 2011

Titanic and the mystery ship - Senan Molony

Die Titanic war ihr Schicksal, RTL 1998

Mythos Titanic – Wolf Schneider

The Night lives on – Walter Lord

The Riddle of the Titanic - Robin Gardiner &Dan Van der Vat

Futility – Morgan Robertson

Berliner Kurier, 2nd January 2017

Schule und Mehr in Alkersum auf Föhr – Anni Haprich-Mommsen

Pictures:

A Myth is Born: The RMS TITANIC ready for launch © public domain

The last voyage ot the TITANIC: Titanic at the docks of Southampton © public domain

TITANIC Destinies: © Photocollage of the author

The Scapegoats of the Disaster: *Untergang der Titanic* Illustration of Willy Stöwer for the newspaper *Die Gartenlaube* © public domain

Thanks

At the end of my fourth TITANIC book, I would like to take the opportunity to thank some important people without whose support this and also my previous books could not have been realized:

I would like to thank my wife Yvonne for the support of my TITANIC passion for many years.

My thanks go to Anka Schlayer from Titanic Connections for her initial proofreading and her great patience in reading that book. She was a great help with some changes in this book.

Many thanks to my proofreader Julie Hanna. She was a great help to realize this English version of my book.

I would also like to thank Simon Medhurst, whose great-grandfather Robert Hichens survived the sinking of the TITANIC, without whose Titanic Gathering 2017 in Belfast I would not have been able to make or even deepen many important contacts in the TITANIC scene.

Author Norbert Zimmermann, born 1970, has been researching the history of the TITANIC for almost three decades and has published four non-fiction books about the world-famous ship. For this book he researched among other things at the original locations in Belfast. Zimmermann is a member of the British Titanic Society (BTS) and the German and Swiss Titanic Society.

More books by the author:

Titanic – Das Ende einer Illusion

The legendary luxury liner RMS TITANIC sank in the icy North Atlantic on 15th April 1912 at 2.20 a.m., killing over 1500 people. This book tells the complete story of the TITANIC, starting with her construction, her maiden voyage with the fateful collision with the iceberg and ending with the discovery of the wreck at a depth of almost 4,000 meters.

ISBN 978-3-8423-5034-2, 252 Pages

Schicksal Titanic

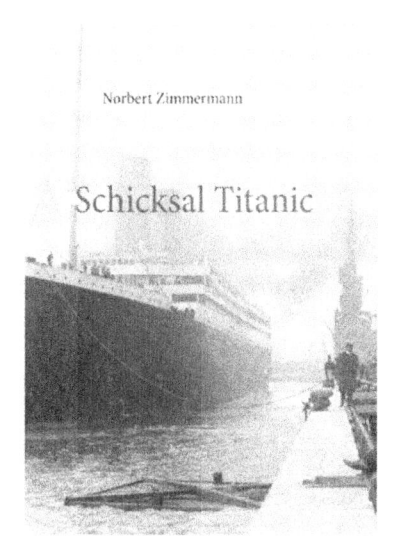

The sinking of the TITANIC was a severe trauma for the survivors of the tragedy. This book tells the stories of the survivors and shows, how one of the greatest shipwrecks of all times was experienced by the victims themselves.

ISBN 978-3-8482-2125-7, 184 Pages

Der zweite Untergang der TITANIC

Over a hundred years have passed since the tragic sinking of the TITANIC on 15th April 1912. However, the legendary ship does not seem to have come to rest. Many questions are still unanswered. Who really found the wreck of the TITANIC? What is the meaning of the open letter to Robert Ballard? What will happen to the recovered artifacts of the TITANIC? This book tries to find answers to these questions, and also ventures a look into the future.

ISBN: 978-3735794062, 124 Pages

Recommended literature on the topic:

Walter Lord
A Night to Remember
ISBN: 978-0-553-27827-9

David Haisman
"I'll see you in New York"
ISBN 0-6463-3236-8

David Haisman
Raised on the Titanic – An Autobiography
ISBN 0- 646-33265-1

David Haisman
TITANIC – The Edith Brown Story
ISBN: 978-1-4389-6182-8

Donald Lynch, Ken Marshall
Ghosts oft he Abyss
ISBN: 0-306-81223-1

Daniel Allen Butler
Unsinkable: the full story of the RMS Titanic
ISBN 978-0-306-81110-4

Susan Wels
Titanic: Legacy of the World`s Greatest Ocean Liner
ISBN: 978-0-7835-5261-3

James Cameron
Mission TITANIC
ISBN: 978-3667102393

Malte Fiebing
TITANIC (1943): Nazi Germany`s version of the disaster
ISBN: 978-3844815122

Lawrence Beesley
The Loss of The SS Titanic